REFLECTIONS ON
MUSICAL MEANING AND
ITS REPRESENTATIONS

MUSICAL MEANING AND INTERPRETATION
Robert S. Hatten, editor

Reflections ON MUSICAL MEANING AND ITS REPRESENTATIONS

Leo Treitler

Indiana University Press

Bloomington & Indianapolis

This book is a publication of

Indiana University Press
601 North Morton Street
Bloomington, Indiana 47404–3797
USA

iupress.indiana.edu

Telephone orders: 800–842–6796
Fax orders: 812–855–7931
Orders by e-mail: iuporder@indiana.edu

⊖ The paper used in this publication meets
the minimum requirements of the Ameri-
can National Standard for Information
Sciences—Permanence of Paper for
Printed Library Materials, ANSI
Z39.48–1992.

Manufactured in the United States of
America

Library of Congress Cataloging-in-
Publication Data

Treitler, Leo, [date]-
  Reflections on musical meaning and
its representations / Leo Treitler.
    p. cm. — (Musical meaning and
interpretation)
  Includes bibliographical references and
index.
  ISBN 978-0-253-35632-1 (cloth : alk.
paper) — ISBN 978-0-253-22316-6 (pbk. :
alk. paper) 1. Music—Philosophy and
aesthetics. 2. Music—History and criticism.
I. Title.
  ML3845.T78 2011
  781.1'7—dc22

2011011588

1 2 3 4 5 16 15 14 13 12 11

In remembrance of conversation with
Siegmund Levarie.

CONTENTS

ACKNOWLEDGMENTS

I wish to express my gratitude to the John Simon Guggenheim
and the Andrew Mellon foundations for their
support of the work on this book.

Robert Hatten, as series editor, Maureen Epp,
as copy editor, and Ji Yeon Lee,
as my assistant, have contributed to
whatever virtues it may have.

INTRODUCTION

The introduction to a book of this sort, one would think, should offer an explanation for the collection of essays on such seemingly diverse subjects in a single volume. As diverse as the subjects are the occasions for which they were written and the publications in which most of them first appeared (chapters 6 and 7 are published here for the first time): scholarly conferences and their reports (chapters 1, 7, 8, 11); publications honoring colleagues (chapters 3, 4, 9, 12); invited contributions to journals or anthologies (chapters 2, 5, and 10); and lectures for interdisciplinary academic institutes (chapter 6). So when Robert Hatten invited me to submit such a collection for the series he edits, Musical Meaning and Interpretation, I welcomed the opportunity to bring together these scattered writings, for I believe the diversity of vantage points from which they address their topics closely approximates the range of approaches—"historical, theoretical, philosophical, critical, semiotic, hermeneutic, cognitive"—identified in the announcement of the series. I hope that bringing these essays together enhances the meaningfulness of each in the light of the others.

The chapters have been ordered here so that following the first, each picks up from the preceding an aspect of its perspective. Thus the first chapter, written originally as a contribution to a conference among philosophers and music scholars under the title "Music and Meaning," explores the resources and limitations of language for representing and interpreting music. The second continues the concentration on language with a critical consideration of the tradition of regarding music to be uniquely ineffable, a notion that provokes the question, "What can we expect of language's ability to represent our world?" The resource of metaphor has a prominent place in both chapters. The third chapter surveys and reflects on Beethoven's use of language for both representation and interpretation in his scores, a duality that is manifested in the interchangeable use of the labels "performance marks" and "expressive marks" in commonplace reference to such indications in his scores. Considered as a kind of musical notation, these indications reflect on the markings that we commonly call "notation" an expressive aspect, a consideration that is taken up in the sixth chapter. The fourth and fifth chapters continue from different perspectives the implications in the score for performance.

Focus on musical notation begins in the sixth chapter with a pursuit of the epistemology and semiology of notations and their sources—especially language and its notation—through history. It takes a side glance at the exploitation of the meaningfulness of musical notation for conveying non-musical meanings. The seventh chapter takes an historical view of the relation between music writing and the musical work. Both chapters six and seven entail reflection on music writing in the light of the making of visual art.

The last five chapters comprise a section of the book most nearly concerned with "meaning" in the commonplace usage of the word. I have brought back chapter 8 from an earlier collection because it answers to my aspirations for a kind of interpretation of musical works that would be responsible at once to musical content, dramatic control, and social and political context of both content and circumstances of creation, myth, and history. Chapter 9 is a more recent, deeper study of the same work as it displays—but does not promote, much critical interpretation to the contrary—archetypal attitudes regarding gender roles and identities held in the culture of which it is a product.

The final three chapters are linked in conveying my beliefs about the obligations that are attendant upon the enterprise of interpreting works of music as bearers of meanings about the worlds in which they were created. They are obligations of clarity about exactly what is being claimed: Is it that infused meanings are supposed to have been held by the contemporaries of the works or newly discovered by the interpreters? Are they held to be immanent to the works? Are they claimed to be conveyed through the experience of the works, which they inform, or are they deduced from the works or from other sources? And they are obligations of plausibility: Is knowledge of such meanings within the grain of knowability in the musical domains for which it is claimed? Is there evidentiary support for the meanings claimed? Is that question even relevant to the enterprise of interpretation?

Almost all of the essays that have had earlier publication have undergone some revision. Chapters 5, 10, and 11 have been the most substantially revised.

REFLECTIONS ON
MUSICAL MEANING AND
ITS REPRESENTATIONS

PART ONE

Language

1

LANGUAGE AND THE
INTERPRETATION OF MUSIC

Talk about music has turned again to its possibilities as a conveyor of meaning. As past skepticism about such possibilities has been driven in part by a persistent belief in music's ineffability, this re-opening entails renewed accommodations between music and language. The nature of such accommodations is the subject I address here, with attention to two main aspects: first, assumptions about the nature of language communication that we take as the standards for assertions about what and how music can and cannot mean; and second, the correspondences that are drawn between music and language. Unexamined habits and assumptions and undefended dogmas about both aspects abound in the discourse on this subject.

Reading a story not long ago by Gabriel Garcia Marquez in *The New Yorker* magazine, I was stopped by this sentence: "Inside the lights burned in the middle of the day and the string quartet was playing a piece by Mozart, full of foreboding."[1] The formal discourse of my field of musicology, operating under no matter what scruples, under regimes modern or postmodern, has tended to shut out such characterizations of music as irrelevant and meaningless. When I read that sentence my mind was swept into a fantasy in which Marquez is reading the story aloud and has just come to that sentence. At once a squad of young men and women rush up to him, outfitted in boots, breeches, and vests of black leather. Their leader hands Marquez a summons and they take him off in manacles. I shall pick up this fantasy again later on.

Marquez's transgression violates some of the most influential answers that have been given to the question of musical meaning—answers identified sometimes as transcendentalist, sometimes as formalist. As far apart as those two thinking styles now seem—one idealist, the other positivist—they were once (in the early nineteenth century) two sides of the same efforts to rescue wordless music from the threat of being empty and meaningless. Music is said to be otherworldly and inscrutable, to demand exegesis and to defy it. In the very posing of the question of meaning there is implication of its pointlessness, of the impossibility of finding answers. Cunning theories have been erected in defense of this negative conception which, as I mean to suggest here, has been misdirected in its isolation of music as *uniquely* indescribable.

The pointlessness of the question was proclaimed by Robert Schumann in an 1836 issue of his music journal, *Neue Zeitschrift für Musik*. Under the title "Chopin's Piano Concertos," he plunges before long into this outburst:

> Away with music journals! . . . The music critic's noblest destiny is to make himself superfluous! The best way to talk about music is to be quiet about it. . . . For the last time, away with music journals, this one and all the rest!

That much is signed "Florestan," Schumann's impetuous alter ego—his Shadow, to place him in the Jungian tableau. Part 2 of the article begins,

> If things were ordered according to that lunatic Florestan, one could call the above a review and let it stand as an obituary for this periodical.

The author of this second part is identified as "Eusebius," Schumann's other, more cool-headed persona. He continues,

> We, ourselves, may regard our silence as the ultimate homage . . . due partly to the hesitancy one feels when confronted with a phenomenon one would prefer to approach through the senses.

The ambivalence is a Romantic characteristic. The enthusiasm for speaking of music was countered by an affirmation of the difficulty or impossibility of doing so, delivered more as a tribute than a lament. Eusebius continues with reluctance—"if we must explain in words . . ."—into a panegyric to Chopin in which words do not fail him. He glides with ease and relish through the most rich, exuberant language that crescendos to the unforgettable metaphor, "Chopin's works are cannon buried under flowers."[2]

Felix Mendelssohn, in a famous letter of 1842 written in reply to suggestions from a relative about the meanings of some of his "Songs without Words," turns the matter around in a stunning way:

> There is so much talk about music, and yet so little is said. For my part, I believe that words do not suffice for such a purpose. . . . People often complain that music is too ambiguous; that what they should think when they hear it is so unclear, whereas everyone understands words. With me it is exactly the reverse, and not only with regard to an entire speech but also with individual words. These, too, seem to me so ambiguous, so vague, so easily misunderstood in comparison to genuine music . . . The thoughts which are expressed to me by music that I love are not too indefinite to be put into words, but on the contrary, too definite. . . . The same words never mean the same things to different people.
>
> Only the song can say the same thing, can arouse the same feelings in one person as in another, a feeling which is not expressed, however, by the same words. . . . Words have many meanings, but music we could both understand correctly. Will you allow this to serve as an answer to your question? At all events, it is the only one I can give, although these, too, are nothing, after all, but ambiguous words![3]

The letter is often cited for its assertion about the preciseness of music's expression, but it is for its far more radical assertion about the opposite effect of language communication that I cite it here. It is not music's ineffability that makes for the difficulty of talk about its meaning, Mendelssohn writes, but the ambiguities, vagueness, and inconsistencies that are inherent in the practice of language communication. Mendelssohn has here touched the heart of the problem of musical meaning, and the source of much disagreement and confusion. His insight here anticipates the pragmatic perspective on language use that is owing to Ludwig Wittgenstein, expressed, for example, in this passage:

> We are unable clearly to circumscribe the concepts that we use, not because we don't know their real definition, but because there is no real "definition" to them. To suppose that there *must* be would be like supposing that whenever children play with a ball they play a game according to strict rules . . . Why then do we in philosophizing constantly compare our use of words with one following exact rules? . . . The answer is that the puzzles which we try to remove always spring from just this attitude towards language.[4]

Carl Dahlhaus might seem at first to dispute Mendelssohn about this fundamental matter. But what he writes is really a refinement.

> The feelings that music possesses with the determinacy extolled by Mendelssohn prove to be not impulses existing outside and without music and whose sounding portrayal is musical, but rather *qualities that are feelings at all only as they are expressed by music.* That they cannot be translated into language—that language does not reach them—accordingly means simply that *they can be what they are only in musically expressive form;* it in no way means that language remains behind music in the characterization of real feelings because it is poorer and more undifferentiated. *Music is not the more specific representation of impulses that are also comprehensible linguistically, but instead the different expression of different feelings* [my emphases].[5]

This has the consequence that qualities or characters that are commonly labeled "extramusical" are precisely the opposite; they can only be musical. And that in turn renders the familiar claim that music can have expressive qualities only in a metaphorical sense rather meaningless, as I shall argue further on.

Mendelssohn's skepticism about the assumption that language expressions have a precise and stable reference from one speaker to another would throw suspicion as well on rigorous theories of musical meaning that depend on that assumption, and leave us to make formulations that are sketches of our understanding in the effort to convey our apprehensions to one another. We would be obliged to recognize such sketches for what they are and to practice tolerance in place of the customary dogmatism. And we would be well advised to try pragmatic descriptions of our use of language in talking about music in place of prescriptive theorizing. We should give serious attention to the writings of those who are skilled in the imaginative and creative use of language—that is, writers of poetry and fiction—whose use of language is often more subtle and versatile than those who are skilled in theorizing, and who may be more concerned with representing through language their experience of music.

I share Mendelssohn's skepticism, and I believe in the consequences that flow from it. If I therefore turn now to what is perhaps the most explicit and musically concrete effort to formulate a theory of musical meaning with a claim to rigor that has been put forward in recent years by a music scholar, it is in order to show how, even through the posture of rigor, and even where the explicit aim is to demonstrate how musical meaning works, the tools of language have been so blunted by a combination of rhetorical and doctrinal motives that language has been drained of the potency and versatility that can be the positive side of the ambiguity that Mendelssohn identified.

I have culled from Kofi Agawu's *Playing with Signs: A Semiotic Interpretation of Classic Music* a basic vocabulary of the main predicates through which its author seeks to identify the modalities of musical meaning: denoting, embodying, expressing, representing, symbolizing—all ways of linking the concrete musical event to something other than itself, ways in which music is supposed to correspond to other things. My purpose is to see whether it is possible to recognize what is to be understood by these modalities, and especially how they are differentiated from one another—in short, whether it is possible to recognize what conception about the modalities of musical meaning underlies the use of language. Emphases in the following citations are mine.[6]

"Measures 72–76 present a concentrated passage of descending fifths, *symbolizing* one high point of the learned style" (p. 107); and "The *alla breve* [passage] *denotes* learned style" (p. 90). "Symbolizing" and "denoting" are treated as synonyms. That seems fair enough, since to denote something is to be a sign or symbol for it. The sign for the note A above middle C denotes the sound 440 Hz according to prevailing tuning standards. Any sign that we would agree upon, regardless of its own shape, size, or color, would do the same job. Less easy to see is that the two music passages cited could be said to be signs for a style—pointing to it rather than *embodying, exemplifying,* or *being in* that style. There are important differences between these two examples that make for the difficulty. First, once we have been led by the sign to the sound 440 Hz, we lose interest in the sign. But we do not lose interest in the passage of descending fifths or the *alla breve* passage once we have been led by them to focus on the concept "learned style." We experience them as aspects of the music, and we would be more accustomed to saying that they embody, exemplify, or are in learned style. By the same token we would be less willing to accept such passages as arbitrary conventions that could be replaced by any others. We would be likely to insist that there are reasons within the character of those passages for their being earmarks of a style we call "learned" (if we have agreed about that convention). And just as they identify "learned style" for us, the phrase "learned style" characterizes them; it sums up the properties for which it is a label. "Symbolizing" and "denoting" lack the reciprocity of "embodying" or "exemplifying." I shall return to this important point and its consequences. If the author really means to say that those passages denote or symbolize "learned style," it can only be because he is unfolding a conception of classic music as a play of signs that signify things beyond themselves—namely styles. The book seems to have been misnamed, for its ultimate subject is the radical conception of classic music as a play of *styles*, for which the music itself constitutes the signs. But just exactly how that can be is baffling because the word "style," as applied to music, is said to be a metaphor—which is to say that music does not literally have or embody style, or is not in a style. Then what those musical passages denote is mystifying, as is the author's notion of "metaphor."

The following passage demonstrates this distancing even more clearly: "*Sturm und Drang denotes* instability" (p. 87). Now, we usually say that "instability"—for example, the instability of a series of diminished seventh chords or of a syncopated passage—is a property or character or condition that we as listeners recognize and even feel. To say that instability is "denoted" by the style *Sturm und Drang* (which we must presumably first recognize as such before we can think "instability") is to go out of one's way to deny that instability can be an experienced condition of music. Consequently it empties the word itself of its suggestiveness, acquired through use, of such feeling or feature. For it says that in identifying "instability" we simply recognize that the music has met certain conventional conditions for the use of that term, conditions that may, again, be quite arbitrary. This is to say something very special indeed about the experience of music and about the language in which we try to describe it. It is understandable, again, from the vantage point of a postmodern attitude toward music as an indifferent play of signs.

Language is used here to hold music at arm's length from the listener but also from meanings that may be attributed to it—to make musical meaning indirect and conceptual and to locate it outside of music. To do so is to construe a concept of the extra-musical. Words are asked to identify not music's properties or the experience of those properties, but abstractions that music *signifies*. That is the doctrinal tendency to which I refer, a tendency to address the question of meaning in music via the semiotic transaction of signifying, hence a tendency to regard "interpreting" as being virtually synonymous with "decoding." A sign of that, so to speak, is the tendency to speak of interpretations of music as "readings." And even though it is most explicit in the semiotic line of interpretive theory with which Agawu identifies his work, it is as much at play in some current hermeneutic theories and interpretations that will be the subjects of the last two chapters.

Another, more arcane use of the word "denote" takes us a step still further into abstraction (the following will require some patience): "Introversive semiosis [as when a first-movement theme is cited in the last movement of the same work] *denotes* internal intramusical reference . . . while extroversive semiosis [for example, the call of a posthorn] *denotes* external, extramusical, referential connection" (p. 132). A definition of "semiosis" is needed: "a process in which signs function as vehicles, interpretants, and interpreters [interpretants and interpreters would both be things or persons that interpret]."[7] How are the roles of subject and object in each pair determined? Could the members of each pair be reversed, for example, so that internal intramusical reference *denotes* introversive semiosis? If so (and I see nothing in the way of the reversal), the equation simply amounts to a translation from the familiar Latin-based "reference" to the less familiar Greek-based "semiosis." But then, too, the purport of those sentences of Agawu's would not be reduced if *denote* were replaced each time by "is equivalent to," or simply by "is." This substitution would, however, remove the confusion—indeed incoherence— that is created by asserting that a signifying process (*semiosis*) *denotes* (that is, signifies) a kind of reference (which is a way of signifying). The whole passage seems to be about language, skating on the surface of some idea about music as a signifying process. But it makes no contribution to the question about how music signifies.

Now to the use of the word *represents:* "Measure 32 *represents* some sort of beginning" (p. 106). As beginnings, middles, and endings are also said to be *symbolized* (p.118), then *representing* joins the synonyms *symbolizing-denoting.* There is talk of "representations that Beethoven makes toward sonata form" (p. 118) and of "representations toward the tonic" (p. 124). But "beginnings," "middles," "ends," "sonata form," and "tonics" are properties about which we usually say "this *is* the beginning," or "this *is* on, or in, the tonic," or "this *is* in, or follows, or approximates, sonata form" (qualified as much as you like), but not "this is a representation" of those things. What phantoms would those things be, anyway, if music is only a representation of them?

The furthest extreme is reached in the uses of the word *express.* Dictionary definitions usually begin with the idea of bringing out, stating, showing, or giving manifest form to attitudes, feelings, characteristics, or beliefs that are held or embodied, before moving to the very different sense of signifying something by certain characters or figures (as in "mathematical expression"). Wittgenstein likened musical expression to the expression on a person's face, and in order to make sense of this it is useful to think of Peter Kivy's distinction between "expression" and "being expressive of."[8] Put this second way, it seems to be closer to what we mean in speaking of music as expressive, for it is noncommittal with respect to the fundamental question whether music holds, or contains, what is expressed. In any case, in ordinary usage the term would seem to be resistant to exploitation for any such distancing function as the other terms undergo. But "expression" is straightaway defined by Agawu as "extroversive semiosis" (in other words, signification of external, extramusical objects, such as the call of a cuckoo). It is converted to a term of reference in preparation for the exposition of a theory of musical expression that depends entirely on codes for external reference. What this comes down to is a confusion between denotation and exemplification. With the conversion of "expression" to a term of reference there remains no real differentiation among these terms; they are all interchangeable, and all come down to "signify."

This powerful wish to regard music as a play of signs might arise out of a desire to compensate for the condition of music as it is so often characterized (or out of a determination to dispute the characterization): that it lacks semantic content, that it bears no denotative relation to an object. Whether or not that is so, it has quite radical implications for the way we would address music, were we to follow it consistently, implications that would certainly run counter to the reasons that most of us have for listening to music. I shall try to bring this out first through reference to a work of fiction, then through a simple philosophical analysis.

In Italo Calvino's story "A King Listens," a narrating voice in the second person reflects to the monarch, who has stolen the throne and sealed his predecessor into a dungeon deep in his fortress, how his life has been given over to two purposes only: self-indulgence and the retention of his power. Calvino turns to music to convey how, paradoxically, this self-preoccupation has destroyed the king's sense of self along with the cultural life of his city.

> Among the sounds of the city you recognize every now and then a chord,
> a sequence of notes, a tune: blasts of fanfare, chanting of processions,
> choruses of schoolchildren, funeral marches, revolutionary songs intoned

by a parade of demonstrators, anthems in your honor sung by the troops who break up the demonstration, trying to drown out the voices of your opponents, dance tunes that the loudspeaker of a nightclub plays at top volume to convince everyone that the city continues its happy life, dirges of women mourning someone killed in the riots. This is the music you hear; but can it be called music? From every shard of sound you continue to gather signals, information, clues, as if in this city all those who play or sing or put on disks wanted only to transmit precise, unequivocal messages to you. Since you mounted the throne, it is not music you listen to, but only the confirmation of how music is used: in the rites of high society, or to entertain the populace, to safeguard traditions, culture, fashion. Now you ask yourself what listening used to mean to you, when you listened to music for the sole pleasure of penetrating the design of the notes.[9]

The philosophical analysis begins with an insight that strikes at the heart of the problem: "It is probably more true of music than of any other art that the sign (if we conceive it as such) is not transparent—that is, the sign does not disappear in favor of its function as pointing to the signified."[10] The context of this remark, which is worth pondering over, is a discussion of the way that signs and the things signified are connected through the action of reference, which the author aims to clarify by way of drawing a distinction between two main types of reference relations, as they apply to music: denotation and exemplification. The distinction turns on the direction of the flow of reference between the sign and its referent, and by implication on the question which of the two stands out more in the receiver's attention to the whole process, the sign or the thing signified.

The terminology and the question can be highlighted through a simple example: a cinema marquee with its text as sign for the film(s) that is (are) being shown inside the theater. The reference usually flows from the marquee to the film, from the sign to the signified. The marquee refers to the film; that is its purpose. Although it is possible to think of the film referring to the marquee, it would be quite unusual to take the pair in that way (not, however, for someone making a study of cinema marquees). After we have seen the film and left the cinema, it is the film that will usually occupy our residual attention, the film that we will discuss on our way home. In this sense the sign is transparent to the signified. It is totally absorbed in its signifying function. It is this process that Anthony Newcomb calls "denotation," following Nelson Goodman, and this example is an extreme case of it.[11]

If we think next of the appreciation of a figurative work of visual art—Michelangelo's sculpture *Pietà*—in these terms, we are certainly involved in following a denotative flow of reference from the sculpture to what it signifies: a lifeless male figure draped across the lap of a mourning female figure, identifiable as Jesus and Mary. But appreciation of the work involves us in reflecting back onto the sculpted figures what tradition and experience, and our own reflection and feelings, bring us about the meaning of Jesus's death and Mary's mourning, and about devotion, sacrifice, death, and mourning in general. Such meaning and feelings are *exemplified* by the work, and the reference between sign and signified flows in both directions. We do not lose interest in the sign once our attention has been drawn to the signified; the sign is not absorbed by the signifying process, it is not transparent to the signified. We would be more likely to say that the artwork in this case is an amalgam of sign and signified.

Here is the first couplet of Shakespeare's sonnet 27:

Weary / *with* **toil**,/ I **haste** me / to *my* **bed** /
the **dear** / *repose* / for **limbs** / with *tra* /*vel* **tir'd** /;

There is a flow of reference from each italicized word to a condition, action, or object that it signifies. But the mood that is evoked by the words signifying the speaker's state and the action that follows from it, both of which we know from our own experience, refer back to the words themselves, and especially to the pacing of the prosody. By convention the syllables of sonnets move in iambs. But the poet has contrived to block such movement throughout the first line in order to enact its meaning: trochee and iamb, pause, amphibrach, anapest (accented syllables are bold; forward slashes separate metric feet.) The second line, with the poet comfortably eased into bed, can swing with ease into the iambic rhythm. Not only does the poem denote through the signifiers of its words a state of being and a consequent action, it also exemplifies both through that rhythmic device. The reference flows in both directions.

Can we imagine music that, when considered as signs, is transparent to the things it signifies? There is a film in the Sherlock Holmes series from the 1930s called *Dressed to Kill* (it is not based on an Arthur Conan Doyle story). For a particular gang of thieves and the detectives trying to identify them, the variants in the way a series of music boxes play the same tune constitute an encoded message about the location of a huge fortune. None of the characters displays the slightest interest in the music for itself, and there is no way that grasping the information that it denotes enriches the experience of it for them. But this is an extreme, and an unreal case. Perhaps one would even question whether the performances by those music boxes constitute music at all, any more than does a Morse Code transmission.

But everyone knows of music that delivers coded messages without ceasing to be music. Beethoven's overture to Goethe's *Egmont* opens with a single tutti chord, *forte*, prolonged by a fermata, followed by a succession of ponderous chords in the low strings, altogether "full of foreboding," to cite Marquez again. The rhythm of those chords is recognizable as that of the Spanish *sarabande*, rendered sinister, however, by the *sostenuto* tempo and the dark register of the low strings—an evocation of the despotic rule of the Spanish Duke of Alba over the Flemish people. (I pray that no one will be tempted to say that this opening is a metaphor for the Duke of Alba or his despotic rule.)

In the second-act finale of Mozart's *Le Nozze di Figaro* the gardener Antonio reports to the Count that he has seen someone jump from the window of the Countess's chamber. He suspects correctly that it was Cherubino. But Figaro, trying to cover for Cherubino, pretends it was he. Antonio produces evidence that it was Cherubino: the document certifying the latter's commission in the army, which Antonio found at the place where Cherubino landed (m. 609). Figaro casts about for a way of explaining why he would have had the document in his possession, and as he does so the orchestra modulates steadily, as though groping for a chord of resolution. And just as Figaro finds his explanation, under prompting from Susanna and the Countess (the document lacked an official seal), the orchestra finds its harmonic clearing (a cadence on the dominant of B♭ major, m. 671). The flow of reference in both directions is apparent here. The orchestral music, giving off a purely musical sense of searching for a way out, enlivens Figaro's search, and we transport the feeling of this man caught in a lie, desperate to find a way out—a feeling we surely all know from childhood—back to the music. In doing so we invest the feeling that the music gives off with that concrete content of human action and feeling. It is the two-way flow that creates the humor.

The passages from Beethoven and Mozart show that music, even at its most specifically denotative, is never reducible to a play of signs. The pseudo–Sherlock Holmes case shows that when music has an exclusively denotative function, a function of nothing but a play of signs, it is at least questionable whether we would consider it music at all.

The conclusion is that music is not transparent, and arraying the semiotic vocabulary to have all musical signs pointing to the conceptual signified somewhere outside the music is at odds with our experience. If music signifies, its sounds do not fade for us once its work of signifying is done. This observation is profound, for the contradiction that it reveals is a risk everywhere in the recent zeal to regard music as cultural, social, or political practice—a zeal that is understandable, to be sure, in view of the long neglect of such associations. But the tendency has been toward the drowning out of music by meaning.

If we think of Beethoven's marking for the slow movement of his Piano Sonata op. 10, no. 3, *Largo e mesto* (Example 1.1) as both an instruction for performance and a description of its character, the difference between explaining musical expression as a matter of denotation and of exemplification is this: on the first view (denotation) the focus would be on the "mournfulness" that the music signifies; on the second (exemplification) it would be on the music in its mournfulness, which the performer is asked to bring out; the music as performed would be said to exemplify mournfulness. It is the notion of musical expression as exemplification that I want to pursue now. There will be more to say about "*Largo e mesto*" in the third chapter.

EXAMPLE 1.1

Goodman makes a further distinction. He allows that "sadness" is a property that a painting can possess and exemplify, but he observes that paintings are insentient objects that cannot literally feel sad. If a painting possesses and exemplifies the property of sadness, which does not come naturally to it, it does so by acquisition or borrowing—the sort of borrowing that is commonly identified as metaphorical transfer. This he contrasts with properties that paintings can literally possess and exemplify, such as yellowness. Hence expression in art is for him a matter of "*metaphorical* exemplification." Volumes have been written about "metaphor," but a simple dictionary definition can be a helpful point of departure. The *Random House Dictionary of the English Language* defines "metaphor" as "A figure of speech in which a term or phrase is applied to something to which it is not literally applicable in order to suggest a resemblance, as in 'A mighty fortress is our God.'"[12]

Goodman's line of reasoning and the distinction to which it leads can be tried on Beethoven's *Largo e mesto* movement. It cannot *be* mournful literally because it isn't sentient. Its mournfulness is a result of borrowing from a source that *can* be mournful by way of suggesting a resemblance. Then we must be making a reference to literally mournful things when we hear the sonata movement as something like them, just as the performer must do in following the direction to play it mournfully. Is that what happens? What can such reference points be? They must be human feelings, for only in human feelings can mournfulness "literally" reside. But if we don't perceive the piece as mournful in itself, we don't know enough to search out something literally mournful for comparison. It must be that we are reminded by the piece of something literally mournful. What might that be? A dirge or a funeral march? Surely not, as these, too, can be mournful only by dint of metaphor. Not even a mournful face, which, after all, is not sentient but can only express the mournful feelings of the mind or heart within or below, can be a touchstone for mournfulness. We are told that elephants mourn their dead, the sign of which is that they gently touch the skulls and tusks of the deceased with their trunks. Perhaps when Dr. Karen McComb of the University of Sussex, who has made this discovery, hears the *Largo e mesto* movement she is reminded of that behavior, leading her to conclude that the piece is mournful. Is it any wonder that the philosopher Stephen Davies has written, "Just what 'metaphorical exemplification' amounts to in musical expression is so obscure that the account is deprived of explanatory power"?[13]

At the root of this failure, of course, is Goodman's initial elementary misstep, thinking that when we characterize a painting as sad or a day as gloomy we can't mean it literally because paintings and days have no feelings. Then building on that strange notion, he has us borrowing those qualities from some source that can feel them literally and presuming that we catch the incongruity of the juxtaposition. Are we conscious of an incongruity in speaking of the mournful tone of that sonata movement, and is that awareness what conveys the character of the movement to us? Goodman serves metaphor better in providing his own highly imaginative and witty characterization of the phenomenon that is at the same time an exemplification of its effect: "A metaphor is an affair between a predicate with a past and an object that yields while protesting." The force and the beauty of this metaphor result from the subtlety with which the foreign domain is insinuated, in the cognitive jolt that comes from the juxtaposition of the contexts of semiotic analysis and an erotic scenario, and in the sharpness with which it delivers at the same time the definition that is its cognitive content. Such juxtaposition of incommensurates to achieve a precision of meaning together with an aesthetic kick is the point of true metaphor. Compare "This mathematical proof is sprung with the force of a mousetrap" with "Oh, what a gloomy day this is." Some musical effects work like metaphor, as I shall shortly suggest, but they are special; musical expressiveness in general—for example the mournfulness of Beethoven's sonata movement—is not dependent on "metaphorical exemplification."

That "mournfulness"—but interestingly only in the Italian version, *mesto*—has long been regarded by practitioners of music as a phenomenon securely in music's semantic field is clear from the appearance of the word *mesto* in pedagogical writing about music as a performance indication right into the twentieth century, and as a specifically musical term in music dictionaries.

We can try to account for the feeling of mournfulness that the *Largo e mesto* movement exemplifies in terms of its musical details: tempo, the dark register and voicing of the opening, the tendency to move to the subdominant harmony, the insistent reiteration of the chromatic dyad C♯–D within D–C♯–D and F–C♯–D (see Example 1.1). In the same way we can try to account for the gloominess that the day exemplifies in terms of its visible aspects: the gray sky, the mist and rain, the bare trees with only the lifeless brown leaves of oaks hanging on. But these are not exercises that we go through in experiencing the mournfulness and the gloom directly.

But wait—"dark register and voicing?" I must have meant, "literally," "low register and dense voicing." But wait—can there be anything *literally* low or dense about a musical sound, any more than there can be dark voicing? I seem to be stepping in quicksand here. "High" and "low" are acquired names for immanent properties of musical sounds that have nothing in common with high and low moods, high and low numbers, or high and low mountain peaks, but in each case we accept those designations without hesitation as natural to their respective domains—as "literal," not "metaphorical" designations. (I believe they were acquired as names for a musical property with the invention of musical notation in Western Europe in the ninth century.) We assume too much when we make an easy assessment about "literal" meanings. But when we speak of dark musical sounds, I believe we mean the experience of darkness as a peculiarly musical, sonic quality arising from tempo, rhythm, voice leading, instrumental sounds, and harmonic relations, an experience not mediated by thoughts of things that are "literally" dark, like Rembrandt's painting *The Night Watch* prior to its cleaning, or a moonless night, or the mood of a jilted lover. Whether we recognize in those darknesses some overlapping fringe of affective quality is less easy to say than has been pretended for a very long time. Whether the quality of darkness is transferred from *The Night Watch* or a moonless night or a jilted lover's mood to Beethoven's sonata movement is not really the question that is up for review. It is whether such a claim has any meaning. What does it really mean to say that the character of that movement can be dark only in a metaphorical sense? Frank Sibley writes, "The warmth or chill of music is only audible; it is not the warmth or chill felt in bath water or seen in smiles."[14]

George Lakoff and Mark Turner have shown what is entailed in the notion of "literal meaning" and the consequent distinction between "literal" and "metaphorical" meaning.[15] On that notion ordinary, conventional language ("literal language") comprises expressions that are semantically autonomous—that is, they are meaningful completely on their own terms without venturing outside their clearly delineated semantic fields. Because they are objective, expressions in ordinary language are capable of making reference to objective reality. Metaphor would stand outside ordinary language so conceived. How dubious the idea is that a boundary between two such sharply delineated uses of language is observed in practice is demonstrated by the very habit of claiming descriptive language about music to be necessarily metaphorical, in other words, that such language cannot be semantically autonomous, that it reaches almost immediately outside the semantic field of music (note the underlying premise, again, of a duality of the "musical" and the "extra-musical"). In this explicit form it is a claim with roots in the famous remark of Eduard Hanslick, that "all the fanciful portrayals, characterizations, circumscriptions of a musical work are either figurative or perverse. What in every other art is still description is in music already metaphor." The eighteenth-century philosopher Thomas Reid seems to have been on to Hanslick's observation. He wrote "In harmony, the very names of concord and discord are metaphorical and suppose some analogy between the relations of sound, to which they are figuratively applied, and the relations of minds and affections, which they originally and properly signify.[16] A moment's reflection will confirm this idea, but it has meaning only on the premise of a definitive boundary between literal and metaphorical language. What language, on this premise and given the concept of "literal," can fall within the semantic field of music? The naming of tones and tone complexes—scales and chords—but not their identification as high or low, or their movement of any kind, or their constitution as lines or phrases, or their points of tension or relaxation, or their implications, or their style, grammar, or syntax (the last three designated by Agawu as metaphorical because of their original reference to language), or their character or expressive attributes.

So narrow a mapping of the semantic field of music implies an underlying duality of the musical and the extra-musical on which the duality of the literal and the metaphorical is dependent as its rationalization. Rather than framing this subject as a philosophical exercise with the aim of drawing sharp lines of demarcation within such dualities, we may do better to recognize in them the face of particular moments in the history of discourse about music.

A duality of literal and metaphorical language meaning, linked particularly to the duality of science and poetry, was taught by writers of antiquity and of the early Christian era (see chapter 2). Long before Hanslick issued his famous proclamation, music was parsed from the very beginning of the Western tradition of writing about it into aspects that can and those that cannot be described in words. The unidentified author of the *Musica enchiriadis* (Handbook on Music), written around 900, wrote that "this discipline [of music] does not at all have a full, comprehensible explanation in this life," and identified those aspects about which "we *can* judge . . . distinguish . . . , adduce . . . , give some explanations": tones, intervals, modes, properly made melodies. But then, "in what way music has so great an affinity and union with our souls—for we know we are bound to it by a certain likeness—we cannot express easily in words."[17] Other writers soon after resorted just exactly to metaphor in the effort to break the silence about the ineffable aspects. In identifying an area of the ineffable in the musical domain—even if only in despair over a failure—and separating it off from an area open to objective verbal exposition, those early writers opened a bi-chambered space that could be value-laden in shifting and sometimes see-sawing, sometimes competing dispositions through history according to intellectual temper, inclination, fashion, and need. If the ineffable aspects of music were a frustration and a challenge in the Middle Ages, the ineffability of music could be associated in the nineteenth century with its transcendental nature and its position as the ideal art for some, while for others it was something to be shunted aside in favor of positive (formalist) language. Both were ways of identifying what was truly musical, and by implication what was extra-musical, both answering to the challenge of redefining the status of an instrumental music around 1800 newly independent of language, imitation, and functions related to the institutions of church and state authority.

The alternative to clinging to these dualities is to take a remark like Marquez's at face value, accepting the "foreboding" character of a Mozart string quartet as a property that music can exemplify in its own way if anything can, and one that we can experience in an unmediated way, analyzing that property, if we like, in terms of the finest details of the musical materials and processes that are its component elements—just as we would analyze the character of a *drohendes Gefahr* that Arnold Schoenberg portrayed in the first part of his "Begleitungsmusik zu eine Lichtspielscene," op. 34. That is, after all, what the achievements of a century of practice in musical analysis should have prepared us to do.

Marquez's aperçu is intuitive. He is one of those "talented laymen," as the art critic and historian Irwin Panofsky wrote, "in whom the faculty of synthetic intuition in the interpretation of art may be better developed than in erudite scholars."[18] The most gifted of such laymen, as far as music is concerned, was surely Marcel Proust. Consider how, in these passages from *Swann's Way*, Proust follows the registers through which music is presented to us and through which we re-present it—from perceived qualities, through conscious interaction with impressions, feelings, and outward associations (of which there are strikingly few in the passage), to reflection—even musical analysis—synthesis, and recollection.

> The year before . . . he had heard a piece of music played on the piano and violin . . . and it had been a source of keen pleasure when, below the delicate line of the violin part, slender but robust, compact and commanding, he had suddenly become aware of the mass of the piano part beginning to emerge in a sort of liquid rippling of sound, multiform but indivisible, smooth yet restless, like the deep blue tumult of the sea, silvered and charmed into a minor key by the moonlight. But then . . . suddenly enraptured, he had tried to grasp the phrase or the harmony . . . that had just been played and that had opened and expanded his soul, as the fragrance of certain roses, wafted upon the moist air of evening, has the power of dilating one's nostrils . . . Scarcely had the exquisite sensation which Swann had experienced died away, before his memory had furnished him with a transcript, sketchy, it is true, and provisional, which he had been able to

glance at while the piece continued, so that, when the same impression suddenly returned, it was no longer impossible to grasp. He could picture to himself its extent, its symmetrical arrangement, its notation, its expressive value; he had before him something that was no longer pure music, but rather design, architecture, thought, and which allowed the actual music to be recalled.[19]

We prize metaphor, not only for its ability to impart meaning in the most precise way but even more—at its best, at least—for the way in which its incongruities affect the intellect (Goodman's metaphor for metaphor), the emotions (Shakespeare's line "How sweet the moonlight sleeps upon this bank"; *The Merchant of Venice*), the senses (Proust's metaphor for the impact of the piano sound: "the liquid rippling of the piano sound . . . silvered and charmed into a minor key by the moonlight"). Metaphor inhabits a realm where imagination, not logic, rules. Donald Davidson begins his essay "What Metaphors Mean" metaphorically: "Metaphor is the dreamwork of language."[20]

Music is capable of metaphor-like effects, entirely within its own idiom. The second movement of Franz Schubert's Trio no. 2 in E♭ Major, D. 929, *Andante con moto,* begins with a long, discursive, lamenting theme in C minor accompanied by a trudging figure that, even though it seems a touch too fast (*con moto;* we learn why only in the finale), registers as the tattoo of a funeral march: repeated chords, accent on the fourth beat followed by an anacrustic dotted rhythm—with drum role if there were a drum, all conventional gestures that could be heard throughout the nineteenth century in music recognizable as funereal (Example 1.2).

EXAMPLE 1.2

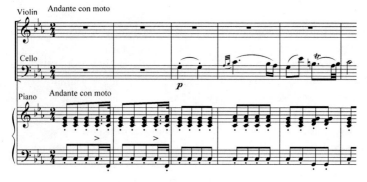

That theme, made only for repetition and closed in on itself, alternates with a soaring, expansive theme in the relative major key that undergoes a vigorous, affirmative development; it seems as though it might be capable of lifting the movement out of the hopelessness of the opening music, but in the end it always slumps back into that music. The movement has the aspect of circular, obsessive thinking (Example 1.3).

EXAMPLE 1.3

The finale, *Allegro moderato,* is one of those endless rondos of Schubert's that seem to modulate through more keys than there are, this one going on in an endless patter of mindless energy (Example 1.4). Toward the middle of the movement the piano's right hand converts its simple triplets to a hemiola, the violin in pizzicato chords and the left hand of the piano together take up the tattoo from the second movement, and, as if out of the depths of the unconscious, the cello steps forward to play the morose theme of the second movement *sotto voce.* It is as though the persistent memory of this is what all that patter had been meant to suppress (Example 1.5). (The reason for the faster-than-funeral-march tempo of the second movement now appears: it is that the cello must be able slip right into its theme without the lurch of a tempo change.) The meaningfulness of this music is immensely enriched through this conspiracy of incompatible realms, producing as powerful a metaphoric effect as any that I can think of in language. Metaphor is as normal a source of meaning for music in its own domain as it is in language in *its* domain. Often what we call motivic work or thematic transformation is musical metaphor; opera abounds in it. Musical metaphor works directly within the musical domain, not indirectly through signifying processes that refer to "extra-musical domains." Music inhabits the mental realm in which metaphor communicates. We have been reading that the expressive effect of music is metaphorical. It is worth considering that the expressive effect of metaphor is musical.

EXAMPLE 1.4

EXAMPLE 1.5

Schubert recalls the first theme of the second movement a second time near the end of the finale, making an end to the piece through that return. By the simple device of opening the third phase of the theme, which until now had always looped back to the beginning, into the major mode (changing G♭ to G♮; Example 1.6), he emancipates the piece from the sense of entrapment with which the second movement had closed, a sense that is reinforced by a single failed attempt at escape near the end (Example 1.7) and from which the scherzo and finale had seemed simply to walk—or skip—away.

EXAMPLE 1.6

EXAMPLE 1.7

What I am responding to here is a narrative dimension in the piece, and I say this in the face of serious questions that have been raised about the interpretation of music as narrative. Comparing music with literary narratives, critics of such an idea call attention to certain differences: the absence of a narrating voice in instrumental music, the inability of music to speak in the past tense, the location of the narrative in the description rather than the music (like the confusion about the location of metaphor—in the music or the description), the inconsistencies about agency in musical "narrative." Narrative accounts of music follow, now musical elements such as keys and themes, now persons, such as the listener as he or she moves through the piece or the composer as he or she composes it. There can be no question about these differences, which are all owing to the differences between music and language. But that has not deflected composers and critics from their interest in something like a narrative dimension in music.[21]

Carolyn Abbate has made strong representations against such interpretations. She reminds us of the distinction articulated by Plato (in the third book
of the *Republic*) and Aristotle (the *Poetics*) between the diegetic (epic or narrative) and mimetic (dramatic) modes of representation in poetry,[22] and she
asserts that music is more like the latter than the former, more like enactment
than narrative. But we should also remember how theorists since Plato have
observed that in practice the two modes are frequently conflated.[23] If clas-
sificatory exposition identifies them as ideal types, that does not oblige the
poet to compose every line as strictly one or the other. Nor is it self-evident
that the distinction between narrative and drama is transposable to music.
Interpreters who speak of musical narrativity do so not in the light of such
an assumption but rather with reference to properties that music shares with
both narrative and drama.[24] We need to operate here with a suppleness of language use that allows us to speak, for example, of certain events in a narrative as "dramatic." In any case, if music is to be described on the basis of any
such system, it seems particularly odd to choose an ancient system that had
no place for lyric. The discussions about musical narrative have been mainly
about music of the eighteenth and nineteenth centuries—a time when lyric
had a place in such classifications along with narrative and drama, and when
the descriptive mode entered prominently into musical composition.

Abbate declares that music is mimetic, and then identifies all the properties
of the diegetic mode of poetic presentation that it cannot, in consequence,
have. Chief among these, for her, seems to be that music has no past tense—
it "traps the listener in present experience and the beat of passing time"—
whereas narrative is by definition "a tale told later, by one who escaped to the
outside of the tale."[25] The reader need only turn back to the narrative passage
cited earlier from Italo Calvino's story to be reminded that tense cannot be
counted on as a criterion for deciding what is and is not narrative.

As another reminder, I note that throughout this discussion I have followed the convention—literally inaccurate—of narrating with verbs in the
present tense an event that is in the past—Abbate expressing the views that
I am just now considering.

The grammatical categories of "present" and "past tense" contribute to the
way events in literature strike us in relation to our many-faceted and many-
layered time consciousness, but they do not by any means alone determine
that experience. The consistent use of past tense in the following narrative
from the beginning of book 22 of Homer's *Odyssey*, "Slaughter in the Hall"—

a veritable model of diegetic presentation—does not prevent the poet's vivid language from making its events strike us as a fearful present. The story carries us along as we follow its telling, reflect with the poet, peer into the minds of the actors, and anticipate:

> Odysseus ... trained a stabbing arrow on Antinous ... just lifting a gorgeous golden loving-cup to his lips, about to drain the wine—and slaughter the last thing on the suitor's mind: who could dream that one foe ... would bring down death on himself, and black doom? But Odysseus aimed and shot Antinous square in the throat and the point went stabbing clean through the soft neck and out—and off to the side he pitched, the cup dropped from his grasp as the shaft sank home, and the man's life-blood came spurting out his nostrils—thick red jets ... The suitors burst into uproar all throughout the house when they saw their leader down. They leaped from their seats, milling about, desperate, scanning the stone walls—not a shield in sight, no rugged spear to seize.[26]

If we are going to compare music with narrative literature, we must take care to compare their performance (the reading—even if silent—of narrative literature is a kind of performance in real time) or their contents, not the performance of one with the contents of the other. If it is said that music "traps the listener in present experience and the beat of passing time," then that refers to its performance, and the same may be said of the performance of literary narrative, as the experience of reading the passage from the *Odyssey* surely shows. With both we want to know what happens next, and interruptions of any kind in the performance will create tension. It is just as true of both that when the performance is over we can both replay it in our minds and create non-temporal portraits of the totality of it, as we do after we have seen a film that has particularly engaged us.[27]

The difference that Abbate has tried to identify with her misplaced emphasis on tense is in the elements that are unfolded in the two arts: events or utterances preserved in language, and tone configurations. But like literary unfoldings, musical unfoldings can refer to their own pasts and futures, that is, to past and future moments in their unfoldings—through memory (the reflection over a pedal in the coda on the first theme of the first movement of Mozart's G-Minor Symphony, as an event or a thought in the distant past) and implications, respectively. Sometimes literary unfoldings can seem very like music in that respect (I think especially of Samuel Beckett's work, for example "Krapp's Last Tape"). There is not much point in comparing the two in terms of the morphological property of tense in the elements that are unfolded, since the elements of musical unfolding lack that morphological property altogether. But that is no new discovery, and it is hardly relevant to the consideration of narrativity in music.

The issue about musical narrativity is linked to the one about literal and metaphorical language in a critique by Jean-Jacques Nattiez.[28] Nattiez's answer to the question of his title ("Can One Speak of Narrativity in Music?") would be "Yes, but one shouldn't." Music cannot *be* narrative, he writes, and adds at various points the qualifiers "strictly speaking," "in itself," "in the strict sense of the word," "properly speaking." Of course he is circling around the concept, taken "literally," and he touches down with the declaration that the *idea* of a musical narrative is therefore a metaphor (probably intending, rather, that the characterization of any musical work as a narrative would be a metaphor). That dictum rests on another: "the trope of music as language needs to be resisted."

That remark demands a pause. When it comes to relations between music and language, and critiques of claims about such relations—whether in considering how language has been set to music in particular cases, in the efforts to compare the structures of music and language on a theoretical level, in the efforts to compare their modes of communication, or in attempts to apply methods of language analysis to the analysis of music (or vice versa)—care ought to be taken to be clear about the register of language to which music is being compared and what it is about music that the comparison is meant to illuminate; specifically whether the attention is primarily to semantics, phonetics, or syntactics. Nattiez's dictum can seem surprising, when fifteen years earlier he had published his *Fondements d'une sémiologie de la musique* (1975), a study with its roots in structural linguistics.[29] But Nattiez's later injunction was directed at a temptation to interpret music on the model of a parameter in the semantic domain of language—story telling—projecting, in a sense, a semantic domain onto music. Such differentiation can help evade a possible conflation of Nattiez's *sémiologie* with Agawu's "semiotics," discussed above, which aims to illuminate music's meaning—in a word, semantics. I quote from Allan Keiler's paper "Two Views of Musical Semiotics":

> One distinction that has been suggested for organizing the different
> kinds of activity understood as semiotic, and useful enough for musical
> semiotics, is that between (1) semiotics as a science of signs, or of systems
> of communication, and (2) any attempt at analyzing some domain of inter-

est (for instance myth, ritual, or musical systems) with the help of techniques borrowed from linguistics . . . About the first, as it applies to the semiotics of music, I would agree with [Nicolas] Ruwet . . . "I don't really see what one gains by considering music as a system of signs or of communication, by speaking of musical signifiers and signifieds or of musical semantics."[30]

But the trope of music as language has in fact not been resisted through the ages by critics aiming to understand musical practice. And historians of music cannot afford to ignore it, and have not, fortunately, done so. A few specifics:

Medieval writers from the beginning of the pedagogical tradition took as their model for explaining the discipline of music (the *ars musica*) the ancient discipline of grammar (the *ars grammatica*), which concerned itself with language and speech.[31] The same author of the *Musica enchiriadis* cited earlier described the musical system as a constituent hierarchy on the model of the constituent hierarchy of language. Quoting in the translation of Powers in "Language Models and Musical Analysis,"

> As the elementary and individual parts for the speaking voice are letters—syllables composed of them form nouns and verbs and they [in turn] the text of complete speech—so *phthongi*, which are called *soni* ["sounds"] in Latin, are the bases of the singing voice, and the content [*continentia*] of the whole of music comes down to them in the final analysis. From the coupling of *soni* [are formed] *diastemata* [=Latin *intervalla*] and from *diastemata* are formed *systemata* [=Latin *constitutiones*] . . . [The] lesser parts [of melodies] are the *cola* and *commata* of singing, which mark off the song at its endings. But *cola* are made by two or more *commata* coming together . . . And the *commata* are made by *arsis* and *thesis,* that is rising and falling [intervals].[32]

The "*cola* and *commata* of singing," in other words, are the counterparts in melody of the hierarchical levels in language of clauses bearing the same designations—which are also the names of the punctuation marks that set them off. A hundred years or so later a writer known to us only as Johannes wrote,

> Just as in prose three kinds of distinctions are recognized—which can also be called pauses . . . so also it is in chant . . . In prose, where one makes a pause in reading aloud, this is called a colon; when the sentence is divided by an appropriate punctuation mark, it is called a comma; when it is

brought to an end, it is a period. . . . likewise, when a chant makes a pause by dwelling on the fourth or fifth note above the final, there is a colon; when in mid-course it returns to the final, there is a comma; when it arrives at the end there is a period.

He demonstrated this, parsing the words of a traditional chant, the antiphon *Petrus autem servabatur*: "'Peter therefore' (colon) 'was kept in prison' (comma) 'but a prayer was made' (colon) 'for him without ceasing' (comma) 'of the church unto God.'"[33] Powers provides a transcription of the melody to that text from an early source,[34] showing that its phrasing exactly corresponds to the phrasing of the words in the way that Johannes described in the last sentence of the passage cited.

Analysis has shown that this principle is the key to the hierarchic phrase structure and the tonal grammar of melodic tradition current in his time and well beyond.[35] But this is not only a matter of structure and grammar. In this practice punctuation and musical articulation play the same role. In marking the syntax of language in its enunciation they enhance the understanding of its semantic contents.

Fritz Reckow, in his 1976 article "Tonsprache," gives an overview of the conceptual and historical aspects of what he calls "the global parallelization of language and music." Wye Jamison Allanbrook has written of the modeling of melodic phrase structure in eighteenth-century music on language phrase structure.[36] Elaine Sissman has presented a conception of musical form based on rhetoric in the same period.[37]

This literature, along with much else on the ways in which music has been modeled on language, may have given Nattiez a last-minute second thought about narrative in music: "There is no smoke without fire," he writes at the end of his essay.

Béla Bartók's *Mikrokosmos* comprises 153 "progressive piano pieces" in six volumes. They are published with titles in Hungarian, French, German, and English. Bartók provided only the Hungarian titles; the translations were made by his friend Tibor Serly. Bartók named no. 142 in volume 6 "Mese a Kis Legyröll," "A Story about a Little Fly." The published French title is "Ce que la mouche raconte," or "What the Fly Recounts." Note the difference: Bartók's title presents the piece as a narrative. Who is the narrator? Perhaps Bartók, perhaps the performer. In the French, the fly is the original narrator, perhaps as reported by Bartók or the performer; but the present tense "raconte" favors the fly as narrator. The published German and English titles seem to nail that down: "Aus dem Tagebuch einer Fliege" and "From the Diary of a Fly," in the first person. None of the titles presents the piece as an enactment, as would "A Day in the Life of a Fly," although that might be the more precise way of characterizing the experience of it, and there are some suggestions of that in the "performance" or "expressive" marks written into the score.

At a certain moment there is an increase in tempo, indicated by a metronome marking and the word *Agitato* above the system. Between the two staves at that point are the words *molto agitato e lamentoso*. The moment is easily recognizable in performance. Also above the system at that point are the Hungarian words "Jaj, pokhalo!!"—"Yikes, a spider web!!" Ten measures later, above the system, are the words *con gioia, leggero*. A linguistic *mélange* of performance direction, characterization, and enactment; narrative, lyric, drama, inseparably conveyed by the music, exemplifying what Mendelssohn put his finger on, the insufficiency of language to say precisely what it is that music does, making dubious the classifications of poetic categories as tokens of what we experience. In our ordinary exchanges of language we take the *words* that are uttered by our fellow interlocutors as clues to what they have in mind to convey to us, not as fixed and invariable coinage.

Hayden White writes of the "cognitive contents" of musical works.[38] Reacting to the way the harmonic progress of the first movement of Beethoven's Seventh Symphony is prefigured in its introduction as a "prolepsis" (recall Marquez's "foreboding," but notice the difference in stance between "prolepsis" and "foreboding"; White was addressing a scholarly conference), he calls that a "narrational" relationship. The awareness of such categories, he suggests—others are "actions," "events," "conflicts," "development over time," "crisis," "climax," "denouement"—is a kind of tacit preknowledge, like the knowledge of a mother tongue. The point of the comparison is that a mother tongue is the language we speak and understand most directly, in the least mediated way, because we begin to learn it from the beginning of our consciousness, or before. And that is when we begin to learn those categories of experience, which are to us intrinsic qualities. We know them in a non-discursive as well as discursive way. This is the "structural reciprocity" between the temporality of human existence and narrativity to which Paul Ricoeur refers when he writes, "I take temporality to be that structure of existence that reaches language in narrativity and narrativity to be the language structure that has temporality as its ultimate referent."[39] In like manner, narrativity in music is that structure that has temporality as its ultimate referent.

Mikrokosmos vol. 6, no. 144 is entitled "Minor Seconds, Major Sevenths." Nevertheless I experience it, just as much as the "Fly" piece, which might have been called "Overlapping Whole-Tone Segments," in terms of the same sorts of "narrativizing" categories, but not at the expense of the minor seconds and major sevenths, which are controlled in a very beautiful way. It is marked *Molto adagio, mesto,* by the way.

Neither the narrative nor the formalist title alone can reveal what either piece is all about. There are other titles in the *Mikrokosmos* that suggest sonorities ("Bagpipe"), genres ("Peasant Dance"), styles ("From the Island of Bali"), actions ("Wrestling"), characters ("Merry Andrew"); different emphases, but none tells what the piece is all about, and none excludes the other categories. One could associate a different aesthetic or historiographic theory with almost every category. But the lesson I draw from *Mikrokosmos* is that these aspects do not compete but coexist in music, and they ought not to compete in the interpretation of music. Music is protean and its meanings span the range of human action and experience.

POSTSCRIPT

The various ways in which the concept of metaphor has been brought into the inquiry about musical meaning and expression are given an exacting and thorough analysis by Robert Hatten in his essay "Metaphor *in* Music."[40] Two fundamental positions in that analysis resonate with my reflections about this subject in the preceding pages.

First, we can make metaphors *about* music by confronting *words* from different subject domains with one another—"the mass of the piano part ... silvered and charmed into a minor key by the moonlight." And we can make metaphors (or metaphor-like effects, as I prefer) *in* music by juxtaposing moments from different domains of music with one another—the moment in the finale of Schubert's E♭-Major Trio when the theme of the second movement emerges against the background patter of the finale, or the moment in the first movement of Mozart's Symphony no. 40 in G Minor when the strings reminisce, *sotto voce,* about the principal theme over a pedal. But if we attach to a piece of music a word or words meant to characterize the music, it makes no sense to think either that we have made a metaphor because we have conjoined an expression from the verbal domain with one from the musical domain, or that in thinking we have done that, we have explained how the word characterizes the music. Nor does such a maneuver offer any gain in general understanding about musical meaning or expression, or the explanation of such understanding.

Second, true metaphor is creative; it creates new meaning not evident in either of the component terms that are conjoined. At its best metaphor cannot for that reason be paraphrased. This is an aspect of what Hatten identifies as the "interactive" theory of Max Black and Carl Hausman.[41]

Hatten begins his essay by citing George Lakoff's notion of the characterizations of concepts in terms of prototypes and exemplars, Ludwig Wittgenstein's notion of family resemblances among the different extensions of terms, and Umberto Eco's notion of a semantic space within which meanings form networks, with the implication that "metaphor" should be understood with similar breadth of meaning. In that spirit my focus is on the affect or impact or feeling of metaphor in language, and I try to recognize that kind of impact in music. I believe it can be very strong (perhaps the strongest I can think of as I write this is the moment in act 1 scene 3 of Alban Berg's *Lulu,* where the Prince, who is planning to marry Lulu, sings about his happiness at the prospect as a solo violin plays the tune of Wagner's Wedding March from *Tannhäuser.* The first four notes of the third phrase of the tune just happen to coincide with the first four notes of the tone row of Dr. Schön, who has more complicated plans about Lulu's marriage, and the violin, by way of irony, just continues the row. See chapter 8). I prefer calling such musical effects "metaphor-like" in order to avoid being bound to a set of defining criteria. Given the frequency of its occurrence, the effect of metaphor is to be seen as one of the major resources of music and music criticism.

BEING AT A LOSS FOR WORDS

1

In a brief text frequently transmitted as the last chapter (19) but occasionally also as the prologue to the *Musica enchiriadis* (Handbook on Music), written about 900, which counts as one of the founding documents of medieval European writing about music, the author laments: "[A]s in other things that we discern only partly and dimly, this discipline [of music] does not at all have a full, comprehensible explanation in this life." He goes on to enumerate the aspects of the discipline that can be explained, ticking them off as though they were child's play. "To be sure, we can judge whether the construction of a melody is proper, and distinguish the qualities of tones and modes and the other things of this art. Likewise we can adduce, on the basis of numbers, musical intervals or the sounding together of pitches and give some explanations of consonance and dissonance."

And then comes the point of the whole passage: "But in what way music has so great an affinity and union with our souls—for we know we are bound to it by a certain likeness [the word 'certain' itself suggests uncertainty]—we cannot express easily in words." The author grasps at an explanation nevertheless when he continues, "[I]t is necessary that the affects of the subjects that are sung correspond to the effect of the song, so that melodies are peaceful in tranquil subjects, joyful in happy matters, somber in sad [ones], and harsh things are said or made to be expressed by harsh melodies." But he concludes that we can see this affinity only in part and dimly: "Although our judgment can be exercised in such matters, there are many things the explanations of which are hidden in secrecy from us."[1]

This striking passage calls for reflection on its epistemological background. The *Musica enchiriadis* author's acknowledgment of the imperfect understanding "in this life" of the discipline of music, particularly with respect to the conception of "music's affinity and union with our souls" which "we cannot express easily in words" and the explanation of which "is hidden in secrecy from us," may be elucidated by way of Saint Augustine's conception about the nature of understanding and the limited capacity of words to promote it. What is reflected here is the Augustinian doctrine that knowledge or understanding is generated internally by the mind of the knower, not transmitted from without. The extreme statement of this doctrine is that "there is no teacher who teaches man knowledge except God."[2] This applies as well to doctrine that is transmitted from without and which must be similarly internalized through reason, otherwise it is no more than belief. "What I understand I also believe, but I do not understand everything that I believe."[3] As for words, "The utmost value I can attribute to words is this: they bid us to look for things [that they stand for], but they do not show them to us so that we may know them."[4] If the *Musica enchiriadis* author's words are indeed indebted to the Augustinian understanding of understanding, then we can understand that the doctrine about music and the soul was for him a belief, but one that he could not explain because he did not know it.

2

The fourteenth chapter of the *Micrologus* by Guido of Arezzo (ca. 1100), entitled "On the Tropes and on the Power of Music," begins with a lament like that of the *Musica enchiriadis*. Referring to a specific demonstration of the second part of his title (the story of David and Saul), Guido writes, "This power is fully clear only to Divine Wisdom; we, to be sure, have learned something of it, but it is veiled."[5] (He had already hinted at the obscurity of his subject by characterizing as "miraculous" the entry of the sweetness of things through the windows of the body into the heart).

Turning back to the ninth century, Aurelian of Réôme is another writer who addressed himself to the qualitative description of music. His declared task is the very practical one of discoursing on "certain rules of melodies called tones and tenors" for his brethren in the monastery. (This is essentially what Guido intends with the first part of the title of his fourteenth chapter, "On the Tropes"). As one approach to the project, Aurelian describes a domain that he identifies first as "voice" (*vox*), then as "tone" (*tonus*), then as "sound" (*sonitus*). "Musicians," he writes, "have divided its classes in fifteen parts."

> First the hyperlydian kind; second the hypodorian; third, song; fourth, arsis; fifth, thesis; sixth, sweet voices that are thin and intense, loud and high; seventh, where there are clear voices which sustain fairly long like the trumpet; eighth, where there are thin voices, like those of infants or musical strings; the ninth is fat, as are the voices of men; tenth is where the voice is sharp, thin, and high, like strings; eleventh, where there is a hard voice that is emitted violently, like hammers on an anvil; twelfth, where the voice is rough; thirteenth, in which the voice is blind because it stops as soon as it is emitted; fourteenth, where the sound is tremulous; fifteenth, where the voice is perfect: high, sweet and loud.[6]

If classifying is cutting up at natural joints, as Socrates says in Plato's *Phaedrus,* then the body joined together of these parts seems truly grotesque.

Edward Nowacki has shown the way to unscramble Aurelian's classification. It is a conflation of elements of the concepts of *tonus* and *cantus* in chapter 19 of the "De musica" in Book 3 of the *Etymologies* of Isidore of Seville (ca. 560–636).[7] Isidore defines *tonus* as "the high enunciation of the voice" and also as the "variation and quantity of a harmonia [which has connotations of what we call 'mode']." "Musicians," he continues, "have divided the tones into fifteen kinds, of which the hyperlydian is the last and highest and the hypodorian is the lowest of all." So here begins Aurelian's model. (Isidore's model may have been the *De musica* of Cassiodorus [ca. 485–580], where fifteen such *tonoi* are listed.[8]) Next Isidore proceeds to "song" (*cantus,* Aurelian's third category), which is "the voice changing pitch, for sound is even-pitched; sound precedes song." The principal properties of song are "arsis, elevation of the voice, ... and thesis, lowering of the voice" (Aurelian's fourth and fifth categories), then Isidore proceeds to the qualities of the even-pitched voice. He lists ten, and those are the last ten of Aurelian's list of the "parts of the classes of tone." Tacking them on willy-nilly to the first five items in his list allowed him to reach the obligatory number fifteen. This clarifies the method through which he construed his classification, but it makes it seem all the more zany, and makes one wonder even more what in the world he could have thought he was classifying.

Perhaps it is true that Aurelian was in disgrace for some unknown offense and that he wrote his treatise primarily in order to regain the favor of his abbot, as Lawrence Gushee has written.[9] In any case his analysis is in effect an enactment of the difficulty of talking about the qualities of music by producing a piece of nonsense, perhaps in an effort to bluff his way out of his difficulties. With this interpretation I am searching for meaning in the passage not so much in its contents as in the fact of its being uttered, as a speech act or illocutionary act, aimed at achieving a certain purpose. I refer here to the philosopher J. L. Austin's conception.[10]

The *Oxford English Dictionary* has a word for "bluffing one's way through something by talking nonsense." The word is "bullshit." That is what Aurelian's classification is. It can't be verified or falsified; it is neither illuminating nor deceitful; it doesn't make any sense except when considered as a speech act, more specifically bullshit, with certain intended effects.

The philosopher Harry Franklin, in his book *On Bullshit,* the most well-known of a recent spate of writings aiming to theorize the concept of bullshit as a category of language communication, puts it that the essence of bullshit is its indifference to the question of true or false in distinction to the notion of lying, which implicitly acknowledges a truth by claiming its opposite.[11] The object of bullshit is thus more to create a certain impression than to inform or to misinform.

The way to speech act theory and bullshit theory was opened by a turn in the philosophy of language that I have still to speak of. The current interest in bullshit theory, I have no doubt, is a response to very worrisome political and cultural conditions, which provide the context, more broadly, for a proliferation of writings in England and North America on truth. (A former Vice President of the United States proclaimed several years ago that "the insurgency in Iraq, if you will, has about run its course." To say that was an untruth would not be false, but it would fall short of catching the illocutionary significance of the utterance in a discourse in which speakers are indifferent to truth and in which the political effectiveness of language trumps inquiry into what is or is not so.)

Returning to Guido, despite the resonance of his concluding words with the lament of the *Musica enchiriadis* author, he is hardly at a loss for words when it comes to gaining access to the mysteries of music. On the contrary, he displays the most virtuosic, I would even say sly, manipulation of the resources of language.

First there is metaphor. The "tropes" of his title are the various melodic idioms of the modes, each with its own discrete character, or "face" (I mean that as a metaphor, not as a literal translation of *facies*. But Guido means it as a metaphor as well, as he indicates with his phrase "so to say, the individual features of these tropes.") The face is what looks out on the world and what the world principally recognizes about its possessor. And recognition as an empirical act—specifically through hearing—is the point of the fourteenth chapter's opening. But the metaphor is then put in the service of the next resource, analogy, by way of its de-metaphorization, to coin a term (is "coin" in that sentence a metaphor? Actually not. It was a verb, meaning "to make or stamp" before it was adapted for the piece of money that was coined.) The recognition of the tropes by their features is likened to the recognition of the nationality of men by their features, but now we are reading "faces" literally in retrospect.

To work this trick Guido is exploiting the dichotomy of the literal and the metaphorical, which was invented by Aristotle—invented, not in the sense that he invented the concepts of literal and metaphorical meanings, but that he asserted their opposite workings in language and declared them to be appropriate to the language of what he held to be opposite intellectual enterprises, specifically physics and poetry, respectively. Nothing can make this more apparent than the following remark from the *Meteorologica*: "Empedocles' notion of the salt sea as the sweat of the earth is 'adequate, perhaps, for poetic purposes', but 'inadequate for understanding the nature of the thing.'"[12] Another, still more restrictive remark, comes from the *Topics*: "Every metaphorical expression is obscure."[13]

But Aristotle could also say, in the *Generation of Animals,* that "the Gods use a good metaphor when they jokingly call white hairs the mould and hoarfrost of old age,"[14] and even more interesting, he anticipated a very modern view of metaphor in writing, in the *Rhetoric,* "When the Poet [Homer?] calls old age stubble, he produces a new idea, new knowledge."[15] That suggests for us the interesting question that has been debated through the ages, with answers enacted now in one direction, now in the other: Does the interpretation and explanation of music call for a language of "physics" or one of "poetry"?

Guido straddles the question. His next move is back into the domain of metaphor. One trope is characterized by its broken leaps, another as voluptuous, another as garrulous, another as suave. Am I right to invoke "metaphor" here? How are those designations metaphoric? Can melodies make "broken leaps" "literally?" If they cannot, do we speak "literally" when we speak of melodic movement? Can melodies be voluptuous "literally"? If they cannot, can they be beautiful "literally?" What kind of language does the interpretation and explanation of music call for?

What is the difference between "voluptuous" and "beautiful"? "Voluptuous" seems to pinpoint a particular kind of beauty, and Guido uses it because of his interest in speaking of the "discrete faces" of the different tropes. His motive contradicts Aristotle's judgment about the "obscurity" of metaphor. Guido chooses metaphor for the preciseness of its predication. But that raises the question again whether Guido's characterizations should be judged according to the standards of scientific or those of poetic language. If there is a dichotomy of the literal and the metaphorical—my "if" here is emphatic—there is certainly a question about the location of the boundary dividing them.

The experiential or phenomenological nature of Guido's analysis is brought home by the analogy with the other senses and their objects—sight, smell, and taste. But this passage goes beyond perception to effect: the hearing is delighted, the vision rejoices, the sense of smell is caressed, and the tongue exults.

3

A sort of backhanded justification of metaphor was provided by a follower of Aristotle's strictures against metaphor in the discourse of science, and, interestingly enough, it is for its use in a subject domain to which Guido addressed himself in chapter 14 of the *Micrologus*. I refer to Galen, the second-century writer on medicine. Heinrich von Staden has written,

> Galen, aware that one of the more treacherous obstacles faced by science is its own textuality—that science cannot do without language but that language constantly threatens to ambush the scientist, Galen repeatedly turns to aspects of the relation of science to language in his medical writings . . . Several of his treatises are devoted exclusively to language.[16]

Confronting a challenge to his deployment of the literal/metaphorical dichotomy from things for which there are no names—anonyms or ineffables—Galen writes,

> After all, since all tangible things have names, it is lengthy rubbish to introduce other names for them on the basis of metaphors. In the case of smells, admittedly, there really are not names for all the qualities (he means literal names), and one might therefore allow that, by transferring (*metapheronta*), we use words that belong elsewhere. . . . [F]or a person who has already acquired acquaintance with the nameless thing, it is permissible, for the sake of succinct clarification, to indicate the thing that is being spoken of by means of words based on metaphor.[17]

In other words, metaphor is permissible for the initiate as a shortcut to instant clarification—for example, Guido's persons who are well trained in the recognition of tropes, or who are familiar with the habits of different peoples.

Galen confronts yet another challenge to his conception of the literal/metaphorical dichotomy: words that can have multiple meanings or that can be coupled with other words to denote widely different things. His example is the word "hard," as in a hard voice, a hard life, a hard wine, a hard wind, hard to bargain with, a hard task, a hard person. His response to the challenge is rather weak: "It is not literally and primarily that we say each of all the other things (which we call hard) is hard, but we name them thus both accidentally and by transference from some similarity."[18] The similarity of a hard life to a hard task may seem self-evident, but that of a hard wine to a hard wind, and of those together to a hard task and a hard life is not. There we would have to resort to "accident," which is no explanation at all. In any case, Galen appeals to the authority of both Plato and Aristotle. Von Staden puts it that

> [b]oth authors discovered one meaning of each of the two words (hard and soft), at least when one uses them literally and not figuratively, seeing that there will be a countless multitude of meanings in the case of metaphors, and not only countless meanings of these two words but also of all other signifiers.[19]

Galen would probably have been critical of Guido's characterizations of the tropes. Such quality words as voluptuous, garrulous, luxuriant, and suave are like "hard," potentially qualifying a wide range of things. But that is just what makes them available for the characterization of music. Plato, recall, found a metaphor that targeted with the utmost precision what it is we want in a classification scheme.

4

The condition of the univocality of words is a sine qua non for the literal, and underlying both is a conception of language meaning that stymied the *Musica enchiriadis* author, that Guido, followed by commentators on music through the Middle Ages and into the age of humanism, defied and circumvented, and that remains embroiled in controversies about the nature of language to the present. It is the conception of a fixed one-to-one link between words and the things they name. This conception, in the words of Saint Augustine's narrative about his learning of language as a child, was brought onstage by Ludwig Wittgenstein in his *Philosophical Investigations* as the jumping-off point for the exhaustive problematization of that language conception that is the enterprise of his book. The core of Augustine's narrative from which one might get the impression that he held such a language conception is the account of how his elders named some object and accordingly moved toward something.

> I saw this and I grasped that the thing was called by the sound they uttered when they meant to point it out . . . Their intentions were shown by their bodily movements, as it were the natural language of all peoples: the expression of the face, the play of the eyes, the movements of the other parts of the body, and the tone of voice which expresses our state of mind in seeking, having, rejecting, or avoiding something. Thus as I heard words repeatedly used in their proper places in various sentences I gradually learned to understand what objects they signified; and after I had trained my mouth to form these signs, I used them to express my own desires.[20]

It is with this passage that Wittgenstein begins the *Philosophical Investigations*.[21]

For the record we ought to consider just how fairly Wittgenstein has represented Augustine's language concept in adapting it to his purpose. Burnyeat speaks of a "creative misprision" and characterizes Wittgenstein's representation as a "stalking horse"[22] for the language conception he aims to undermine.

Citing the same passage from Augustine's *Confessions* at the beginning of his *Brown Book,* Wittgenstein writes that "Augustine, in describing his learning of language, says that he was brought to speak by learning the names of things. It is clear that whoever says this has in mind the way a child learns such words as 'man,' 'sugar,' 'table,' etc. He does not primarily think of words like 'today,' 'not,' 'but,' 'perhaps.'"[23] Such words are swept aside by Augustine as "something that will take care of itself," as Wittgenstein puts it. This marginalization allows him to attribute to Augustine a conception of language meaning according to which "[e]very word has a meaning. This meaning is correlated with the word. It is the object for which the word stands."[24] It also encourages Wittgenstein to say of this concept that it "has its place in a primitive idea of the way language functions," and even that "it is the idea of a language more primitive ['simpler' in *The Brown Book*[25]] than ours." But Augustine meant that all words—including "today," "not," "but," "perhaps," "if," "from"—are names. That is, they name or refer to something that may be a state or condition; for example, "perhaps" and "if" can refer to a condition of uncertainty. Augustine manifestly thought of "name" with a broader sense than that of labels for concrete objects or persons. With this understanding the grounds for regarding Augustine's language and his notion of language function do not appear so readily as "primitive."

Wittgenstein's Augustine describes language teaching by "ostension." But Augustine's epistemology suggests something less elementary:

> No word shows me the thing it signifies. No word taken singly tells me what it signifies or anything about what it signifies ... [N]othing is learned by its own sign. If I am given a sign and I do not know what it is the sign of, it can teach me nothing. If I know what it is the sign of, what do I learn through the sign? ... [T]he sign is learned from knowing the thing, rather than the thing itself being learned when the sign is given.[26]

This resonates with Wittgenstein's remark: "When we say 'Every word in a language signifies something' we have so far said nothing whatsoever."[27]

Among the multitude of theories that are informed by something like the basic language conception of Wittgenstein's Augustine is the theory that Wittgenstein himself submitted in the *Tractatus logico-philosophicus,* according to which every meaningful sentence has a logical structure that corresponds to a logical structure of the world and is either an elaboration of another simpler sentence or a concatenation of simple names. Every sentence is a picture of a possible state of affairs, which must, as a result, have exactly the same formal structure as the sentence that depicts it. This conception of an exact and fixed correlation between language and the world has become known as the "picture theory" of language meaning, following Wittgenstein's own words: "A proposition is a picture of reality."[28] One therefore derives conclusions about the nature of the world from observations about the structure of sentences. The world consists primarily of facts corresponding to true sentences, rather than of things, and those facts, in turn, are concatenations of simple objects corresponding to the simple names of which the atomic sentences are composed.

This conception differs from the Augustinian one principally in the nature of the connection between sentences and the realities they depict—isomorphism in the conception of Wittgenstein's *Tractatus*, association in the conception of Augustine. What they share is their provision of a foundation for a conception of literal meaning for a language whose function is reference or signification and description, based on a concept of meaning that predicates a fixed relation between language and reality. Aristotle's reservations about the use of metaphorical language in argument and physics can be seen as arising out of an underlying conception of language as a system of signifiers.

5

The essence of Wittgenstein's retraction of this idea that is embodied in his later *Philosophical Investigations* is a view of language as a creative activity on the part of both sender and receiver. Sentences are not to be taken as pictures of facts, and the simple components of sentences do not all function as names of simple objects. "One cannot guess how a word functions. One has to look at its use and learn from that."[29] The meaning of words is not elucidated by attending to the unique and fixed links between words and things or words and facts or sentences and states of affairs, but by attending their use in the stream of life. "To imagine a language means to imagine a form of life."[30] Understanding language is similarly not a matter of following linguistic rules as though they were logic machines that churn out applications independently of us; it is an ability to act creatively in response to language, to create meaning in exchanges that Wittgenstein calls "language games."[31] In this conception language is limited to neither a single underlying logical structure nor a uniform function. It is a host of different activities, used to describe, report, inform, affirm, deny, speculate, command, ask, tell stories, play—to act, entice, urge, provoke, incite, and much else. No unitary account can be given that explains the whole working of language in terms of a single theoretical model. The term "language game" is meant to bring into prominence the fact that the speaking of language is an activity.

I believe that my reading of Guido's fourteenth chapter shows him stirring up an imaginative understanding in the reader, without necessarily being open to Aristotle's and Galen's charge that metaphor grants license to read many meanings into the same expression—the charge of multivocality.

I'll illustrate that with a passage from the very essay on Galen that I've cited. Near the end of his essay von Staden writes,

> To secure scientific truth, one must . . . not only conduct scientific investigations according to proven logical and methodological principles, but also, in Galen's view, *ferret out* [my emphasis]—(may Galen pardon a wild animal metaphor for human scientific activity) and thus expose, the metaphors of precursors, recent and distant.[32]

Whatever Galen might have thought of this metaphor, it seems that von Staden is playing a little ironic language game of his own. His use of the word "ferret" summons to our mind's eye the sharpest, most precise possible image of Galen's frenzied and zealous digging for the metaphors of his precursors that have, he charges, caused so much confusion and imprecision. No single non-metaphorical word could possibly provide as vivid a representation of the activity. The three words that I have just used ("frenzied zealous digging") do not approach the animation of "ferret." It is like the difference between a motion picture scene and its verbal description. Nor is there risk of our heaping multiple meanings onto the metaphor.

I would like to underscore this point with a drawing (Figure 2.1). I would call it a visual metaphor. I've learned something important from it and others like it. It is that the effect of metaphor depends, among other things, on our reading every word in a metaphor literally. This is a central point in a number of modern theories about metaphor. It somewhat undermines from one side the dogma about the opposition between the literal and the metaphorical. It is undermined on the other side by the observation that language—and not just language about music, as Hanslick implied—is through and through

FIGURE 2.1. "Flying in the face of reason."
Drawing by Mary Frank. Used by permission.

metaphorical. This attitude to language, I think, supports an understanding of metaphor not as direct conveyor of meaning but as stimulus to its creation by the listener or reader.

Returning once more to Guido: with his observations about the effects of sensory stimulation he moves into the subject indicated by the second part of his title, the power of music; and it becomes clear why he treats the two subjects in the same chapter. And for this he brings on the figure of allegory. Stories of extreme events are adduced as testimony to this power—no mention of Orpheus and Eurydice, but events that might be reported by a journalist or in a book on music therapy: a madman cured of his madness by music, a man brought to the point of rape by one kind of music and then made to back off at the last moment by another kind. Whether or not it was so intended, such episodes in the mortal world ask for and imply the possibility of explanation, in contrast to the Orpheus legend, where events are under the control of supernatural forces. But no explanations are forthcoming, and Guido registers that with the remark I've already cited, that this power is fully clear only to divine wisdom. The sense that he has come to the limit of what can be explained is made explicit in the concluding sentence: "But as we have touched upon something—even if only a little—of the power of this art, let us see what is required in order to make good melodies."[33] In other words, let's stop complaining and get down to brass tacks.

6

The counter-openings of Schumann's article on "Chopin's Piano Concertos" (see chapter 1) embody a theme that shadows the history of music in Western culture: the urge to speak of music and the lament that one cannot do so; the retreat into silence, the limits of language, the appeal to reason, to the imagination, to the senses, to poetry when one tries nevertheless. But if language is inadequate for describing the qualities and experience of music, then it is no better suited for describing phenomena and experiences in many other realms of life. The fault may lie less in the shortcomings of language than in our expectations of its role—more specifically in the assumption that it functions as a medium of cognition for knowledge that may not be verbal.

Undermining that assumption was an objective of the Hungarian chemist, medical doctor, and philosopher Michael Polanyi in his book *Personal Knowledge: Toward a Post-Critical Philosophy*. In his introduction he writes, "We can know more than we can tell . . . We know a person's face, and can recognize it among a thousand, indeed a million. But we usually cannot tell how we recognize a face. So most of this knowledge cannot be put into words."[34] Two phenomena mentioned by Polanyi about which we have tacit knowledge will provide an immediate sense of what he was identifying: keeping our balance when riding a bicycle, and the sound of a clarinet.

The essential insight about the uses and limitations of language embodied in this challenge is central to the *Philosophical Investigations*. There Wittgenstein wrote, "Compare knowing and saying:

how many feet high Mont Blanc is—
How the word "game" is used—
  How a clarinet sounds—

If you are surprised that one can know something and not be able to say it you are perhaps thinking of a case like the first. Certainly not of one like the third."[35]

Polanyi's first example, face recognition, is more telling. I invite the reader to pursue it by way of three thought experiments.

1. You are asked to visualize a face so well known that it has achieved the status of an icon—say, Marilyn Monroe's or Albert Einstein's face. I believe the image presented to the mind's eye of anyone familiar with either will be very vivid, very distinct. Now imagine that you are asked to write a description of it but without identifying the person. Copies of your description are distributed widely and all are asked whose face you have described. How large do you imagine the percentage of correct identifications will be? This experiment has been performed by a team of cognitive psychologists under controlled conditions, and as you may have surmised, the percentage is always very low.

2. We are all asked to visualize a familiar face whose owner has been specified, and each of us is to write a description of it. We exchange and compare descriptions several times, and many different faces are described. This experiment, too, has been performed with just that result.

3. Here is the most significant experiment: all of us are shown a photograph of an unfamiliar face and told to study it carefully in order to learn its features. Half of us are told to write a description of the face. Then all of us are asked to pick out the photograph we have studied from a large collection of photographs of generally similar looking persons in generally similar environments. Which group is more successful in that task? It is the group that did not write a description, as you might have surmised, and significantly so every time.

All of these experiments and many others like them have been performed by a group under the leadership of Jonathan Schooler, professor of psychology at the University of Pittsburgh in the United States, working in the 1990s. I'll try to summarize what might be relevant to my subject from what they think they have learned.[36]

The apperception and recall of such visual images is under the control of cognitive processes that do not entail verbalization. They are, as Schooler puts it, "non-reportable," "non-verbalizable," or "non-descriptive."[37] We might say they are "ineffable." The domain of such non-verbal cognition is very broad, including the perception of forms, macrospatial relations, taste, smell, hearing—the perception of music, for example—affective decision-making (for instance, the recognition and judging of wines), insight problem-solving, as when we have a sudden "aha" reaction or epiphany, color recognition, emotional states or feelings, and creative activity such as improvising drama or music.[38] Music is far from alone in its ineffableness, which is neither its unique problem nor its unique appeal.

7

Schooler's interpretation of the experiments involving efforts to describe wordless cognition in words is that such efforts interfere with the functioning of wordless cognition. He calls this "verbal overshadowing." The activity of the left brain has interfered with, "overshadowed," the activity of the right brain. When the effort is made nevertheless, the focus is usually on whatever verbalizable attributes that mode of cognition may have, to the neglect of the non-verbalizable aspects. Isn't that just what the author of the *Musica enchiriadis* reports? Every generation of writers on music in the West since the first has had its own focus within the range of what we tend to call technical attributes of the art, or "music theory," that lend themselves to verbal description: pitch, intervals, tone systems, modes, counterpoint, rhythm and meter and their notation, harmony, form. These topics might be thought to constitute the ontology of music. And the increasing dedication to the aim of rhetoric to move the soul in writing about and composing music might be seen in terms of an increasingly successful determination of such writers to overcome language's interference with what they felt.

8

What I have been reviewing here comes together in agreement about one thing: that the simple image that Wittgenstein winnowed as "stalking horse" from Augustine's *Confessions,* of language as words that name things and thereby picture the world, hardly matches the experience of saying and knowing. But what it all comes to in positive terms is less easy to say. It is a bewildering complex of different and sometimes opposing variations on the same subject. If I try to think of a single configuration in which the different voices and what they have to say can be staged, what comes to mind is a Mozartian opera finale in which all the main characters are onstage and all have something to say, whether all together or individually, or in various smaller groupings reflecting their opinions and reactions.

As I imagine the scene, Wittgenstein has given his reading of Augustine in a recitative. Galen sings in canon with Aristotle, "Yes. One word, one thing," but each of them takes off in his own flight of improvisation about the accident of multiple meanings and the possibility of metaphor. The masked *Musica enchiriadis* author, Guido, Florestan, and Mendelssohn—musicians all—protest that it doesn't work that way for music so they hum, like Papageno with his mouth locked shut, the *Musica enchiriadis* author and Guido in especially melancholic tones of lamentation. Guido, however, resolutely breaks off and spins out one metaphor after another, and Aurelian, taking his cue from Guido, enters with a patter song on the theme, "Just say anything." Augustine and Wittgenstein, looking at each other, sing *sotto voce,* "Does he know what he's saying?" The *Musica enchiriadis* author, Guido, Wittgenstein, and Polanyi take up the tune, but in retrograde: "You can know things that you can't say." At the end of the scene Schooler, who hasn't yet been seen, steps forward from the back of the stage with a warning in deep tones like those of Pluto in *L'Orfeo,* "That may be just as well; if you say what you know, your words can muddy the water."

9

The continuation of this history would trace its ups and downs—the ascendancy of rhetoric among the humanists, the effort in the nineteenth century to restrict the domain of the musical to the verbalizable (and to the language of "science," taking up again the question provoked by Aristotle's bipolar attitude about language), with the consignment of everything else said to the category of the "extra-musical," Eduard Hanslick's famous book *On the Musically Beautiful* that bars "the shabby aesthetic of feeling" and language that promotes it; concomitantly and at the other extreme (the poetic), E. T. A. Hoffman describing the unfolding of his novel *Die Elixir des Teufels* in sections that could be marked *grave sostenuto, andante sostenuto e piano,* and *allegro forte,* and his Kapellmeister Kreisler describing how he once bought a coat in the unusual key of C♯ minor, which so alarmed his friend that he hastily had sewn onto it a collar in the more decorous key of E♭ major; language that calls for a fuller exposition about the useful categories of speech acts and bullshit; a sidelong glance at the visual arts, wondering whether—when Constable describes a painting as "pearly, deep, and mellow" and Roger Fry characterizes Matisse's line as "rhythmic" and "elastic"—anyone worries about these qualities as extra-pictorial; an expansion on the fact that language about wine has come up in two such disparate connections as Galen's rationalizations about the multivocality of language and Schooler's experiments about the ineffable.

Speaking of wine is suggestive for the problem of speaking of music. Just now I can only hint at that by quoting the epigraph of Adrienne Lehrer's book, *Wine and Conversation,* one of the most enlightening studies of the uses of language that I have encountered.

> You can talk about wine as if it were a bunch of flowers (fragrant, heavily perfumed), a packet of razor blades (steely), a navy (robust, powerful), a troupe of acrobats (elegant and well-balanced), a successful industrialist (distinguished and rich), a virgin in a Bordello (immature and giving promise of pleasure to come), Brighton beach (clean and pebbly), even a potato (earthy), or a Christmas pudding (plump, sweet and round).[39]

These words call to mind another provocative paragraph in the *Philosophical Investigations:*

> Describe the aroma of coffee.—Why can't it be done? Do we lack the words? And for what are the words lacking?—But how do we get the idea that such a description must after all be possible? Have you ever felt the lack of such a description? Have you tried to describe the aroma and not succeeded?[40]

Lehrer's book reports on a language-user community in which precisely these questions are addressed. The few lines of her epigraph underscore two fundamental principles of language communication: (1) that multivocality (a more accurate word than "ambiguity") of words and word groups is not only common but essential for communication, and that this undermines the notion of a duality of the literal and the metaphorical; (2) that each enduring link between words and referents is invented, arbitrary, and becomes conventional through use, and that the search for the "original" reference of a word or word group—while it may be historically interesting—does not yield a hierarchy of the literal and the metaphorical. Lehrer's study of language about wine shows that words and referents, saying and knowing, are co-creations.

I close with a few beautiful words of E. M. Forster, speaking in an essay appropriately entitled "Word-Making" of the conclusion of the *Andante* of Beethoven's Fourth Piano Concerto: "The strings and winds sink at last into acquiescence with true love,"[41] and wonder why we shouldn't take those words literally.

3

BEETHOVEN'S "EXPRESSIVE" MARKINGS

When Beethoven wrote the words *Largo e mesto* at the head of the second movement of his Piano Sonata op. 10, no. 3, what was his intention? In Italian-English dictionaries those words are translated "broad" and "mournful," respectively. They will also be found in music dictionaries, such as the excellent *New Harvard Dictionary of Music,* which is useful both as a technical and historical lexicon and as a guide to the common usage of musical terms. *Largo* is identified there as a tempo: very slow according to eighteenth-century witnesses, the slowest of the four principal divisions of tempo.[1] Think of "Ombra mai fu," the aria at the beginning of Handel's comic opera *Serse,* a humorous apostrophe to a shade tree, marked *Larghetto* by Handel but now lodged in many minds as "Handel's *Largo,*" thus transposed into a piece of ritual pomp. Beethoven's intention in writing *Largo* in 1798, then, was simply to provide a stage direction, conveying to the pianist the speed at which the piece is to be played. Or is it really that simple and straightforward?

Mesto is in the *New Harvard Dictionary of Music* as well, but without a clue about performance, nothing more than what is offered by the Italian-English dictionary: "sad," or "mournful."[2] The *Harvard Dictionary*'s silence on the question of *mesto* as performance direction is telling. But so is its inclusion of the word in the first place, which makes of it a technical term in discourse about music. Does "mournful" seem like a technical term? Why do we more readily accept the Italian word as such? The English and Italian words have the same meaning, after all. Or do they, really? This little question throws us immediately up against the reality that the meaning of a language utterance is not given just by consulting a lexicon but that meaning is bestowed by the way we use language.

Composers have long written the word *mesto* at the beginnings of their scores, among them C. P. E. Bach, at the slow movement of the fifth of the eighteen sonatas presented as *Probestücke* with his *Versuch über die wahre Art das Clavier zu spielen: Adagio assai mesto e sostenuto;* Joseph Haydn, the slow movement of the String Quartet op. 76, no. 5: *Largo. Cantabile e mesto;* Georg Philipp Telemann, *Sonate metodiche* op. 13, no. 6, third movement: *Mesto;* Beethoven, the slow movement of the String Quartet op. 59, no. 1: *Adagio molto e mesto;* Frederic Chopin, Mazurka op. 33, no. 4: *Mesto;* Johannes Brahms, Trio for Piano, Violin, and Horn op. 40, third movement: *Adagio mesto;* Brahms, Intermezzo in E♭ Minor op. 118, no. 6: *Largo e mesto;* Béla Bartók, the motto that precedes each of the four movements of his String Quartet No. 6: *Mesto;* Bartók, *Mikrokosmos,* vol. 6, no. 144: *Molto adagio. mesto;* Roger Sessions, the opening movement of his Symphony No. 8: *Mesto.*

Before its appearance as any kind of designation in a score, the word appeared in discussions of musical character, a subject as old as any in writing about music in the Western tradition. Jacopo Peri, in the foreword to his opera *Euridice* of 1601, wrote of the mournful (*mesto*) airs of Orfeo, Arcetro, and Dafne, an affect he says he achieved through "the use of false proportions, played and sung without hesitation, discreetly and precisely."[3]

This usage has earned *mesto* its place in music dictionaries. It identifies an item with a long tradition in a vocabulary of musical *affects* that Beethoven inherited and passed on. And since the *affect* to which it refers has so long a musical tradition, it is reasonable to ask whether that tradition includes a style of playing. The *New Harvard Dictionary* seems to imply generally that it would, in its entry "Performance marks," which are identified as "words, abbreviations, and symbols employed along with the notation of pitch and duration to indicate aspects of performance. These may be tempo indications, dynamic marks, technical instructions, marks for phrasing and articulation, and *designations for the character of the piece or section*" [my emphasis].[4]

That requires some thought. I have emphasized the last phrase because on its face it does something strange with language. It says that a word that seems outfitted to *describe* a state of feeling or a character quality *incites* a behavior. There is a chance of learning something about our use of language about music from this sort of thing. The phrase prompts the question, just *how* does a designation of character serve as a performance indication when it seems to say only what the character of the piece is? But first comes the question, does it really even do that? What does it mean to predicate of a sequence of sound patterns that it is "mournful?" To Peri it meant that it comprises certain kinds of imperfect consonances—false proportions combined in certain ways in its constituent harmonies.

I am trying to force out two questions: How is the piece *mournful* (as distinct from some other affective state)? and more fundamentally, How is the *piece* mournful (how can any piece be characterized in terms of an affective state)? Focus on the second: Is it the way we are mournful over the loss of someone close to us? Certainly not, if we mean by that the feeling of mournfulness that we have; music can't have feelings in that sense. But perhaps we mean how someone would describe the way we look and act in those circumstances. Wittgenstein compared musical expression to the expression on a person's face.[5] We don't find out how Peri would have thought about that. He might simply have meant that *mesto* is the name, that is, the label, for the musical character of the "false relations" and the music in which they occur—whatever that character is, it is called *mesto*.

A symposium during the 1972 Congress of the International Musicological Society provoked these reflections for me through its focus on the slow movement of Beethoven's Piano Sonata op. 10, no. 3. Ludwig Finscher, one of the participants, brought fresh language and a correspondingly fresh perspective in his contribution. He asked, "How, in what measure, with what means, does Beethoven's performance designation *Largo e mesto* find its *analogue* in the musical material and process of the movement?"[6] With this formulation Finscher found a way to assuage the frustration inherent in the subject in view of the ambiguous position of such annotations between character designations and performance indications. The important new term is analogue, which poses a relationship between the words of such annotations and the music they annotate that is an alternative to the commonly held conception of a linkage in which "the individual words in language name objects [and the meaning of each word] is the object for which the word stands."[7]

Perhaps it is because we approach the question about the relation between the annotation and the music with tacit expectations born of such an idea of language as picturing the things and states of affairs in the world that the question resists settling: Is it facts about performance or about the music that the words picture, and in either case, what facts? It is a value of Beethoven's practice in writing such annotations that it forces questions that put this conception of meaning in language to the test.

In order to make this account fully reflective of the language concept that is challenged by Beethoven's practice, it must be filled out with reference to an aspect that is implicit in the description already given, but that was made fully explicit by George Lakoff and Mark Turner in their critique of the "theory of literal meaning" in their book *More Than Cool Reason* (see chapter 1). Approaching Beethoven's annotation from the viewpoint of such a theory, we would expect that the movement could be described unambiguously as mournful without dragging that word out of its own semantic reference field (or that it could be performed in a way that could be unambiguously so described). If we cannot obtain general agreement about that possibility it may be because the reference field of "mournful" (or "mournfully") is not unambiguously delineated, or because Beethoven's movement or music in general (or the performance of either) lies outside of that field, or, as I believe, because Beethoven's use of language in such annotations is not governed by such a concept at all.

In any case, no one claims explicitly that a word like *mesto* can describe music in accordance with the expectations of such a conception of language. Instead, there has sprung up a rash of claims—inspired by Eduard Hanslick in the mid-nineteenth century but gone quite out of control in recent years— that the mediation between music and language about it is metaphorical and hardly, if at all, literal. As for the commonplace talk of a duality of the "musical" and the "extramusical" and the corollary labeling of musical meaning or expression as "metaphorical," these linked dualities are in themselves rather incoherent conceptions, yet at the same time perfectly understandable in the evolving context of music conceptions in the nineteenth and twentieth centuries in which they arose and have recently been given new life. Finscher concretized the question: "What *sense* [*Sinn*] do the motive of the first measure and the theme that is developed from it have? . . . Do motive and theme follow a musical type that might at the same time be an expressive type, both individualized in the particular piece?"—again the gesture of positing a conventional duality in order to mediate between its supposedly exclusive sides and thereby to dissolve the boundaries between them. The historian, then, has the task of elucidating the historical background of such an association of character type with musical material and process, whereby Finscher suggests "the melancholy trope, the 'speaking' motivic style, and the speech-like tempo rubato clearly point back to C. P. E. Bach."[8] The factor of history is crucial for this conception, for it establishes the basis for the recognition of such correspondences in practice, as is shown by the brief survey reported at the beginning of this chapter.

These remarks of Finscher are made under the heading *Zum Inhaltsproblem* (On the problem of content). In modern German musical scholarship, the concept of musical "content" (*Inhalt*) has had a special meaning not so familiar to us in Anglophone musical criticism. The sense of it is most closely akin to our word "meaning," and it refers to the analogical relationship between musical materials and processes on one side and character on the other. At the time of the discussion in Copenhagen, the idea that the word "content" should refer to anything other than the notes and their patterns would have been thought strange by musical scholars in North America.

One of the principal differences between the histories of musical studies and of the study of visual art is that art history has, on the whole, not been constrained by so narrow a conception of its objects. The art historian Erwin Panofsky has explicitly denied what would have been the exact counterpart of the view of the musical object that held sway at the time he was writing: "Anyone confronted with a work of art, whether aesthetically re-creating or rationally investigating it, is affected by its three constituents: materialized form, idea (that is, in the plastic arts, subject matter) and content. The pseudo-impressionistic theory according to which 'form and color tell us about form and color, that is all,' is simply not true."[9] This reveals as too simple and too superficial the attribution of the more constrained critical practice in music history, as compared to art history, to music's lack of an explicit semantic content.

In the same essay, Panofsky articulated a conception of the artwork comprising its idea—"the meaning to be transmitted or . . . the function to be fulfilled"; its form—which may be in balance with the idea but can eclipse it; and its content—which emerges the more clearly, the more the idea and the form are in balance. Content, as opposed to subject matter, wrote

Panofsky, is a matter of "the basic attitude of a nation, a period, a class, a religious or philosophical persuasion—all this unconsciously qualified by one personality, and condensed into one work." It "may be described . . . as that which a work betrays but does not parade." If either idea or form is emphasized or suppressed relative to the other, the revelation of content will be obscured. "A spinning machine is perhaps the most impressive manifestation of a functional idea, and an 'abstract' painting is perhaps the most expressive manifestation of pure form, but both have a minimum of *content*."[10] We may not have seen so elegant a formulation regarding the musical work, but judging from recent writing about music, we are, it seems, at least ready to try.

In modern music criticism, the subject of musical content has been of no greater concern to anyone than it was to Heinrich Schenker, and the concept has perhaps never been given a richer, more passionate, and more moving portrayal than Schenker gave in his earlier writings.[11] Schenker's reputation in the United States has been based largely on his later work, particularly the *Fünf Urlinie-Tafeln* and *Der freie Satz*.[12] The theory embodied in these works has been characterized by Ian Bent as Schenker's "mature theory," but that should be taken only in the chronological sense of "later."[13] The doctrine of "Schenkerism," for which these works constitute a foundation, amounts to a decontextualization of Schenker's theories that is exemplified by Allen Forte's remark, in his introduction to the 1979 translation of *Der freie Satz*, about Schenker's "polemical and quasi-philosophical material." "Almost none of [this] material," Forte notes, "bears substantive relation to the musical concepts that he developed during his lifetime, and, from that standpoint, can be disregarded."[14]

It is in earlier interpretive writings, such as the monograph on Beethoven's Ninth Symphony and the explicatory editions of the last piano sonatas, that Schenker articulated a conception of musical "content" and an elucidatory style that runs quite counter to the reductionism of Hanslick.[15] The core of that concept, in Schenker's words, is "the life of tones (*Tonleben*)."[16] It must be distinguished from the relatively lifeless conception of "the combination of tones" in the theories of early formalist writers like Johann Friedrich Herbart (1776–1841), just as Schenker's conception of form as *Gedankengang* (the procession of thoughts), which defines content, must be distinguished from *Formenlehre* (the study of conventional forms), against which he polemicized all of his life.

The life of tones coincides with the human feelings of the composer; they cannot be separated. About Beethoven, Schenker writes: "Both worlds—those of the life and of the tones—flowed into one another, without losing their identities in one another."[17] But "the composer" in Schenker's conception is, I think, not to be thought of as the biographical or the historical Beethoven; it is the composer whom Edward T. Cone has posited in *The Composer's Voice* as a virtual persona.[18] But what has all this to do with "expressive marks" in Beethoven's scores? For one thing, Schenker both presents his account and represents the work itself as narrative. What he follows is the *Hauptfabel*, the main plot, the *Fortsetzung des Melos*, the continuity of the melodic thread (this anticipates recent discussions about music and narrative). Also he suggests that when Beethoven writes *espressivo* in a score it is often as a marker of that continuity—something like Schoenberg's *Hauptstimme* marking, which says, "Here is the main voice." That is a mark of the strength of Schenker's belief in the inseparability of expression and content. An equally strong indication of that is his provocative claim that if the Ninth Symphony had no dynamic signs, we would be able to enter them exactly as Beethoven himself did.[19] This is because of the integration of dynamics with cadences, modulations, the separation and binding together of formal sections.

Such annotations as I have interpreted in the sense of correspondences between words and sounding music Schenker interprets in the sense of the flowing together of the life of tones and human life. Perhaps the outstanding instance is the interpretation of the annotations in the *Adagio* of the Piano Sonata op. 110, which follow this sequence: *Recitativo, Cantabile, Arioso dolente, Perdendo le forze, dolente, Poi a poi di nuovo viventi, poi a poi tutte le corde, poi a poi più moto.* The expression *poi a poi* identifies the spiritual-physical feeling, the sonority, the movement as aspects of the same phenomenon. Here is Schenker's language:

> Where before [i.e., in the first *arioso*] the breath had always extended
> long enough here [in the second *arioso*] it is now shortened, yet because
> it lacks endurance, it suddenly breaks off and must begin a second time
> and repeats the tone that it cannot sustain, still expressively striving for
> clarity . . . Quite incomparable in figurative gesture are the abbreviations
> in bars 120–21; the breath, for which strength seems to stream in from a
> mysterious source, can already carry the tone that it wants to achieve,—it
> suddenly breaks off there in the last possible moment and looks toward the
> goal that nevertheless seems so certain to it.[20]

Schenker speaks repeatedly of both sides of the narrative—the verbal and the sounding-musical—as programmatic. These annotations function as programs, not in the sense of the historical duality of program-versus-absolute music, which runs directly counter to his conception, but in a sense that transcends the boundary between them. The work's content is the interrelation of the verbal program with the sounding music; they are parallel representations of the content.[21]

Schenker's conception comes alive especially against the background of a Romantic conception in which it is rooted and that has even deeper roots in the music concept of the Baroque. It is well articulated in a breathless publication of 1810: Johann Wilhelm Ritter's "Fragmente aus dem Nachlasse eines jungen Physikers." I cite a short passage:

> Tones are creatures that understand one another, just as we understand them. Every chord can be an understanding of tones among themselves and can come to us as an already constructed unity; . . . a chord becomes an image of a spiritual fellowship, love, friendship, etc. . . . Harmony, image, and society. There simply cannot be any human relationship, no human story, that cannot be expressed through music. . . . The spirit that speaks in music is the same as ours. . . . Besides, in tone we have to do with our image and likeness. . . . In tone we are dealing with our equal. All life is tone, and all music is as life itself, at least its image . . . But it must be possible to elevate music to the absolute complement of humankind so that everyone's understanding would be easily opened . . . Everything that can enter a person's thoughts can be expressed in in speech, and what a person can express, tone also expresses. . . . Human and tone are throughout equally inexhaustible, and equally unending in their work and their essence. Man's being and effect is tone, is language. Music is likewise language, universal; man's first. The existing languages are individualizations of music; not individualized music, but such as stand to music as the individual organs stand to the organic whole.[22]

If the reading of the word *mesto* as a performance mark depends on its correlation with the tradition of a particular affect or expression, then what of the word *serioso*, which appears for the first time in history at the head of the third movement of Beethoven's String Quartet op. 95 (1810), marked *Allegro assai vivace ma serioso*. This word did not exist in the Italian language at all until Beethoven invented it. He created it to refine further an already nuanced annotation (why he would have called for *ma* rather than *e* will become apparent presently), and on its face the resulting annotation could not possibly refer to a conventional affective or performance type. That holds for many of the annotations in Beethoven's scores that, even if the words themselves were not inventions, are new in such a role with Beethoven.

Beethoven's oeuvre marks a pivot in the history of the use of words alongside notation as musical signs, and he was well aware of and impatient with the ambiguity surrounding their use. In a letter written in 1817 to Ignaz von Mosel, a Viennese conductor, composer, and writer on music, Beethoven declares himself happy to share von Mosel's views about tempo indications that have survived from the "barbarous age of music," "for what could be more contrary to good sense, for example, than *Allegro*, which once and for all means 'cheerful' [*lustig*] and yet how very far we often are from the idea of that tempo, so that the piece itself says the very opposite of the indication."[23]

The Piano Sonata in F Minor, op. 57 (1804), known as the "Appassionata," is marked *Allegro assai* but would hardly be apprehended as "very cheerful"; the first movement of Brahms's Clarinet Sonata in F Minor, op. 120, no. 1 is *Allegro appassionato*, the second is *Allegro amabile*; Beethoven wrote *con amabilita* at the beginning of the Piano Sonata op. 110. He argues, then, for doing away with these indications altogether and replacing them with metronome marks. He did not anticipate that he would himself later use a metronome marking for the beginning of the "Hammerklavier" Sonata op. 106, which demands a tempo impossible of execution (quarter note = 138), effectively as a character indication, or that he would break his promise to his publisher Schott to provide metronome marks for the String Quartet op.131, with the outburst "hohl der Teufel allen Mechanismus" (the devil take all mechanical devices).[24] Beethoven goes on in the letter to Mosel: "It is a different matter when it comes to the words designating the character of the composition. These we cannot give up, for while the beat is actually more the body, these [words] themselves already have reference to the spirit of the piece."[25] This ambiguity about annotations could still produce the swerve at the end of the entry "Performance marks" in the *New Harvard Dictionary of Music*, from "tempo indications, dynamic marks," and so forth, to "designations for the character of the piece or section," and then to the reference to the entry "Expression marks," where, however, the conundrum is only sharpened. "Expression marks" are identified as "symbols and words or phrases . . . employed along with musical notation to guide the performance of a work in matters other than pitches and rhythms. Such marks in general affect dynamics, tempo, and articulation." But then, "the use of the term expression in this context is somewhat misleading, since whatever the nature of musical expression, it does not result exclusively or even principally from those aspects of music specified by 'expression' marks. See 'Expression marks.'"[26]

Explaining the word *allegro*, the *New Harvard Dictionary* picks up the ambiguity about which Beethoven complained. The entry first translates it as "merry, lively," then "fast," and then continues: "Although the term has been used since the seventeenth century to indicate a fast or moderately fast tempo and is the single most widely used term for such a tempo since the eighteenth century, it continued to be used into the eighteenth century as an indication of character or mood without respect to tempo."[27]

Anton Schindler, Beethoven's amanuensis and first biographer, describes a conversation he says he had with Beethoven in 1823, the subject matter of which, at least, lies in the neighborhood of these questions. Now that Beethoven biographers from Thayer to Solomon have unearthed so much inaccuracy, misinformation, and downright forgery in Schindler's record of Beethoven, their condemnation of Schindler rings with moral outrage, and the idea of calling on him as a witness can evoke scorn. But his claims, even when they are demonstrably false, are nevertheless primary historical data and must be taken into account, to be sure with all due perspicacity, in sketching a picture of what musicians thought and thought about in his day. He says when he asked Beethoven why he hadn't "indicated the poetic idea of this or that movement" from his sonatas to help the listener, Beethoven answered that the time in which he wrote his sonata was a more poetic time than the present (1823). Such indications would therefore have been superfluous. Everyone at that time felt from the *Largo* of the third Sonata in D, op. 10 the portrayal of the spiritual condition "of a melancholic person, with all the various nuances of light and shade in the image of melancholy and its phases, without requiring an annotation as the key to that."[28]

This is indeed inaccurate on its face, at least because Beethoven did "indicate the poetic idea" of the piece with an annotation that corresponds to the "spiritual condition of a melancholic person." It is nevertheless instructive that Schindler, if not Beethoven, believed that such annotations correspond to "the poetic idea" of the movement—not so far removed from Beethoven's words "character" and "spirit" in the letter to Mosel. In that sense they constitute programs; and Schindler, if not Beethoven, believed that the purpose of writing such annotations was to help the listener apprehend the poetic idea of the music. This belief is carried out in the practice of printing them on programs. Finally, Schindler, if not Beethoven, believed that such annotations were needed more in 1823 than in 1798. His explanation was that 1798 was a more poetic time; listeners could recognize the poetic idea of a piece then, but no longer in 1823. The historian oriented to the relationship between the audience and the composer might interpret the same remark in the sense that by 1823 (indeed by 1817) Beethoven had outstripped the conventional affective vocabulary of the eighteenth century in his music, and that listeners could not be expected any longer to recognize its poetic ideas; that is why they needed those annotations.

A well-documented case of the introduction of a neologism, so to speak, into the affective vocabulary of Beethoven's musical culture is the case of the spread of religious content in secular music.[29] Nietzsche described the feelings as "religious after-pains" in *Menschliches, Allzumenschliches:* "However much one thinks he has lost the habit of religion, he has not lost it to the degree that he would not enjoy encountering religious feelings and moods without any conceptual content as, for example, in music."[30] Composers throughout the nineteenth century wrote *religioso* or its equivalents into their scores. Such characterization was sufficiently common that an *American History and Encyclopedia of Music,* published in London in 1908, includes the term *religioso,* defining it as "religious, pious, devout, solemn."

A *Musikalischen Conversations-Lexikon* has the entry *Religiös:* "Solemn; a performance indication that calls for an execution corresponding to a reverent, pious mood. For vocal works of religious content such an indication is not needed because the text gives the necessary instructions. In contrast for instrumental works it is needed if the performance is to succeed in the sense and spirit of the composition."[31] In the finale of the Ninth Symphony, just after the transcendental setting of "Brüder! überm Sternenzelt muss ein lieber Vater wohnen," the chorus sings, "Ihr stürzt nieder Millionen?" Here (mm. 62–7ff.) Beethoven wrote above the orchestral score an annotation in which performance indication and character designation resonate off one another: *Adagio ma non troppo, ma divoto* (Slow, but not too much so, *but* pious). I emphasize the second "but" because it gives the really interesting twist to the annotation.

Beethoven signaled religious mood in the heading for the second movement of the Pastoral Symphony: "Shepherd's Song (or Idyll): Benevolent feelings together with thanks to the Deity following the storm. Allegretto."

At the head of the third movement of the String Quartet op. 132, he wrote: "Sacred song of thanks to the Deity from one who has recovered, in the Lydian mode." Among sketches for an uncompleted symphony, he wrote, "*Adagio Cantique*—religious song in a symphony in the old modes—Lord God we praise thee—alleluia," evidently a note to himself about the character the piece was to have, written before the notes that the performers would play were written.[32] (He went on in these annotations: "In the *adagio* a text from Greek mythology. *Cantique Eclesiastique*—in the *Allegro* a celebration of Bachus.")

There are annotations with references to feelings not in the religious domain that read like titles but that seem even less like performance directions—at least in any direct way: *La malinconia,* at the head of the fourth movement of the String Quartet op. 18, no. 6; or *Der schwer gefasste Entschluss* written at the head of the fourth movement of the String Quartet op. 135, followed immediately by *Muss es sein?* and then later twice by *Es muss sein!* This movement follows one marked *Lento assai cantante e tranquillo.* The annotations in op. 135 read like a narrative of the changing states of a restless and reflective spirit. They are verbal counterparts of the musical narrative. That is the sense of Schenker's interpretation of the verbal descriptions that Beethoven provided in the *Arioso dolente* of op. 110.

Beethoven wrote *Le-be wohl* at the beginning of the Piano Sonata op. 81a, which, independently of his intention, has taken on those words (and even more their transformed French counterpart, *Les adieux*) as its title. They correspond recognizably to the musical post-horn imitation with which the piece opens. The hyphen that Beethoven set between the two syllables of "Le-be" is as though the words would be sung. But they are not. Only the performer can recognize the whole brief annotation as a subtle and complex communication (subtler than writing *parlando* over a Bagatelle of op. 33). Beethoven's words in a sketch for the last movement of the Ninth Symphony—"Nein, diese . . . erinnern an unsre Verzweifl" (No, these . . . call up our disp[air])[33]—can have been addressed only to himself, but that is so of the musical notation in the sketch as well. Those words are part of the score, and they enact in the verbal medium the search for the last movement that is enacted in the notational medium; it is multiple representation. The relationship is one of analogy, correspondence; not description.

There is something less than satisfying about the attempt to locate the meaning and purpose of such annotations in the loop that winds from "performance mark" to "expressive mark" and back—not merely because those concepts, difficult as they are to pin down, don't quite grasp the practice, but also because the practice seems both richer and finer than the grain of those concepts. There are two fundamental underlying causes for this failure: on one side, the inadequacy of the Aristotelian language concept and its progeny, the "picture theory" and the "literal meaning theory," for explaining how such instances of language function; and on the other, the adoption of a dichotomy of the composition and the performance that underlies the very designations "expressive mark" and "performance mark."

The musical concept that is framed by this dichotomy was set out in Eduard Hanslick's book *Vom Musikalisch-Schönen* (*On the Musically Beautiful*). "Philosophically speaking," wrote Hanslick, "the composed piece, regardless of whether it is performed or not, is the completed artwork."[34] This is to say that it exists outside of ourselves, apart from our experience of it. Formalist writers on music aesthetics since the very early nineteenth century had been asserting that the beauty of music could be apprehended through reading the score alone. It did not need to be heard, hence it did not need to be performed. The work resides in its notation, according to this view, and that is the other side of the dogma that the work's notatability is the bona fides of its coherence.

But the premise that the composed piece, apart from its performance, constitutes the musical artwork, Hanslick goes on, "ought not to keep us from giving consideration to the division of music into composition and reproduction." While "the musical artwork is formed" (and resides in its notation), it is "the performance that we experience" and by implication, the work that we contemplate. The further implication is that the beauty of the musical work is not a matter of experience, for beauty is the property of the work, not of the performance. Hanslick writes, "The composer works . . . for posterity"—the work is enduring, unchanging—"the performer [works] in impetuous flight . . . , for the moment of fulfillment." But then he challenges that as a rhetorical device, teetering on the edge of his position. "Of course the performer can deliver only what is already in the composition; this demands not much more than playing the right notes. Some say that the performer has only to fathom and reveal the spirit of the composer. Fair enough. In the instant of recreation, however, this very assimilation is the work of . . . the performer's spirit." Hanslick is trying to have his cake and eat it too. He must be able to account for the work as form and as a fixed, autonomous object of contemplation and analysis on one side, and for what he freely calls "the subjective impression of music" and the display of feeling and physicality on the other. But the work is not affected by such display. "To the performer [I believe he means only to the performer] it is granted to release directly the feeling which possesses him through his instrument, and breathe into his performance the wild storms, the passionate fervour, the serene power and joy of his inwardness. The bodily ardour that through my fingertips suddenly presses the soulful vibrato upon the string, or pulls the bow, or indeed makes itself audible in song, in actual fact makes possible the most personal outpouring of feeling in music-making. . . . The emotionally cathartic and stimulating aspect of music is situated in the reproductive act." But none of this affects the being of the work.

In the realm of musical signs, nothing can better provoke a second, skeptical look at Hanslick's confident splitting of music into composition and performance than a practice that seems at first thought unquestionably to belong in the second realm: Beethoven's practice of writing fingerings into the scores of his music for piano. This has in fact been closely studied, with interpretations reported in a reflective and imaginative essay by Jeanne Bamberger,[35] but its significance goes well beyond Beethoven's piano scores, as the author recognized. A few citations can give the sense of it.

> [Following Beethoven's fingerings, the pianist realizes] the musical gesture at once in a physical gesture. Beethoven's fingering seems to "speak" to the performers . . . on this direct level of intimacy—an immediate kinaesthetic sense of a passage can lead the player to a greater musical understanding of that passage. For this reason the fingering must often be read as part of the composition itself. . . . What is important in Beethoven's fingering is . . . the psychological effect which results from the relationship between the pianist's hearing, his gesture, and his actual performance. . . . The physical gesture of the performer's hand becomes a sort of sound analogue.[36]

Bamberger cites as examples the instruction to change fingers—from fourth to third—on tied notes in the Sonatas opp. 106 (the third movement, *Adagio sostenuto. Appassionato e con molto sentimento*, m. 164) and 110 (the third movement, *Adagio ma non troppo. Recitativo*). In both cases, it is the fourth finger on a relative upbeat and the third on the following downbeat to which the preceding is tied—in short, a syncopation. She writes, "Beethoven's fingering helps the performer to realize the great expressiveness of these two passages—to feel restlessness and motion where neither melodic nor harmonic motion are involved."[37] A similar case that she does not mention (her essay is limited to the piano sonatas) is the fingering 4–3 on tied notes in the right hand of the piano part at the beginning of the scherzo movement of the Sonata for Cello and Piano in A Major, op. 69. The pianist comes down *fortissimo* with the fourth finger of the right hand alone on the upbeat and changes to the third on the downbeat, in solidarity with the left-hand chord on the downbeat.[38] This limping syncopation is the core musical idea of the whole scherzo. To be sure, the fingering in all three cases is an instruction to the pianist. But it would make no difference to the listener if in any of them the pianist were to ignore it and fail to change fingers on the tied note. The fingering is an intimate communication to the performer about the music.

A wonderful demonstration of how the sense of a poetic text is projected in its musical setting and translated into the physicality of a fingering is given by the conclusion of Beethoven's song about the flea (text from Goethe's *Faust*). The last words are, "Wir knicken and ersticken wenn einer stickt" (If one [flea] pricks us we will crush it and choke it). Descending dyads in the piano right hand are slurred but played with the thumb. Bamberger cites what Paul Mies wrote about this: "The resulting rapid tearing away of the hand, sliding thumb, and aural effect all combine to mimic most accurately the crushing of the flea." In the end Bamberger writes: "Beethoven provided fingering where he felt, at the moment, that this was the best way to explicate the structure and to communicate his expressive intent. Explication in the long run is not limited to the particular passage that is fingered; I found . . . [she is a pianist] that my focus of attention kept expanding outward into the work as I considered the implication of the fingering in any one moment of that work."[39]

Explication for whom? Communication to whom? No one in particular and everyone. The fingering is part of the score that denotes the work, and the work is everything that is denoted in the score. If someone protests that these fingerings are nevertheless prescriptive signs for the performance and that if they have any expressive effects it would be only through the performance detail that they specify, we can move to yet another apparent performance mark that is impossible to execute (see Example 3.1). Such things occur in piano writing by Schumann, Brahms, Debussy, Berg, and Webern, among others (see chapter 6). One recognizes the swell of feeling on seeing these hairpins on the sustained sound, but what they communicate and how the performers might manifest that is open to different possibilities. It surely marks a significant moment in the form and the harmonic progress of the piece, the recognition of which by the performers would affect the performance beyond the moment itself. It might prompt a rhythmic hiatus, or perhaps even a bodily gesture.[40]

EXAMPLE 3.1

Such notations help us to think about the question, To whom were Beethoven's annotations addressed? As with any communication, without considering that question we can hardly assess their meanings. And we can scarcely hope to find an answer by considering them only in the context of the present-day transmission of music through anonymous scores, digital recordings, simulcasts, and huge concert halls. In contrast to today, music in Beethoven's Vienna was heard primarily in private homes and semipublic salons. The transmission of music was mainly an intimate affair. This sociocultural situation must be considered together with the fact that the works most provided with the sorts of annotations I have been describing are the solo and chamber works and songs—mainly with piano, Beethoven's own instrument—and those least provided with them are the large orchestral works. What is suggested is that they constituted some sort of intimate discourse about the music or even part of the music addressed to the intimate circle that included the composer, the performer or performers, and such listeners as had access to them, and perhaps also to that transcendental realm of music that Schopenhauer struggled to describe. To whom, after all, was that annotation in the sketch for the last movement of the Ninth Symphony addressed? Perhaps to whomever the words "Le-be wohl" at the beginning of the Piano Sonata op. 81a are addressed. In both instances, the words and the sounding music are multiple representations of those ideas, which we hold as intentional, not real, objects, although they are embodied in both the words and the sounding music.

The conclusion from all of this must be that the "expressive" or "performance" marks are more than autonomous signs with prescriptive reference to the performance. They are integral parts of the score that denotes the music, and they participate in the multifarious modes in which the score's denotation functions. The music consists of all of the qualities that are denoted by the score. If one speaks of the music as structure, and the score as denoting structure, then that does not discriminate between formal and affective properties. In order to understand this, one must clear away yet another false dichotomy. Carl Dahlhaus has put this in a way that has implications for our conception of what is musical:

> That hermeneutics and the aesthetics of feeling are grounded purely subjectively and that the aesthetics of form . . . are in turn objectively grounded, are assertions that persistent repetition has vested with the appearance of the obvious. . . . They are nevertheless questionable.[41]

Dahlhaus continues later in the same essay with an understanding that was cited in the first chapter: "The feelings that music possesses . . . prove to be not impulses existing outside and without music and whose sounding portrayal is musical, but rather qualities that are feelings at all only as they are expressed by music."[42] *Mesto,* in other words, identifies a known and specifically musical quality, and we should not look to the feelings we have on mourning a loss or to the expression on a basset hound's face to capture it. We seem, after all, to have no difficulty accepting "sharp" as a term for a musical quality or property heard, but is it that we make the link between the word and the quality or property by way of a deviation to qualities in other domains of experience that share the use of the word "sharp"—for example to a razor's edge, a piquant sauce, an acute conundrum, a witty person? If "sharp" is a loanword in musical terminology, which of those other domains is its home base? What is it that razors and conundrums and sauces and wits and raised pitches have in common that serves as the track on which the word "sharp" glides easily from one domain to the other? And if its use in musical terminology is based on some such shared quality, why have only speakers of English recognized that sharing? Why does the word corresponding to "sharp" have musical connotations in no other language? It does not seem right to act as though the answers to these questions were obvious.

When reading from the label or a guide that the wine we are about to drink has hints of blackberry and vanilla, we do not expect to taste something like vanilla ice-cream with blackberry sauce poured over it. We neither have in our mind's taste buds images of absolute vanilla and blackberry flavors that we integrate with wine taste as a mental act; nor do we borrow those flavors mentally from vanilla ice-cream and blackberry sauce (or from vanilla beans and blackberries). The qualities "vanilla" and "blackberry" as nuances of the taste of wine made from cabernet sauvignon grapes can exist only as they are embodied in specimens of that wine variety, just as the quality *allegro* exists only through its enactments in particular pieces. If there is skepticism about that, consider the description of a Hungarian wine given in the very extensive catalog of the Swedish State Liquor monopoly: "tastes of cellar earth and leather." A catalog prepared by a wine dealer in New Jersey offers a Romanian pinot gris with a flavor of "candied clementine." It seems safe to guess that the writers of those descriptions did not have reference to the tastes they had experienced on eating cellar earth, leather, and candied clementines; or if they did, they did not expect the prospective buyer to recognize those tastes from *their* experience of them. We have to learn to recognize the referents of the words "blackberry and vanilla" in cabernet sauvignon, of the words "cellar earth and leather" in Hungarian Egri Bikaver, and of the words "candied clementine" in Romanian pinot gris. Having once learned them, we are alerted by those words to experience their referents.

In the same way, we have to learn what the referents of words like *mesto* are in music, and having once learned them, we are alerted by that word to experience its referents. Such a state of alertness, or mind-set, corresponds to the *Stimmung* (as the *Musikalisches Conversations-Lexikon* of Mendel and Reissmann put it) in which expressive marks like *religioso* place the performer, from which to deliver a corresponding performance, but which would also be aroused in a listener who is aware of the annotation, and in which he or she would be prepared to receive the music.

But that emphasis consigns the language of the annotation too exclusively to the domain of performance (listening is a kind of performance, too) as prescriptive signs. It tends to obscure the role of the language as an alternative medium of signification, working together with the notation in the awesome task of representing music—another way of thinking about "the language of music."

PART TWO

Performance

THE IMMANENCE OF
PERFORMANCE
IN MEDIEVAL SONG

Music has been thought of in two alternate ways—as object, and as event.

We construe from our scores works—we even call them structures. But the very aspects that we call structural can, with a shift of attitude, be recognized as performance events without depriving them of their place as content. Performance as *content* of music is what I want to talk about. And I shall look for help in articulating this idea by considering performance as content in music's sister arts.

I might appear to be fumbling with a tautological notion here. After all, music is a performance art, and works of music are realized through time in performance. But is it really self-evident to all that it is primarily in performance that music's values are manifested? Not, it seems, when there is a background of philosophers and critics locating musical beauty in the configurations of tones, which for some do not even need to be heard to have their effect. Struggles over the ontology of music are written in and between the lines of aesthetic philosophy, music history, and music theory.

I'll let the discourse about this be exemplified by Roman Ingarden's prestigious book, *The Work of Music and the Problem of Its Identity*.[1] The work is *dif-*

ferent from its performances, writes Ingarden. It possesses neither the temporal nor the spatial localization characteristic of real objects. It is not a process,
since all its parts exist simultaneously. The work is a schematic construct, and
as an object of aesthetic cognition the work reveals itself as characterized by
a *quasi*-temporal structure, since it contains a number of phrases or parts
that succeed each other in a determined order, but which we apprehend as
coexisting all at once, not in real time.

This conception is encapsulated in a brief formulation about musical form
that occurs in the book *Esthetics of Music,* by Carl Dahlhaus:

> Insofar as music is form, it attains its real existence, paradoxically ex-
> pressed, in the very moment when it is past. Still held firm in memory, it
> emerges into a condition that it never entered during its immediate pres-
> ence; and at a distance it constitutes itself as a surveyable plastic form.
> Spatialization and form, emergence and objectivity, are interdependent:
> one is the support or precondition of the other.[2]

Such a synoptic idea of form has conditioned much of the analysis of music that is practiced in our critical literature and academic training. My word
"synoptic" merely follows upon Dahlhaus's language: "at a distance," "sur-
veyable," "plastic," "spatialization," all of it betraying our culture's prioritizing of the visual sense over the aural and attributing to it the virtue of "ob-
jectivity" that it would, by implication, deny the aural sense. Notice that
we say "synoptic" with ease. We do not say "synaural." We say "I see what
you mean," not "I hear what you mean." We say "you and I see eye to eye"
to indicate that we are in agreement; we do not say "we hear ear to ear." It is
interesting to contemplate the paradox of a culture that embeds this value
system in its languages while at the same time producing art works (poetic
and musical) that address the aural sense. A consequence of this paradox is
the neglect of sound in discourse about poetry and music. It is fashionable
now to speak of interpretations of music as "readings," rarely as "hearings."
The sound values of poetry are virtually ignored in its analysis. I suspect
this relates to the fashion for "conceptual" art, but pursuit of that connection would take me too far afield. If I guess accurately what someone is
thinking I may be told I have "read" her mind, but never that I have "heard"
her mind. Yet in ancient Chinese culture the latter would have been quite
normal, and precisely as an aspect of the prioritizing of sound among all the
senses.

That brings me back to the idea of performance as content of music, which I would like to introduce with reference to that culture. The most noble of ancient Chinese instruments was the qin (or "ch'in"), a zither-like instrument with seven strings that are stopped with the left hand and plucked with the right. R. H. van Gulik, in his foundational monograph *The Lore of the Chinese Lute,* writes about this instrument:

> [F]rom a remote time the lute was set apart as the inseparable companion of the literatus, that engaging combination of official, poet, painter and philosopher, until gradually it became in itself a symbol of literary life, with all of its elegant and tasteful pleasures. The musical properties came to be accessory to the instrument as center of a special system of thought, an ideology fitly encompassing the eclectic tendencies characteristic of the old-fashioned Chinese scholar. [Van Gulik calls the instrument "lute" only by way of comparison with the prominent place of the lute in European Renaissance culture].[3]

The manner of plucking and stopping produced the sound quality in which lay the aesthetic essence of the performance, far more than in the pitch and durational configurations that command our attention in the music of the West. The earliest known notations for the qin (sixth century) are written descriptions of hand positions and movements, a practice that became standard during the Tang dynasty (618–907). As many as 150 distinct signs for hand positions and movements have been identified, which corresponds to the enormous range of timbres that can be produced and gives evidence of the prominent place that timbre occupied in the aesthetic of that tradition. Pitches and durations were at the discretion of the performer. In his book *A Song for One or Two: Music and the Concept of Art in Early China,* Kenneth de Woskin has written something about such notations that could well guide us in interpreting any notation: "The contrast between what Western notations describe about the sound and the ch'in graphs describing the movements of the performer is suggestive of what ch'in masters thought was important to record, and hence what they felt was essential to the performance."[4]

Beginning in the Ming dynasty (1368–1644), qin handbooks include long, illustrated sections in which line drawings of hand positions are placed alongside natural scenes that were understood to correspond to them. The correlates could be birds and beasts (real or mythical), natural scenes or formations, people. Beneath the sketch of the scene or the creature is a poetic

FIGURE 4.1. Drawings representing the song
"Sending a sound through the ancient valley."

invocation of the *essence of the posture*. For example, beneath the illustration
of a figure facing an empty valley (correlated with a particular hand position;
see Figure 4.1) there is a poem entitled "Sending a Sound through the Empty
Valley":

> Long whistle, just one sound
> Rattles the trees and the mountains.
> Following the sound, echoes return,
> In the void of the valley, between here and there.[5]

It is this way of apprehending the feeling of the sound produced by the performance, I think, that identifies performance as content. That is essentially
the subject of the preceding chapter, manifested in the identity of meaning
between "expressive" and "performance" markings in musical scores of the
eighteenth to the mid-twentieth centuries.

Against this background I turn to two items of medieval song—one sacred, one secular—where of course music and language are one. And when I
say language I mean the sound of language, as well as its meaning. Language
shares with music what Wilhelm von Humboldt wrote about it:

Language in actuality only exists in spoken discourse. Its grammar and dictionary are hardly even comparable to its dead skeleton.[6]

Appreciation of the sound qualities of language is evident in the writing of medieval pedagogues on composing songs, of whom I would like to cite two. First, Guido of Arezzo, in his *Micrologus* (ca. 1050):

> Thus in verse we often see such concordant and mutually congruous lines that you wonder, as it were, at a certain harmony of language. And if music were added to this, with a similar interrelationship, you would be doubly delighted by a twofold melody.[7]

And a *De musica* by a writer we know only as Johannes (ca. 1000):

> The first piece of advice we offer about making a melody is that the music shall be varied according to the sense of the words ... [then] the composer must take pains to put together a melody with such propriety that the melody is seen to express what the words sound.[8]

The first of my examples is a Latin gradual, *Sciant gentes,* in a tenth-century Frankish transmission and three Roman transmissions of the eleventh to twelfth centuries (Example 4.1).[9] When studying such a complex we usually ask on what grounds can we consider the individual transmissions to be versions of the same song. And if we can identify such grounds we are inclined to think them as having been as well the grounds of the composition and/or transmission of the song. In this case we can begin by identifying the tonal configuration, essentially the melodic span D through A, with occasional extension down to C and upward to B (flat) and even C, and when the melody moves all the way to the upper C, the A acts as a pivotal tone that divides a lower range of a fifth from an upper range of a third. This is a conventional melodic pattern. It is a basis for making melodies, but it is not unique to this group of chants, nor to the genre of graduals.

Another determinant is the design of the melody for the clear projection and appropriate emphasis of the liturgical text, which was itself arranged for singing. The principal means for doing that was the organization of the language in sense units, and we can see that all the melodic versions manifest the same decisions about that organization: "The people are to know / that your name is 'God' / that you alone are the highest / above all of the earth." The sense units are set to more-or-less complete melodic phrases. In this re-

EXAMPLE 4.1

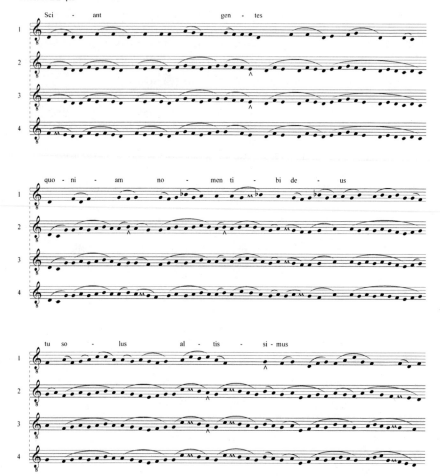

spect the melody plays a role parallel to, but even more explicit and detailed than, punctuation in the performance of language. This parallel was recognized at least as early as the eleventh century. We now tend to think of punctuation as marking off the structural members of sentences. In the Middle Ages it was a kind of notation for the performance of speech—indicating pauses and raising or lowering of the voice. It is hardly surprising that the neumes that were the earliest Western musical notations were for the most part adapted from the signs of this notation for speech. Nor is it surprising that all the melodic versions identify the same sense units. There is some room for variation, but all settings are informed by the language syntax.

There are constants in the pace of the language declamation within the setting of each sense unit, as that is set by the melodic figure carrying each syllable. All opening syllables are given relatively short settings, whereas the syllables "ro-[tam]," "sti-[pulam]," and "fa-[ciem]" in the verse are carried by long melismas in all versions.

The uniformity of all versions with respect to this property is the most compelling sign of a continuing tradition for this chant that seems to go back to a time before the separation of the Frankish and Roman traditions prior to 800 and that was transmitted without writing at least until the Carolingian era in the Frankish regions and at least until the eleventh century in Rome. This is a constant that is far more significant for such a tradition than the melodic outline itself. The declamatory pace seems a property that is immanent in the chant, as much so as the very word-content itself, and it is a property that lies as deep as a performance content.

The poem of the troubadour Jaufre Rudel is spun out around the phrase *amor de loing,* "love from afar" or "distant love," and the differently shaded meanings through which that phrase passes. This "love from afar" is painful. The poem is rich with expressions of desire, and it becomes plain that "love" is not only what the poet feels, it is an epithet for the lady who is the object of his quite carnal desires—the "love from afar" is the exotic woman. The double meaning is focused in stanza VI. The context is the crusade. God, who "established this love from afar," is asked for the power "to see this love from afar, *truly,* in agreeable places," in other words, to consummate the love in "chamber and garden." Once that has been made virtually explicit we can enjoy the irony of the lines, "For no other joy pleases me as much as enjoyment of love from afar" (VII). But that irony, which also has an aspect of mystery or enigma, is implicit throughout the poem.

I.	1.
Laquand li jorn son lonc en mai	When the days are long in May,
M'es bęls douz chans d'auzęls de loing,	I like the sweet song of birds from afar,
E qand me sui partiz de lai	And when I have departed from there,
Remembra·m d'un'amor de loing;	I remember a love from afar;
Vauc de talan enbroncs e clis,	I go sad and bowed with desire
Si que chans ni flors d'albespis	So that neither song nor hawthorn flower
No·m platz plus que l'inverns gelatz.	Pleases me more than icy winter.

II.

Ja mais d'amor no·m gauzirai
Si no·m gau cest' amor de loing,
Qe gensor ni meillor non sai
Vas nuilla part ni pres ni loing.
Tant es sos pretz verais e fis
Qe lai el renc dels Sarrazis

Fos eu per lieis chaitius clamatz.

2.

Never in love shall I rejoice
Unless I enjoy this love from afar,
For nobler or better I do not know
In any direction, near or far.
Her worth is so true and perfect
That there in the kingdom of the
  Saracens
I would, for her, be proclaimed captive.

III.

Iratz e gauzens m'en partrai
Qan verai cest' amor do loing,
Mas non sai coras la·m verai,
Car trop son nostras terras loing:
Assatz i a portz e camis.
E per aisso no·n sui devis,
Mas tot sia cum a Dieu platz!

3.

Sad and rejoicing I shall depart
When I shall see this love from afar,
But I do not know when I shall see her
For our lands are too far.
Many are the ports and roads,
And so I cannot prophesy,
But may all be as it pleases God!

IV.

eBe·m parrá jois qan li querrai

Per amor Dieu l'amor de loing.
E s'a lieis plai, albergarai
Pres de lieis, si be·m sui de loing.
Adoncs parrá·l parlamens fis
Qand drutz loindás er tant vezis
C'ab bels digz jauzirái solatz.

4.

Joy will surely appear to me when I
  seek from her,
For the love of God, this love from afar.
And if it pleases her, I shall lodge
Near her, although I am from afar.
Then will appear fine discourse,
When, distant lover, I shall be so close
That with charming words I shall take
  delight in conversation.

V.

Ben tenc lo seignor per verai
Per q'ieu veirai l'amor de loing,

Mas per un ben qe m'en eschai

N'ai dos mals, car tant m'es de loing.
Ai! car me fos lai pelerís

Si que mos fustz e mos tapís
Fos pelz sieus bels huoills remiratz!

5.

I consider that Lord as the true one
Through whom I shall see this love
  from afar;
But for one good that befalls me
  from it,
I have two ills, because she is so far.
Ah! Would that I might be a pilgrim
  there
So that my staff and my cloak
Might be seen by her beautiful eyes.

VI.	6.
Dieus qe fetz tot qant ve ni vai	God who made all that comes and goes
E fermęt cest' amor de loing	And established this love from afar,
Me don poder, qe·l cǫr eu n'ai,	Give me the power, for the desire I have,
Q'en breu veia l'amor de loing	Quickly to see this love from afar,
Veraimen en locs aizís,	Truly, in agreeable places,
Si qe la cambra e·l jardís	So that chamber and garden
Me resemblęs totz temps palatz.	Might always seem to me a palace!

VII.	7.
Ver ditz qui m'apęlla lechai	He speaks the truth who calls me greedy
Ni desiran d'amor de loing,	And desirous of love from afar,
Car nuills autre jǫis tant no·m plai	For no other joy pleases me as much
Cum jauzimens d'amor de loing;	As enjoyment of love from afar;
Mas sǫ q'eu vuǫill m'es tant ahis	But what I want is so difficult,
Q'enaissi·m fadęt mos pairis	For thus did my godfather decree my fate,
Q'ieu amęs a non fos amatz.	That I should love and not be loved.

VIII.	8.
Mas sǫ q'ieu vuǫill m'es tant ahis ...	But what I want is so difficult ...
Toz sìa mauditz lo pairis	May the godfather be cursed
Qe·m fadęt q'ieu non fos amatz!	Who decreed my fate that I should not be loved![10]

The word "loing" (far) is truly a semantic and sonic emblem for the whole rich and subtle turn. It is a bell-like ostinato, a performance effect inscribed in the song as key to its meaning. (You need to hear all the verses to get the effect.)

AFTERWORD

Another approach to the evasive conception that I've been grasping at was suggested to me by a review in the *New York Review of Books* by Andrew Butterfield of an exhibition of paintings by Tintoretto at the Prado Museum in Madrid.[11] The review's title—"Brush with Genius"—enjoys a *double entendre* that is thematic for the article, through which numerous sentences like the following stream: "The brushwork is *evident* and *animate*, flickering with highlights and shadow across the surface of the skin" [my emphasis].

FIGURE 4.2. Drawing/collage by Henri Matisse, *Nude with Oranges*, 1953. © Succession H. Matisse, Paris/Artists Rights Society (ARS), New York. Photo credit: Erich Lessing/Art Resource, N.Y. ART 45945.

Such sentences convey a judgment that the author sums up in these words: "painters did not always think that brushwork should be seen, and it was Tintoretto more than any previous artist who made it a central part of the artist's repertoire . . . [and] a stylistic feature in the history of art from Rubens and Rembrandt to Franz Klein and Willem de Kooning."

What is the gain from this, that its invention is reckoned so heavily to Tintoretto's credit? Speed, economy of means, and an impression of liveliness; or as Butterfield puts it, "the idea that art should be a form of energy made visible," a principle that, he says, inspired the instigators of the Baroque. Well beyond the Baroque, it is known of de Kooning that however long he may have worked over a painting, his aim was to have it inspire the feeling that one is witnessing the moment of its creation, as if to defeat the tendency of "the finished work," as Walter Benjamin had put it, to be "the death mask of the inspiration."[12]

Butterfield writes that "it is the boundless creativity of the invention and the prodigious strength of the execution that gives [Tintoretto's] pictures the pulse of life." The magic effect of experiencing both invention and execution simultaneously and inseparably has long been represented for me by a painting of far simpler means, Matisse's 1935 painting "Nude with Oranges" (Figure 4.2). We cannot stop seeing the line and the dots as the brush in motion and punctuation, but through our own contribution to the image we make them the outlines and anatomical details of the spaces and then the volumes of a two- and then three-dimensional representation of a woman's body. For me the most amazing effect is the simple loop of the line that suggests the head, looking over the right shoulder in a gesture of cool disengagement. The solid oranges—I mean the word to denote both the fruit and the colors—make a statement of a formal nature, as oranges tended to do in Matisse's paintings from early on. Against the play of line, they assert that this is a painting and present themselves as decoration, not to be related to the figure in any narrative way. Even more stunningly, in the Chinese ink drawing (Figure 4.3) we make a cloak of the swooping brush that overwhelms the petty details of the figure's head and feet, without letting go the experience of its grandiose gesture.

The interpretations of this chapter reflect back to an item in the first chapter, Shakespeare's sonnet 27. Shakespeare has contrived through the control of meter to have the poet's physical state block the obligatory iambic rhythm

賜大學士傅以漸
順治乙未仲冬朔日

at first, forcing a stop in the midst of the first line. But then the gate is lifted to allow his rush, through the iambic flow, to the desired bed and rest. The performance aspect, manipulating the conventions of the sonnet form, enacts the idea of the words. The two collaborate, they are in balance, to make the meaning of those lines. There is no understanding the metrical scheme as a "formal" device. Only through performance in real time—enunciated or silent—can the poem be *experienced*.

FIGURE 4.3. *Facing.* Drawing by the first Qing emperor, Shunzi (1638–61), *Bodhidharma Crossing the Blue River on a Reed,* 1655. NMOK-293. Photo credit: Used by permission of the Museum of Far Eastern Antiquities, Stockholm/Östasiatiska Museet.

5

EARLY RECORDED
PERFORMANCES OF CHOPIN
WALTZES AND MAZURKAS:
THE RELATION TO THE TEXT

A recent contribution to the literature on commercial popular music by Albin Zak carries the title *The Poetics of Rock*.[1] The author uses the word "poetics" with deliberation in the sense of its etymology in the Greek verb *poiein,* to do or to make, and in this he follows Igor Stravinsky's explanation of his title, *The Poetics of Music in the Form of Six Lessons:* "The poetics of music is exactly what I am going to talk to you about; that is to say, I shall talk about *making* in the field of music."[2] Indeed he follows a much older tradition, represented, for example, by the thirteenth-century writer who left us a detailed description of the musical practice associated with the cathedral of Notre Dame in Paris: "Master Leoninus ... so it has been said ... *made* the great book of organum on the Gradual and Antiphonary to enrich the Divine Service."[3] Zak's book is about making in the practice of rock music.

Of course when we speak of the "poetics" of art—as in Aristotle's *Poetics* or Stravinsky's *Poetics of Music*—we have in mind, especially since the eighteenth century, an association with aesthetics—concern over the experience, the interpretation, the criticism of art—and concern with its rhetorical edge, the effect of art. Zak makes that association explicit in his book, which stirs new thought about one of the main preoccupations of aesthetics, the ontology of art, inseparable from poetics since the inception of formal thought about it. The core idea of his book is that in the domain of rock music it is the recording that is the artwork, the recording that is made, in the sense of *poiein,* the imprint of compositional activity, the object of aesthetic experience and the source of rhetorical effect.

So far outside of the habit in which recordings are represented as just that, faithful *records* of performances which in turn are renderings of scores, which in their turn are representations of works, this ontology has far-reaching implications for the picture we hold of the institution of music and its dynamics. Reflection about it can throw open our understanding of these states of music and their differentiations and interdependencies in ways not unlike the challenges posed by the phenomenon of improvisation, especially if we think of the making of a rock recording as itself a kind of performance act, as Zak encourages us to do. Performance has not usually found a place in the center of study within that accustomed picture. The focus has been on music as object, not as process.

This chapter focuses on performances of waltzes and mazurkas by Chopin in recordings made in more or less the first three decades of the twentieth century, as they relate to corresponding scores. Ultimately the question will be, What conception about the music's ontological status as music seems to underlie the relationship? With this focus I mean also to be supporting the case for recordings as primary objects of study in the pursuit of some of the most fundamental music-historical questions that confront us.

The technology of gramophone recording was introduced in 1877. As early as 1904, Enrico Caruso's recording of "Vesti la giubba" from Leoncavallo's *Pagliacci* became the first recording to sell a million copies. As far as I know, the earliest commercially released recording of any music by Chopin was made in 1902, of the Mazurka op. 67, no. 4, by Alfred Grünfeld (1852–1924). In recent times recordings from the epoch then initiated, based on player-piano rolls and acoustic and electric recordings, have been remastered and released in increasing numbers. By now we have the complete recordings of the following pianists of the first recorded generation in remastered form: Ferruccio Busoni, Alfred Cortot, Ignaz Friedman, Leopold Godowsky, Alfred Grünfeld, Josef Hofmann, Mischa Levitzski, Vladimir de Pachmann, Ignaz Paderewski, Raoul Pugno, Sergei Rachmaninoff, Moriz Rosenthal, Josef Lhevinne, Simon Barere, Harold Bauer, and Arthur Friedheim.

In his later years Vladimir de Pachmann (1848–1933) took to introducing his performances, telling audiences what he would play and, sometimes, how he would play it. Introducing a recording of the D♭-Major Waltz op. 64, no. 1, the "Minute Waltz," he says, "At first I play it like it is written down. Afterward the slow movement a little slower than usual and afterward *staccato* à la Paganini, and then again à la Chopin *legato* and finish the Waltz."[4] Now Pachmann was so eccentric (the critic James Huneker dubbed him "The Chopinzee"[5]) that there might be a temptation to write him off as an unreliable witness for any performance tradition. Harold Schonberg writes, "[I]t is hard to conceive how he could ever have been taken seriously.[6] But the sorts of things that he did in this performance are no more eccentric than what we can hear from Paderewski, Rachmaninoff, Rosenthal, Barere, Hofmann, and Cortot, even if we find the inventions of this group more tasteful than those of Pachmann. And my notion is that we ought to take all of them seriously as witnesses to a musical conception that is simply different from the one that prevails today, different in ways that touch not only on performance in relation to the text, but also on the practice of musical composition and the nature of its products, and on scholarship regarding all of these angles of the musical economy.

In addition to the matters of articulation and tempo that Pachmann identifies in his introduction, he extends Chopin's four-measure opening wind-up to seven measures and adds the following figure to the left hand in mm. 29–33 and 117–21:

EXAMPLE 5.1

I'm interested in his claim to play at first "like it is written down," a loaded phrase, indeed, whose unpacking in different ways has been one of the leading continuous themes in the historiography, theory, and philosophy of Western art music. Consider Pachmann's extension of the vamp at the beginning of his performance, which he evidently regarded as being within the bounds of "playing like it is written down." Rachmaninoff, whom Schonberg dubs "The Puritan," extends the opening vamp to six measures at the beginning and to seven in the reprise. Perhaps they are enacting an idea about the passage that Jean-Jacques Eigeldinger attributes to Chopin in his book *Chopin: Pianist and Teacher as Seen by His Pupils:* "It should unroll like a ball of yarn."[7] Rachmaninoff's segue from the "slow movement" into the reprise is sentimentalized by an extreme *allargando* and *rubato* and by the continuation of the grace notes on each downbeat, which creates a kind of barber shop cadence:

EXAMPLE 5.2

In something like Pachmann's intensification of the scenario shown in Example 5.1, Rachmaninoff alters the dramatic scenario in the op. 18 Waltz, again with an *allargando* and with an added bugle call in the right hand, recalling the opening in mm. 49 and 157.

EXAMPLE 5.3

The right-hand trill that prepares the reprise in the "Minute Waltz" (mm. 69–72) has something like the effect of a drumroll that tightens the tension in the circus just before the aerialist leaps into a mid-air triple somersault. In another recording,[8] Pachmann enhances that effect, taking the trill in the left hand and making a spectacular flight in the right hand:

EXAMPLE 5.4

Such displays abound in early recordings of Chopin: the addition of flourishes that are not indicated in the score at all, like this last one; the chromaticization of something that was originally diatonic, which sacrifices tonal definition to bravura or to the haze of chromatic shading, or both. Here Paderewski chromaticizes in triplets what Chopin wrote as a diatonic run with two eighth notes to the beat that concludes the second section of the C♯ Minor Waltz op. 64, no. 2. In this case the point seems not so much to be pyrotechnics but a way of making the passage sublimate imperceptibly, going up in a wisp of smoke (Example 5.5 at letter A). Cortot and Rachmaninoff have different ways of giving a hurried quality to this passage. Cortot drops the third beat of every measure in the left hand (at letter B in Example 5.5). Rachmaninoff creates an inner voice by emphasizing the last note of every measure in the right hand, raising the melodic action to the higher metrical level that he has thus identified. But he does this by violating the direction of the score, which instructs him to play the last note of each measure most softly (letter C in Example 5.5).[9]

EXAMPLE 5.5

Another favored stunt is the doubling of a passage that is written as a single line. In the op. 42 Waltz, the right hand at mm. 222–28 rises in a climactic frenzy out of the whirligig second theme. Chopin doubles the first two eighths of each measure. Rachmaninoff, in a recording of 1923, jacks up the excitement one notch by creating a hemiola out of that doubling (Example 5.6). Simon Barere raises it two notches, spectacularly doubling at the octave through the whole passage. Rachmaninoff doubles at the sixth in the passage at mm. 240–43 in the same 1923 recording of the op. 42 Waltz. In 1938 Josef Hofmann recorded the "Minute Waltz" in thirds. Rosenthal did it, too, but went Hofmann one better by combining the main theme, in thirds, with the theme of the middle section. These displays take us to the edge of Brahms's arrangement of the op. 25, no. 2 Étude in sixths (to be sure, as a sort of super-étude), and to Debussy's remark that "the attraction of the virtuoso for the public is very like that of the circus for the crowd. There is always a hope that something dangerous may happen."[10]

EXAMPLE 5.6

Chopin's own attitude about the authority of his texts seems not to have been a simple matter. Eigeldinger's reports on the testimony of witnesses to his playing of his own music make clear that he did not hesitate to add ornaments, change harmonies, or make formal alterations during performance, and that impression is reinforced by his annotations in the scores of his music used by his pupils and by variants in presentation copies, copies prepared for publishers, and sketches and drafts.[11] At the same time, however, there are indications of the most meticulous proofreading on Chopin's part during the process of publication.[12] His own variations in the writing or playing of what is in the score presumably would not have been regarded by him as violations of the principle of playing "like it is written down," any more than Pachmann's inventions would have seemed violations to him.

John Butt calls attention to a phenomenon of the relationship between the notation of music and its performance that we can find throughout the history of music writing, and that offers a way of understanding this seeming contradiction in Chopin's behavior. It is when "a certain perfection or 'finish' was expected in the notation of the music for its own sake, while its performance entailed a different set of conventions which may, at times, have gone against the perfection of the notated music."[13] Butt's references extend from "contrapuntal correctness" in the notation of Renaissance polyphony to the highly detailed performance indications in scores of Bartók and Stravinsky, which the composers did not necessarily observe in their own performances. This range can be extended and filled in: Nino Pirrotta, writing about a musically nonsensical polyphonic fragment at Foligno, Italy, declares, for example, "The clash of G against F . . . is a joy to my musicologist's eye, if not to my ear, as evidence that the writing down of the piece had nothing to do with the requirements of its performance";[14] Susan Rankin, likewise writing about a specimen of early notated Italian polyphony, asserts that "the music as notated would not make sense in a performance."[15] I report a case of chant in two parts with extremely neat mensural notation in a fifteenth-century book in Cividale, Italy, of which the individual characters are correctly drawn. The problem is that they don't add up: neither voice works out mensurally, and the two cannot be made to fit together.[16] There are chant manuscripts written in the tenth century in the monastery of St. Gall, where the scriptorium observed high standards of correctness and thoroughness, with notations that are extremely detailed with respect not only to note groups and their alignment with words but also to nuances of performance (voice production, duration, pitch inflection). Such notational detail would have been redundant as prescriptive signs in a culture in which performers were still trained from childhood in an oral tradition; it reflects, instead, a high standard of correctness and finish in the graphic representation of singing (see chapter 7 regarding notational finish and performance).

Butt writes that this category of relation between notation and performance can be found in "many more repertories and compositional styles; indeed it should perhaps be tested, at least, for virtually any music we encounter."[17] The spectacular effects brought off in early recordings of Chopin's music are not always just a matter of circus; they project the performer's sense of the piece.

The biggest climax of Chopin's op. 42 Waltz follows the run that Rachmaninoff plays in sixths (mm. 240–43). Moriz Rosenthal plays it like a man out to bring the house down, figuratively but also literally (mm. 244–61). This climax is followed again by the whirligig theme. This time when Rosenthal begins the descent in m. 274 he is swept away, and when his right hand comes crashing down it plunges three octaves and two measures too far (Example 5.7).

EXAMPLE 5.7

It would be misleading to say that Rosenthal is violating the spirit of the piece. If he can't bring off his sense of it within the bounds of what is in the score, he acts beyond them. After listening for a while to recordings from this period, the experience of shock wears off somewhat. We begin to regard the score as a highly detailed *vade mecum* for the performance, but one that neither exhausts nor limits the possible.

I believe that this seemingly paradoxical situation is an entry to the aesthetic condition of Chopin's music, which was inherited by the generation of pianists whose performances I have been citing. It is worth considering the recordings of this generation as the sounding manifestation—in a way the flip side—of the conception that was forced to our attention by a notational practice in chapter 3 and now presents itself again from the vantage point of a performance practice. At the same time they not only mark the end of the ascendency of that conception, they should probably be regarded as contributing to its end in the practical—if not in the philosophical—sense. Underlying both practical contexts is the aesthetic doctrine that Hanslick gave philosophical framing in *Vom Musikalisch-Schönen* (*On the Musically Beautiful*) in a passage cited and interpreted in chapter 3. It bears citing again (without interpolation) in the context of the present chapter.

> The act in which the direct emanation in tones of a feeling can take place is not so much the fabrication as the reproduction of a musical work. That, philosophically speaking, the composed piece, regardless of whether it is performed or not, is the completed artwork ought not to keep us from giving consideration to the division of music into composition and reproduction . . . To the performer is granted to release directly the feeling which possesses him, through his instrument, the serene power and joy of his inwardness . . . The composer works slowly and intermittently, the performer in impetuous flight; the composer for posterity, and the performer for the moment of fulfillment. The musical artiwork is formed; the performance we experience.[18]

This calls to mind a distinction drawn by François-Joseph Fétis in his review of Chopin's first concert in Paris, which took place on February 26, 1832. Although complaining of "too many colorful modulations, so much confusion in linking phrases that it sometimes seems as though one is hearing an improvisation rather than a written composition," Fétis compared Chopin to Beethoven, who "wrote music for piano, while Chopin's is "music for pianists," something "we have long been searching for in vain . . . I find in M. Chopin's inspirations the sign of a formal renaissance that could eventually exercise enormous influence upon this branch of art."[19] I find in this the implication of a contrast of music concepts that is thematic for this chapter, differentiated by the locating of music in its performance as against locating it in its abstract "workhood."[20]

What has all this to do with the first-generation recordings that are my subject? In 1938 Theodor W. Adorno wrote these words in his ongoing polemic against the culture industry: "Perfect, immaculate performance in the latest style presents the work at the price of its definitive reification. It presents it as already complete from the very first note. The performance sounds like its own phonograph record."[21] The first-generation recordings give us a last glimpse into the opposite relationship, recordings that record a performing tradition. It is a reversal of that relationship that aggravated Adorno. But Adorno was no adept of music's history.

These early records, and the reflections on older traditions, teach us that the meaning of "playing like it is written down"—that is, the relationship between score and performance—must be determined with respect to the practice of each performance community on the basis of whatever clues and information can be garnered about that practice, not on the basis of universal principles about the authority of texts.

That this is suggested by performances in early Chopin recordings is reinforced by a practice that may seem trivial, but its very triviality brings home the point. And it is so common as to be hardly foregrounded in our hearing. It has to do with left-hand accompanying figures in the waltzes, in respect to both rhythm and harmony. In both cases we can think of the measure as a matrix of potential events: playing on the three beats and articulating a chord or two. With respect to rhythm, Chopin may have written something on each beat or on any two of the three beats, but the performer will have his or her own way about that (see Cortot's playing in the op. 64, no. 2 Waltz, Example 5.5, letter C).

With respect to the harmony in the left hand, Chopin writes a chord in a particular position, with particular voicing, in a particular register, but the performers may fill out octaves, play an octave lower, add a passing tone, or reverse chords between measures. In a 1923 recording of the "Minute Waltz," Georg Liebling recasts the pattern of downbeat bass notes (Example 5.8). Josef Hofmann's 1916 recording of the C♮ Minor Waltz op. 64, no. 2 is full of such details (Example 5.9, in each case Hofmann's performance where it differs from Chopin's notation).

EXAMPLE 5.8

EXAMPLE 5.9

We may suspect that the fluid relationship between score and performance that we've seen here is something peculiar to mazurkas and waltzes because of the popular character of their genres, allowing for a more improvisatory performance. This suspicion may be tested with performances of pieces in other genres, for example, the Nocturne no. 5, op. 15, no. 2 in F♮ Major, one of the most frequently recorded Chopin works during the early period. Virtually all the elements are subject to variation in those recordings: individual harmonies, chord voicings and register, ornamentation. Pianists who played those details exactly as written were by far in the minority. Only the basic melodic line and underlying harmonic process are fixed. Examples are too numerous to itemize; I merely draw the reader's attention to a number of recently remastered CD recordings: Raoul Pugno (Pearl/Opal CD 9836); Camille Saint-Saëns (Achophon ARC-106); Ferruccio Busoni (Symposium 1145); Ignaz Paderewski (Pearl Gemm CD 9323); Alfred Cortot (Hunt CD 510 and EMI CDZF 67359 2, disc 6); Mischa Levitzki (AAD CDAPR 7020, disc 1); Josef Hofmann (VAI Audio VAIA/IPA 1047); Sergei Rachmaninoff (RCA Gold Seal 09026-61265-2).

At this point it will be interesting to consider a passage about Hofmann and Rachmaninoff from Harold Schonberg's book *The Great Pianists.*

> It may come as a surprise to hear them called "modernists." As one listens to their records, it is easily apparent that they took more liberty in phrase, tempo, and rubato than do most pianists who belong to the twentieth century proper. But time alters perspective, and modernists they were, in their day. Compared to most of their great colleagues, Busoni included, they took remarkably few liberties, and their performances were models of textual accuracy against the performances of the Lisztianers and Leschetitzkianers. Hofmann and Rachmaninoff represented the first reflection of the modern attitude that the printed note is the all-important guide for the performer. This was something new in history, though today we take it for granted. And as the printed note became more and more important (because of the disappearance of such traditions as improvisation and embellishment and the old idea of the virtuoso as hero), so did the "message" of the composer.[22]

Anton Rubinstein's attitude had been, in his own words, "Just play first exactly what is written. If you have done full justice to it, and then still feel like adding or changing anything, why, do so." But "No!" said Rubinstein's greatest pupil, Hofmann. Hofmann's attitude was that the performer had enough to do to play the notes as written without adding anything of his own.

> I venture to prove to anyone who will play for me—if he be at all worth listening to—that he does not play more than is written (as he may think) but in fact, a good deal less than the printed page reveals
>
> The true interpretation of a piece of music results from a correct understanding of it, and this, in turn, depends solely upon scrupulously exact reading. The player should always feel convinced that he plays only what is written.[23]

"Exactness" and "accuracy" (and their companion pejorative, "taking liberties") are the banner words for this ideology that Schonberg draws from Hofmann's own writing, and what it comes down to is the limitless repeatability of the performance in full compliance with the written score. Rubinstein, who was, after all, a performer and performance pedagogue as well as a composer, testifies to a role for the score in the learning of the piece, but with a binding force that does not carry over to the public performance. This is a way of using scores that we know from the very beginning of the practice of making them in the Middle Ages. The shift from Rubinstein's attitude to what his pupil Hofmann said exemplifies a major piece of Western music history during the nineteenth and twentieth centuries. The contradiction between what Hofmann said and what he did in performance demonstrates the strength of an ideology just as tenacious in what Schonberg writes about Hofmann's playing: "[T]extually it remained breathtakingly accurate. In his best recordings . . . one can take dictation from his playing. Even in the left hand, every value—every rest, every dotted note, every phrase mark is reproduced with blueprint accuracy . . . Yes, Hofmann was a modernist."[24]

I mention—only tangentially, since it is not central to my task here—that this characterization of musical modernism, however inaccurate we may find the listening to be on which it is based, anticipates by about two decades the discourse about the historically informed performance movement as a modernist phenomenon. It is surprising that this viewpoint, and the performance history that it characterizes, has never found a place in that discourse.[25]

In 1910 Ferruccio Busoni wrote the following defense of transcription for a program note for an Artur Nikisch concert in Berlin. He was responding to the frequent opposition aroused by his transcriptions:

> Notation is itself the transcription of an abstract idea. The moment that the pen takes possession of it the thought loses its original form. The intention of writing down an idea necessitates already a choice of time and key. The composer is obliged to decide on the form and the key and they determine more and more clearly the course to be taken and the limitations. Even if much of the idea is original and indestructible and continues to exist this will be pressed down from the moment of decision, into the type belonging to a class. The idea becomes a sonata or a concerto; this is already an arrangement of the original. The performance of a work is also a transcription, and this, too—however free the performance may be—can never do away with the original. For the musical work of art exists whole and intact before it has sounded and after the sound is finished. It is, at the same time, in and outside of time.[26]

There is a parallel expression about literary texts and their contents in Italo Calvino's book *If on a Winter's Night a Traveller.*

> At times I think of the subject matter of the book to be written as of something that already exists: thoughts already thought, dialogue already spoken, stories already happened, places and settings seen; the book should be simply the equivalent of the unwritten world translated into writing. At other times, on the contrary, I seem to understand that

between the book to be written and things that already exist there can be only a kind of complementary relationship: the book should be the written counterpart of the unwritten world; its subject should be what does not exist and cannot exist except when written, but whose absence is obscurely felt by that which exists.[27]

The great performer and composer Busoni has dealt in a more subtle way than the theorist Hanslick with the conundrum of the two faces of music. How different an attitude this is from one that has, I think, been more influential on modern habits of thought, expressed earliest, as far as I know, by Johann Nikolaus Forkel in 1788, that the coherence of music depends on its susceptibility to being notated. He actually put it the other way around, reporting that travelers in distant places populated by "wild and uncultivated" people were unable to write down their music because it was too incoherent to be written down.[28] This dogma about a linkage between notation and order has continued to influence musical studies. Notation is among the controls on the chaos into which music is always feared to be on the verge of erupting.

> Chopin revised habitually. He altered works extensively already when he commenced composing at the keyboard, and he continued to revise when he first notated with pen and paper ideas conceived at the piano. He revamped continuously through successive stages of manuscripts, though addressing different varieties of problems and correcting less frequently in the second or third autograph of the same work. Publication in no way hindered him. He made changes to proofs, as well as to students' copies of his published editions, and he requested publishers to alter printed texts. Chopin's habits have left a complex welter of changes, yet there is more to complicate matters. Though he revised constantly, he did not always do so consistently: sometimes he altered one engraver's manuscript or printed edition, and not another. [These tendencies] in essence make the revisions to a work a part of its aesthetic property.[29]

This is the beginning of Kallberg's essay "The Problem of Repetition and Return in Chopin's Mazurkas." His theme is Chopin's tendency to change the disposition of sections and repetition schemes of mazurkas, not only during the compositional process but also between published editions and autograph scores, and through annotations in student copies and in autograph presentation copies made after publication. Close attention to this opening paragraph suggests that its author was himself struggling with two competing interpretations of the significance of these observations—something that I venture with all due respect for his knowledge of the Chopin sources and the sensitivity of his interpretations in general. It is the implicit conflict between the interpretation of the revisions in a work as "a part of its aesthetic property" and the very use of the word "revisions," which suggests more than the writing down of different versions, especially considered together with the use of the word "problem" in the title and throughout the essay, sometimes in connection with "solution," and with the words "struggles" and "corrections" later in the essay. The general tendency of Kallberg's essay suggests the dominating influence of what I will call the Beethoven sketch-studies paradigm, under which sketches, drafts, and so on are looked upon as witnesses to a struggle to gain control of compositional ideas and materials in striving for a single final and most perfect work (further to this subject in chapter 7). It is with this conception that the idea that revisions are a part of the work's aesthetic property seems to be in conflict. Kallberg clarifies this second idea in his later essay, "Are Variants a Problem?" There he reports on similar types of "revision," and adds the case of the Nocturne op. 62, no. 1, of which Chopin sent off three autograph scores to as many publishers on the same day, scores that do not agree with one another. Kallberg writes, "If Chopin allowed multiple versions of a piece to appear before the public, then this reflects something essential to the constitution of a work of art in the 1830's and 40's."[30] The "aesthetic property" on which he touches in the earlier essay is "a fluid conception of the work of art, a conception that Chopin embraced" along with "poets, novelists, and painters." Specifically, Kallberg cites Friedrich Schiller's *On Naive and Sentimental Poetry,* in which Schiller describes "the modern poet as an essentially self-divided figure, who writes in awareness of multiple alternatives."[31] Under this conception the musical work could therefore be exemplified by notations that do not fully agree with one another. Kallberg's explication is not meant, however, to suggest some Romantic impetuousness—giving over to flights of fancy and lack of discipline. It is a realism about the circumstances under which Chopin worked, including his relationships with his publishers, his pupils, his audience, his patrons. If differences in those relationships called for different notational representations of his works, there was no aesthetic scruple that acted as censor to block such variation in the interest of uniformity. Variation could continue for as long as the circumstances of transmission and reception might change. That is the sense of Kallberg's remark that "composition was an ongoing process with Chopin."

What this arouses us to is that, after all, the bundle of concepts comprising "final," "authentic," and "authoritative version" and "authorial intention" always implies an ideal scenario in which an autonomous composer works alone, in relation only with the work, a scenario in which the composer—if he or she is worthy of our attention—pushes through sooner or later to the achievement of a single best version of the piece, and in which there would be no reason to let different versions stand. To see those concepts as the uniform premise for editing and interpreting all music is tacitly to assume that scenario for all composition, and that is simply false, as Kallberg has shown in the case of Chopin. And what the evidence of first-generation recordings shows is that the performers of rank who made them were still working under the same paradigm. The "modernist" attitude articulated by Hofmann and Schonberg has a history, and it has to be shown why it should be the lense through which any particular tradition is to be viewed, rather than assuming its universality.[32]

Returning to the shifting formal arrangements in the mazurkas that are Kallberg's subject in his earlier essay, that is another type of variant that we continue to find in early recorded performances. An example is Moriz Rosenthal's 1937 recording of the Mazurka op. 67, no. 1. Rosenthal plays mm. 1–26 as in the Henle edition, which is based on the French and German first editions, which are in agreement (there is no surviving autograph). Then he plays mm. 27 and 28 in the altered version of Example 5.10:

EXAMPLE 5.10

When he gets to m. 59 he plays instead what amounts to Chopin's mm. 28 and 29, then jumps back to m. 53 and continues to the end. What it comes down to is that Rosenthal decided that Chopin's ending happens too quickly.

A more complex case involving the composer, the first editor, and several performers is that of the Waltz in G♭ Major, op. 70, no. 1. It is one of five waltzes (opera 69 and 70) published posthumously by Chopin's friend, Julian

Fontana. For all but op. 70, no. 3, autograph scores have turned up after the publication of Fontana's edition, which never agrees fully with any of the autographs. For op. 70, no. 1 there are two autograph scores: one that was in the Yale University library when Ewald Zimmerman prepared his *Urtext* edition of the waltzes for Henle (Munich, 1978) and that he published there as the *Fassung nach der Eigenschrift* along with the Fontana version; and one in a private collection in France, found by Byron Janis in the Chateau de Thoiry near Paris, tied up together with an autograph score of the Waltz in E♭ Major and published in facsimile and transcription by him, also in 1978. All other editions and all recent performances that I know are based on the Fontana version. Note the rhythmic differences in the right hand between this second autograph and the Fontana version (Examples 5.11 and 5.12) One can always recognize a performance based on the Fontana edition right from the start because of this marker.

EXAMPLE 5.11

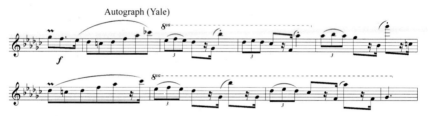

EXAMPLE 5.12

The Yale score is dated 1832, while with the Thoiry score—but not containing it—was found a folder bearing the inscription "Written and given by Frederick Chopin, 1833," in the hand of the great-grandmother of the present owner of the chateau. This would have been one of many cases in which Chopin wrote out a presentation copy of a piece that differs from other autograph copies or editions. There are many differences of detail between the two autographs; the one I want to focus on is a difference in the formal arrangements.

Thoiry autograph	AA BB CC DC DC AA
Yale autograph	AA BB CC DC AA
Fontana	AA BB CC DC DC AA
Cortot	AA BB **AA** CC DC DC AA **BB AA**
Rachmaninoff	AA BB CC DC AA

Fontana's formal arrangement is the same as that of Thoiry, but there are many differences of rhythmic detail between them, so one can't leap to the conclusion that Fontana copied from the Thoiry autograph or some relative of it. The identity of form can be a coincidence, the polygenesis of homologous forms. When Rachmaninoff recorded the piece in 1921 he played it in the Yale arrangement, but not because he'd had a peek at that score. From the rhythmic details it is clear that he was using the Fontana edition, which was the only one then in circulation. Cortot, when he recorded the piece in 1934, played from the Fontana version but added the extensions indicated above by bold letters. In Rachmaninoff's 1923 recording of the Waltz op. 69, no. 2, the situation is like that of his recording of op. 70, no.1: the melodic details show that he played from the Fontana edition but on his own initiative in the form of the Yale autograph (see Example 5.13 and the sectional arrangements shown here):

Fontana and Cortot	AA B A' BA' BA' CC' A B A'
Yale (autograph)	AA B A'CC' A(A)B A'
Rachmaninoff	AA B A'CC' ABA

As long ago in our musical history as 1527, the German music pedagogue Nicolai Listenius wrote of the difference between "practical music," by which he meant, essentially, performance, and "poetic music, which consists in making or constructing, that is, in such labor that even after itself, when the artificer is dead, leaves a finished work."[33] So Hanslick's separation of the two sides of musical creation really has a long history, at least conceptually. Whether it corresponds throughout that history to real historical situations is another question. So far as Chopin's waltzes and mazurkas are concerned, the context of his music included the folk music of the Polish countryside and the popular concert and salon life of early nineteenth-century Paris. This certainly has something to do with the extent to which he chose episodic forms in which the sequence of episodes is governed by ideas of dramatic scenarios that may be as ephemeral as the performance itself. Both Polish and Parisian contexts imply a relation to audiences that would hardly have brought him to focus exclusively on the production of perfect and absolute works for contemplation, isolated from their performance. Today's standards of playing "like it is written down" do, however, suggest a concentration on that side of Hanslick's duality, and early recordings remind us how one-sided and unhistorical that conception is.

We are confronted with two attitudes that have been at play in our musical culture for a long time, now one, now the other dominating, or held simultaneously with respect to different traditions or practices or genres. Neither one can be taken as uniquely and universally defining the conditions for Music. These changing attitudes mark out an essential dimension of music history, and recordings constitute essential evidence so far very much underexploited.

In interpreting changes along this dimension I draw very briefly on two well-known interpretive models: Nelson Goodman's model for the relationships among musical scores and the notations in which they are written, performances, and works;[34] and Thomas Kuhn's model for interpreting changes in the practice of science.[35]

The premise underlying Goodman's model is that scores are characters in a system of signs that signify by referring within a reference field. To understand what that comes down to in detail it is necessary to consider first Goodman's assertion that the primary theoretical function of a score is the authoritative identification of a work from one performance to another. Such identification is a matter of picking out from all performances—from the reference field—those that are performances of the work. The score, then, is the touchstone of what will count as a performance of the work for which it is a score, and the work is nothing other than the class of performances that are in compliance with the score. "Compliance," Goodman writes,"requires no special conformity; whatever is denoted by a symbol complies with it." Translating, the work is nothing other than the class of performances that its score denotes. (We may wonder at the end of this exercise just how much has been said. Nevertheless, putting it in these terms does have some heuristic value. It is naive to expect that we should be able to make mental moves without ever lifting ourselves by our bootstraps.)

The efficacy of all this depends on the distinctness of scores and performances (we must be able to tell one score from another and one performance from another) and a stable linkage between scores and performances. This requirement passes down to the requirement for distinctness of the constituent parts of scores and performances (signs for pitches, durations, and so on, and their respective denotees) and the stability of the linkage between them.

Goodman has spelled out these requirements in very clear operational terms, and in doing so he has provided the clearest explicit formulation of what, in Kuhn's terms, would be called a paradigm for musical practice and interpretation that has been tacitly held as a premise for some part— we cannot say all—of musical practice and interpretation in the domain of Western art music since roughly 1800, at least so far as the relations among works, performances, and scores are concerned. The obvious failure of the performance practice that I have been describing to conform to the paradigm would count, in Kuhn's terms, as an anomaly. And so would Harold Schonberg's report on the performance practices of Hofmann and Rachmaninoff, and Hofmann's own statement of his ideals compared with his practice. They are exact counterparts of the kinds of reports that historians of science produce about the failure of nature to behave in accordance with prevailing paradigms, and of the peculiar struggles of scientists to explain away the anomalies—or to be blind to them. A colleague, when confronted with the sort of thing I have reported here, compared it to variation of intonation in different performances of the same work by different string players using the same score. That trivialization of what are far greater freedoms preserves the paradigm, but one feels the strain of the effort and can wonder just what has been served by it.

There is an important difference, however, between science and history. I would not for a moment suggest that the anomalies we have witnessed are the signs of the breakdown of the paradigm that Goodman described and of the inevitability of a paradigm shift. The anomalies just show us that the paradigm doesn't speak for all of music. The historical world and its interpretation are not subject to the kind of uniformity that is implied in the concept of a paradigm as it was brought in for the explanation of the natural world by science in the first place. For one thing, if we were to shift our attention from the performance of Chopin's waltzes and mazurkas to the performance of ballades and a piece like the Polonaise-Fantasy (op.61), not to mention the concertos, the findings would be quite different, and the investigation of the reasons for that would make an interesting historical study in itself. And for another, even with the performance of waltzes and mazurkas the tradition we have witnessed is over, and the investigation of the reasons for that would make another interesting study. In any case, we need to address the very central question of the relation to the text always with reference to specific local historical forces and circumstances.

PART THREE

Notation

WHAT KIND OF THING
IS MUSICAL NOTATION?

1

The first section of this chapter has been informed, in a way incited, by my reading or re-reading of a number of seminal modern secondary studies[1] and ancient primary ones. In pursuing these sources I follow an intuition about our relation to our musical notation, looking beyond its service as a code system for the performance and explanation of music to an understanding of it as one sign system among others through which we represent aspects of our experience. Such a broad view must open a long view on the history of our musical notation, well back beyond the beginning of the actual practice of writing down music in the Western world during the ninth century. The intuition itself was born, after many years of gestation, of my recognition that a good deal can be understood about the workings of those early notations by regarding them from a semiotic point of view.[2] But that work was limited by its exclusive focus on musical notation, closed to a long history of semiotic thought and to the influence of the heritage of that history in the time of the invention and early uses of notation. My purpose here is to remove that boundary.

One of the more difficult cognitive tasks we can set ourselves is erasing from our consciousness something that has been prominent there during most of our lifetime and then re-emplacing it, but without the baggage of expectations, habits, and associations that it normally carries. The de-familiarizing of musical notation is such a task, and it is what the question of my title calls for. And in order to strip the phenomenon of our music writing of all that we take for granted about it as we settle into a score, we must look back to its earliest inventions and uses in that age of "writing rage" (*Schreibewut*, the great paleographer Bernhart Bischoff called it), the Carolingian ninth century. If we are scrupulous about the risk of undermining the very advantage that this perspective offers by projecting modern understandings onto the new practice, we may be able to catch sight of attitudes that prevailed in the time of the earliest music writers about how graphic systems in general (including language writing and visual arts) functioned and what purpose they served in apprehension, creation, representation, and communication of every kind—in short, in the business of connecting with the world. Then we might glimpse how such attitudes influenced the invention and early practice of writing and reading music.

In modern studies of early music writing in the European Middle Ages, it has been virtually a commonplace to presume that the neumes by means of which liturgical and other songs were recorded functioned as (no more than) mnemonics for their singers (a sampling in Example 6.1). That would likely have been the view of musicians during those early centuries as well, but without my parenthetical qualification, which stands for the far greater expectations that musicians nowadays have of musical notation. This small difference of orthography may be a key to fundamental differences of disposition then and now toward the function of those enigmatic signs and toward the phenomenon of music writing in general, even toward the uses of signs in general—that is, toward the question of my title.

That this presumed role of neumes would nowadays be looked upon as a deficit comes about only with a narrow focus on musical notation, in several senses: (1) Although melodies were represented for centuries by such signs, the other side of the "mnemonic" assessment—that the transmission and the singing of the melodies would have depended also on unwritten processes in collaboration with which the neumes must have been adequate—was long ignored and is still resisted in some quarters; (2) Musical notation has mainly

EXAMPLE 6.1

quando ueni am et appare bo ante fa ciem dei

mei. ℣ fuerunt michi lacrime me

e panes die ac no cte dum dici

tur michi p̄ singulos di es u bi est deus

tu us.

Uinea enim domini sabaoth domus

israel ℣ Cantabo nunc dilecto can

tico: dilecte uine e mee. Dom̄

℣ Vinea facta est dilecta: in cornu in loco uberi Dom̄.

℣ Et edificauit turrem in medio eius et torcular

fodit inea. Dom̄

℣ Et maceriam circumdedit et circum fodit et

been treated as sui generis, without side glances at other sign systems—
notations used in other fields, speech and written language, visual arts—and
without attention to acculturated beliefs about the role of sign systems in
acquiring and imparting knowledge; (3) The assumption that as a system
sui generis, the role of musical notation is just to provide instruction for real
or virtual performance or to encode representations of musical structure.
This amounts to an intellectual isolation of musical notation as a technical
matter confined to just one practice or discipline. Tanay notes as a symptom
the combing of theoretical writings of former times for principles or rules
of notation that can be read as clues to methods of transcription.[3] As another
symptom, she notes that studies of notation have avoided following a shift in
twentieth-century semantics from a "classical referential" conception, with
its "premise that words [this can be generalized to signs] are pictures or imitations fixed to prior objects in the world, to a functional semantics in which
meaning depends on the functional relations among the words [or signs]
themselves [and on their uses, Wittgenstein would have added]." Colish characterizes the same process as a shift from an understanding of language as
"instrumental" to one in which it is "heuristic."[4]

Studies of early notations that dwell on their insufficiency for the exclusively technical role that is identified with "notation" in general and that leap
therefore to a narrow sense of "mnemonic" as second best tend to draw that
assessment into a portrayal of the history of notation in which the practice, or
the technology, develops from a rudimentary state toward its perfection—a
teleological evolutionary view in which the goal is precise explicitness of denotation, and in which stations on the way can be labeled "primitive," "transi-
tional," and so forth. At the same time under such a historiography, the highly
detailed and specific information that is encoded with some early neumatic
writing (see the reference to the Hartker Antiphonary below) may be tacitly
and unquestioningly assumed to have been directed at singers in the interest of the modernist value of closing the space between written artifact and
sounding performance, a conclusion that overlooks the context of a continuing oral practice in which church singers were trained from boyhood, learning by rote from teachers as well as from written sources. That context should
encourage a pause, at least, to consider alternative interpretations of such
abundance of denotation. This caveat will later be generalized to include our
commonplace modern notations. Only under the dubious model of a sharp
dichotomy of orality and literacy, in which each excludes the other, would

such an interpretation be compelling; only then, on the premise that the written sign contains all the information that is in the text, would "reading," as an unmediated move from sign to signified, be the total cognitive act ("Playing like it is written down," chapter 5; what an irony that in the postmodern present the concept of "reading" has taken on just the opposite meaning). That modern scholars, as members of a culture of high literacy, would regard neumes as mnemonics in the sense of *faulte de mieux* while medieval musicians would have regarded the phenomenon of mnemonics to be altogether *comme il faut* conveys much about the two cultures.

My conjecture about the attitude of earlier musicians is based on indications of their participation in a culture that Mary Carruthers characterizes as "fundamentally memorial."[5] But, she continues, "the fact of books in themselves. . . . did not profoundly disturb the essential value of memory training until many centuries had passed." She cites Thomas Aquinas:

> A thing is said metaphorically to be written on the mind of anyone when it is firmly held in memory. Things are written down in material books to help the memory.

Books, that is, function as mnemonics. Carruthers comments "If my study achieves nothing else, I hope it will prevent students from ever again dismissing mnemonics and mnemotechnique with the adjective 'mere.'"[6]

This is not to be taken as an indication that the culture had not yet reached a condition of full literacy. It shows, rather, the misleading influence of the idea of such a dichotomy. More than a millennium before Thomas Aquinas, Cicero wrote,

> Memory . . . is in a manner the twin sister of written speech and is completely similar to it though in a dissimilar medium. For just as script consists of marks indicating letters and the material on which those marks are imprinted, so the structure of memory, like a wax tablet, employs places and in these places [joins] together images like letters.[7]

Such remarks begin to mark out the philosophical background for the invention of musical notation in the Middle Ages and for medieval reflections and teaching about notation. That this was the context of belief and practice for the early history of music writing is confirmed by the way that some of the commentators present writing and remembering as collaborative or as analogues.

A much-cited passage from the widely transmitted *De harmonica institutione* by Hucbald of Saint Amand (840–930) would seem to substantiate the modern impression of the inadequacy of neumes as mnemonics. But the full passage in its context is quite in the spirit of those from Cicero and Aquinas, confirming, rather, their sense of the collaboration of written signs and memory. Hucbald proposed that the alphabetic letter names of pitches and other signs regarding performance details be placed near the figures of the neumatic notation so that "there will be clearly on view a full and flawless indication of the truth." And he justified that precaution, writing that "the memorial aid is scarcely able to attain its goal; for the signs always guide the reader by an uncertain trace."[8]

In evaluating Hucbald's proposal, we need to take note of the fact that it did not get much traction in practice following its circulation. Why not? Some likely answers will suggest themselves if the reader will try to imagine "reading" music from a score in which the identification of pitches depends on the labeling of their signs with letters of the alphabet. What is the difference? First, letters are abstract. Their ordering as the alphabet is arbitrary and contributes no information regarding the relations or groupings or sequence of any item that they may be assigned to signify, including musical pitches. They are no more inherently suggestive of musical sounds or their properties or their relations to one another than they are suggestive of such aspects of speech sounds, to contradict an ancient and widespread misapprehension to which I must return.

Second, writing letters along with the neumes and other signs would indeed have put on view "a full and flawless indication of the truth," but it also would have obstructed rather than facilitated the fluent reading that neumes seem designed to encourage. These have from the start in the ninth century an iconic aspect, a correspondence between the contours of note groups representing melodic gestures and the up-and-down movement of the singing voice. The survival value of those mnemonic features surely accounts in large measure for the evolutionary success of neumes and their successor signs—ultimately our commonplace notation—especially when they were fixed onto a grid. Our notations on the staff retain that correspondence.[9] Identifying pitches with alphabetic letters, on the other hand, emphasizes a note-by-note enchainment—a distortion of the melodic idea that parallels the distortion entailed in the ancient and tenacious dogma that speech is comprised of the discrete sounds represented by the individual letters of the alphabet, which has still to be discussed here.

In this respect European musical notation embodies from its beginning to the present a principle that we have inherited from antiquity about representation through signs, namely the principle of mimesis. It is articulated in Plato's dialogue *Cratylus,* through Socrates' mediation in the debate between Hermagoras and Cratylus over the question whether the names given to things are natural by way of mimesis (Cratylus) or arbitrary and conventional (Hermagoras). Colish succinctly summarizes the position to which Socrates drives his interlocutors through his merciless questioning:

> The relationship between words and things is one of imitation; and this verbal mimesis would not be possible unless there really were a natural resemblance between words and things [and even the likeness between the letters by which words are comprised and the things that they name, I must add, along with the assertion that "names which are rightly given . . . are images" of the things named].[10]

However, writes Plato,

> realities are to be learned and sought for, not from names [which imitate them] but much better through themselves . . . No man of sense can put himself and his soul under the control of names and trust in names and their makers to the point of affirming he knows anything.[11]

Colish summarizes, "For Plato, the sensuousness and ambiguity of verbal signs is understood in the context of an epistemology of two worlds, a world of ideal forms and a world of tangible realities, which mirrors the ideal forms imperfectly at best."[12] This holds not only for verbal signs but for signs in general.

It is Plato who first placed the concept of mimesis under detailed scrutiny, and it is he who focused at the same time on the inevitability in that process of flawed knowledge, illusion, deceit, counterfeiting, corruption, seduction, and enchantment, obscuring the difference between appearance and reality, between truth and falsity, and appealing to the inferior, irrational part of the soul. The full force of this dour assessment is unleashed in the latter part of book 10 of *The Republic,* which is about deception through the eye and the ear by painting and poetry, with the conclusion that they should be banned. Why is this of interest? Because we find here the wellspring, not only of the conception of mimesis but also of the standard of absolute, other-worldly truth that mimesis cannot achieve and that marks for Plato the threshold between the real and the spectral. Something resembling that strong conception of "truth," even if it is not confined to another world, recurs throughout the history of representation and of what is expected of it. After all, Hucbald's expression that "there will be on view a full and flawless indication of the truth" seems like a stiff way of saying something like "there will be a reliable or accurate score." His expression seems to hint at something more than that.

Gombrich and Havelock have independently noted the coincidence of Plato's life span—427–347 BC—with the period that realized a zenith of evolutionary developments in ancient Greek culture, in practices achieved through mimesis. Gombrich writes of "the Greek revolution," "the heroic sprint of those discoverers who were active between 550 and 350 BC," "artists who discovered new effects to increase illusion and lifelikeness," naming Phidias (480–430 SBc), Zeuxis (born 464), and Apelles (352–308). He writes,

"The writers of the Renaissance echoed anecdotes that extolled the powers of painting to deceive the eye, the very character which made Plato disapprove of art and prefer the immutable laws of the Egyptian canon."[13] Havelock writes of what Harris calls the "writing revolution."[14]

> Between Homer and Plato, the method of storage began to alter, as the information became alphabetized and correspondingly the eye supplanted the ear as the chief organ employed for this purpose. The complete results of literacy did not supervene in Greece until the ushering in of the Hellenistic age, when conceptual thought achieved as it were fluency and its vocabulary became more or less standardized. Plato, living in the midst of this revolution, announced it and became its prophet [it being understood that the role of prophet subsumes that of critic].[15]

Identifying the period in which a decline in the influence of mimesis has been noted, Gombrich evokes the concept of revolution again: "It is one of the gains we owe to the great artistic revolution which has swept across Europe in the first half of the twentieth century that we are rid of this type of aesthetic"[16] (an aesthetic that holds "representational accuracy" in the visual arts as the highest value). Tanay writes of the shift during the twentieth century from a "classical referential semantics" to a "functional semantics,"[17] and Wittgenstein renounces in the *Philosophical Investigations* (1945) the "picture theory of language" that he had earlier embraced (see chapter 2).

Plato's ambivalence from the start is apparent in his outspoken distrust of writing and the staging in writing of his philosophical analyses in the form of spoken dialogue. Harris implies that this is disingenuous, asserting that "the careful organization of a Socratic dialogue, let alone the organization of connexions between one dialogue and another, is the kind of organization which not even a Plato can undertake without at least jotting down a few notes."[18]

Such a priori judgments are residuals of the deep-seated attitude that we saw in the citation of Johann Nikolaus Forkel in chapter 5, holding writing to be essential to logical thought and notation to be essential to coherent music. How alive this attitude remains regarding music is demonstrated by the six-volume *Oxford History of Western Music* (Richard Taruskin, 2004), to whose contents only notated music—the "literate tradition"—is admitted; the vast domain of unwritten practices is excluded from the domain of Western music. That most reviews have raised no questions about that exclusiveness and its far-reaching implications for the treatment of the "literate tradition" is further affirmation of the tenaciousness of such dogma. What turned Plato so against the imitative arts? Most approaches to this question emphasize either the negatives that I have itemized above, or the positive emphasis on *la vrai vérité* that imitation cannot attain. Another approach suggests itself when I recall the experience one can have in Athens at the Parthenon or in the National Archeological Museum of the "revolution" about which Gombrich writes, as if life has been breathed into the marble and the nostrils of horses flare, the veins on their bodies stand out, and wind blows women's garments. It is not difficult to imagine a man of Plato's strong beliefs perceiving what he saw as threatening, seeing men pretending to be gods, and writing about "the art of conjuring and of deceiving by light and shadow and other ingenious devices . . . having an effect upon us like magic."[19]

If the artwork to which he was reacting strikes us with the power of its illusions, we can try to imagine how much greater would have been the effect on its contemporaries. People who heard the pinched, crackling sounds of the recordings of Adelina Patti during the first decade of the twentieth century are reported to have said that it seemed as though she were in the same room with them.

Mimesis is a factor in Aristotle's conception of language and knowledge, but without Plato's ambivalence. Colish refers to "Aristotle's certainty that signs, including words, may be accurate tokens of the things they represent," and she cites Cicero's adoptions of this assurance.[20] Modrak's account of Aristotle's conception is centered on this passage from his *De interpretatione*:

> Spoken words, then, are symbols of affections of the soul and written words are symbols of spoken words. And just as written letters are not the same for all humans, neither are spoken words. But what these primarily are signs of, the affections of the soul, are the same for all, as also are those things of which our affections are likenesses.[21]

According to Aristotle's realist epistemology, Modrak writes,

> The human mind is so related to the world that the mind is able to grasp the basic categories of reality. The impact of the world on us through our senses and intellect produces the concepts, which provide the foundation of knowledge and language, for not only are empirically produced concepts the bases of science, they also serve as the intentional content of the internal states that words symbolize. When one acquires a natural language, one acquires a classification scheme that is embodied in these internal states and is isomorphic with the things that are. Since these objects have stability, senses of words are stable and, for general terms, reference is fixed by sense, so that human beings equipped with language are able to refer to and describe real objects. . . . Aristotle believes the relation between a phoneme [the spoken word] and a meaning [affection] is conventional. The meaning is the intentional content of the psychological state for which the word stands. He holds, nevertheless, that the relevant mental states (meanings) . . . are likenesses of extramental states of affairs. The crucial contrast here is between *convention* as the explanation of how sounds carry meaning and a natural relation . . . rooted in the *likeness* between a meaning and a reality [my emphases].[22]

The words I have emphasized resonate with Wittgenstein's formulation of the "picture theory of language," which he transmitted in the *Tractatus Logico-Philosophicus* and, as I've noted above, retracted in the *Philosophical Investigations*.

What is left open is the question of the relation between the spoken word, which expresses the affection by convention, and the written word, which is symbolic of the spoken word. Is that by way of convention or of likeness, as Plato held? Does it matter? The remarks of two successors to Aristotle show that the question is moot and that the attempt to sort it out can yield confusion:

We have in use two languages which have no affinity between them but what custom has established, communicated through the eye by written characters, and through the ear by articulate sounds and tones. But these two kinds of language are so early in life associated, that it is ever after difficult to separate them; or not to think that there is some kind of natural connection between them. (Thomas Sheridan, 1762, Irish stage actor and teacher of elocution)[23]

A [spoken] language and its written form constitute two separate systems of signs. The sole reason for the existence of the latter is to represent the former. (Ferdinand de Saussure, *Course in General Linguistics*)[24]

This passage from Saussure's famous book portrays a confusing ontology for the written language. It is a "form" of speech, yet is separate from it (Cicero simply wrote "written speech"). And it has no other reason to exist than to represent speech.

What counts in Sheridan's comment is that if we believe, albeit mistakenly but consistently and in agreement with our fellows, that there is a natural connection, then that belief is itself a convention. Returning to the "iconicity" of neumes, the belief that the form of a neume is isomorphic with the movement of a melodic segment ultimately depends on conventions assigning directions to the components of neumes. Given such conventions, likeness to a melodic contour is directly legible in a sequence of neumes (Example 6.2). The reading of a series of ten small circles diagonally across a five-line staff as isomorphic with an upward or downward scale fragment (Example 6.3) depends ultimately on conventions assigning vertical and horizontal direction to the writing surface. That I can describe the arrangement of the circles as "diagonal" depends on the same conventions, and our need to remind ourselves of that demonstrates how easily we regard as natural what is ultimately conventional. That is in fact the great advantage of the system. It is the idea of mimesis, the belief in it, that has priority, and that is the product of a long history of thought about signs and signification. It is not as if the reading of that series of circles as moving upward or downward is an empirical observation, for which way, by nature, is "up" or "down" on a horizontal writing surface?

The point has been firmly established by Gombrich with reference to a kind of speech.[25] Certain expressions are used conventionally to represent the sounds made by animals: the rooster says "cock-a-doodle-doo" in English, "co-co-ri-co" in French, "ki-ki-ri-ki" in German, "kiao-kiao" in Chinese. The

EXAMPLE 6.2

EXAMPLE 6.3

expressions chosen have been invented to represent the rooster's crowing mimetically. But that they are conventional is clear from the fact that the same sound phenomenon is represented by different vocables in different languages, no one of them any more natural than any other. Reflection on this phenomenon prompts Gombrich's question, "Is there really such a sharp division between representation and expression?"[26] And we should add, "Is there really such a sharp division between the natural and the conventional in either of these modes of signifying?" These questions are relevant to the uses of musical notation. Gombrich had written earlier, "The likeness that art produces exists only in our imagination."[27] The case of the imitation of animal sounds shows that this observation is not limited to imitation in art. It is true even of photography.

Two of a Kind: Dogs That Look Like Their Owners (1999), a book of photographs is intended to show that "owners and their dogs truly look alike." As we read further in the book's introduction we learn that the suggestion of a likeness is a construction of the authors', out of "physical similarities" but also

FIGURE 6.1. Photograph of Pam and her dog Federico Fellini.

out of their impression that "the owner and his dog shared a disposition—an outlook on life and on the moment . . . the less obvious but ever-present bond that unites them."[28] This book, when its photographs are studied closely, offers as good a portrayal of the complexities and subtleties of the relationship of "likeness" as anything I know. The photograph of Pam and her dog Federico Fellini (Figure 6.1) is my favorite.

The subject arises again in connection with another axiom of the historiography of spoken and written language in the West. It is the tradition that takes the principle of symbolic representation down to the ground level of language, the letters of the alphabet that compose words—in speech. This, too, we hear about first from Plato, again in the *Cratylus*. In speech:

> Just as painters, when they wish to produce an imitation, sometimes use only red, sometimes some other colour, and sometimes mix many colours, as when they are making a picture of a man or something of that sort, employing each colour, I suppose, as they think the particular picture demands it. In just this way we, too, shall apply letters to things, using one letter for one thing, when that seems to be required, or many letters together, forming syllables, as they are called, and in turn combining syllables, and by their combination forming names and verbs. . . . Could a painting . . . ever be made like any real thing, if there were no pigments out of which the painting is composed, which were by their nature like the objects which the painter's art imitates? Is that not impossible? . . . In the same way, names can never be like anything unless those elements of which the names are composed [i.e., letters] exist in the first place and possess some kind of likeness to the things which the names imitate[29]

And later:

> Just as atoms come together and produce every corporeal thing, so likewise do speech sounds compose speech as it were some bodily entity. (Priscianus, *Institutiones grammaticae,* fifth century)[30]

And in writing:

> Fundamentally letters are shapes indicating sounds. Hence they represent things which they bring to mind through the windows of the eyes. Frequently they speak voicelessly the utterances of the absent. (John of Salisbury, *Metalogicon,* twelfth century)[31]

And still further:

Writing [is] the use of letters, symbols, or other conventional characters, for the recording by visible means of significant sounds. (*Encyclopedia Britannica*, 1911)[32]

This is a matter of some interest for the way people have thought about musical notation by analogy with language writing since its very earliest days:

Just as letters are the elementary and indivisible parts of articulated speech, from which syllables and in turn verbs and nouns are formed to create the text of finished speech, so too the pitches of sung speech, which the Latins call sounds, are themselves basic elements. (Anonymous, *Musica enchiriadis*, late ninth century)[33]

I will return to this after the next foray into the early history of such thinking.

Memory and the specter of writing are posed as alternatives in a much-cited passage from the *Etymologies or Origins*, book 3, by Isidore, Bishop of Seville (ca. 560–636):

Music is the art of measurement consisting in tone and song. It is called music by derivation from the Muses. The Muses were so named . . . "from inquiring," because, as the ancients would have it, they inquired into the power of song and the measurement of pitch [or the modulation of the voice]. The sound of these, since it is a matter of impression upon the senses, flows by and is left imprinted upon the memory. Hence it was fabled by the poets that the Muses were the daughters of Jove and Memory. Unless sounds are remembered by man, they perish, for they cannot be written down.[34]

The last sentence is often cited for its negative purport, as evidence that musical notation was not known in Isidore's day. There is abundant other evidence for that conclusion without elevating Isidore's remark as the conclusive proof on the point. We have done so at the cost of undervaluing the passage for its clear expression of an epistemological doctrine that prevailed through most of the centuries when music was written down in neumes. The focus in this passage is on music, but the epistemological doctrine applied to signs of every kind. This passage from Saint Augustine's *Confessions* comes closest to showing that:

A sound . . . is impressed on the mind through the ears, leaving a trace by which it can be recalled . . . [T]he things themselves do not penetrate into the memory. It is simply that the memory captures their images with astonishing speed and stores them away in its wonderful system of compartments, ready to produce them again in just as wonderful a way when we remember them.[35]

Undervalued too, is Isidore's prophetic imaginative act in projecting the use of writing as a sort of potential alternative to imprinting sounds on the memory, even though it had not been, and, he thought, could not be done. It would be as though someone had said in 1950 that "unless sounds are recorded by analog means they perish, for they cannot be digitally recorded" (digital recording began in the 1970s). But Isidore's remark is really right in line with the remarks of Cicero and Saint Augustine just cited, as are the confident assertions by later writers that music could be written down.

His remark implicitly projects onto future music-writing systems the ideal that they would, like the memory on which melodies were imprinted, exactly capture and preserve those ephemeral sounds as they flowed by into the past. That is what would be expected of music writing, but since there is no such practice, preservation must fall to memory. This conjecture is essentially confirmed by Isidore's poetic remark about speech and writing, reported by Carruthers:

> Isidore of Seville, we remember, in words echoed notably by John of Salisbury, says that written letters recall through the windows of our eyes the voices of those who are not present to us (and one thinks too of that evocative medieval phrase, "voces paginarum," "the voices (or sounds) of the pages."[36]

The ideal, again, is mimesis, and it is surely modeled on the conception of the work of memory as it had been articulated by Saint Augustine two centuries earlier in the passage from his *Confessions* cited above and confirmed in Hucbald's aim of achieving "a full and flawless indication of the truth."

The earliest and most explicit coupling of memory and music writing appears in a passage from the *Musica disciplina* by Aurelian of Réôme (ca. 850): "At this point it is pleasing to direct the mind's eye and the point of the pen to the melodies of the verses."[37] "Directing the point of the pen to melodies" suggests notation. "The mind's eye" is a core metaphor of the epistemology of antiquity and the Middle Ages for what we call memory. Sam Barrett cites a passage from Boethius's *De arithmetica*:

> This, therefore, is the Quadrivium by which we bring a superior mind from knowledge offered by the senses to the more certain things of the intellect

... so that by means of the eye of the mind ... truth can be investigated and beheld.[38]

Aurelian reaffirms the role of memory with a metaphor more familiar to us:

> Although anyone may be called by the name of singer, nevertheless, he cannot be perfect unless he has implanted by memory in the sheath of his heart the melody of all the verses through all the modes, and of the differences both of the modes and the verses of the antiphons, introits, and of the responsories.[39]

So far as I know the next firm testimony to the possibility of writing down music came from the anonymous author of the *Musica enchiriadis* toward the end of the ninth century, and with this we pick up again the thread about the alphabet as a notation of speech and the relevance of that to the history of music writing:

> Just as letters are the elementary and indivisible parts of articulated speech, from which syllables and in turn verbs and nouns are formed to create the text of finished speech, so too the pitches of sung speech, which the Latins call sounds, are themselves basic elements, and the totality of music is encompassed in their ultimate realization. From the combination of these sounds intervals are created, and from the intervals, in turn, scales .... [P]ractice will make it possible to record and sing sounds no less easily than to copy and read letters.[40]

Hucbald is more explicit about the alphabetism:

> As the sounds and differences of words are recognized by letters in writing, in such a way that the reader is not left in doubt, musical signs were devised so that every melody notated by their means, once these signs have been learned, can be sung even without a teacher.[41]

The following passage from the *Musica enchiriadis* adds to the clear reference to symbols for notes and to the implication by analogy of the discreteness of individual notes as basic components of melody a hint that the symbols themselves have properties in common with the notes—a mimetic aspect of musical notation:

> The Symbols of the Pitches and Why There Are 18: Since ... nature decreed that there are four sets of four similarly related notes [four tetrachords] so too are their symbols nearly identical.[42]

A mimetic principle for the relation between signs and sounds is called for even more explicitly for the notation of a rhythmic system by the fourteenth-century writer Jehan de Murs in his *Notitia artis musicae:*

> [A]lthough signs are arbitrary, yet, since all things should somehow be in mutual agreement, musicians ought to devise signs more appropriate to the sounds signified.[43]

I. J. Gelb cites two eighteenth-century literary figures with poetic commitment to the parallel proposition for language of a mimetic relation between sign and signified:

> ... this ingenious art of painting words and speaking to the eyes. (Brébeuf)

> Writing is the painting of the voice; the greater the resemblance, the better it is. (Voltaire)[44]

The metaphors, of course, presume an understanding that "to paint" is to render a likeness. And still in the early twentieth century, there is the *Encyclopedia Britannica*'s assertion that writing records the sounds of language. We know that skillful writers can create the impression that one hears their characters speak, just as one sees the landscapes they describe. But that is not the sense of the long tradition through which it has been held that the written language imitates speech. What can it mean in any empirically recognizable sense to claim that written words represent the sounds of spoken words, especially keeping in mind the emphasis on the constituent letters of words that is part of that tradition? Perhaps it was out of puzzlement about this that Derrida saw,

> in the very moment by which linguistics is instituted as a science, a metaphysical presupposition about the relationship between speech and writing.[45]

That presupposition was made long before the institution of linguistics as a science, but that it was made at all is what matters.

One could approach the idea of mimesis between written and spoken language with a concept of "phonetic iconicity,"[46] based on some isomorphism between the two. But before we begin to worry about identifying properties of the two that could be isomorphic, we encounter the question provoked by the *Encyclopedia Britannica* entry about what units of speech (or of "significant sound") are the counterparts of letters, that could be isomorphic with them? That search would be pursued on the assumption that speech is composed of discrete, identifiable sound units—phonemes—each consistently denoted by its own letter or letter combination in the written language. No alphabetic language-writing system meets that standard, with the possible exception of Korean, for which a written alphabet (*Han-gul*) was created in the fifteenth century with the intention, at least, of meeting that standard. Fourteen consonant signs and ten vowel signs are associated with like numbers, respectively, of standard sounds. (I am unqualified to speak to the actual stability of the system as to regional variation and historical evolution, and so on). The intention, at least, parallels that of the International Phonetic Alphabet, but with a living language. The Korean system was established in 1446 under the original name *Hunmin chong-um*, "the correct sounds for the instruction of the people." It is worth knowing about these two systems, because they do display, at least in their designs, what is claimed for all languages using an alphabet under the ancient doctrine of alphabetism. Harris writes,

"The great mistake about the alphabet is the persistent belief that it constitutes eo ipso a phonetic notation [for speech]."[47] The following observations of two linguists make clear why this is a mistake:

1. "A definable, systematic variant of a phoneme is called an allophone. Let us see what we mean here by 'definable, systematic variant.' Consider some variant s of the phoneme /s/. In the words sill, still and spill, each [s] is slightly different because it is spoken as tied to a different following sound, and the same differences occur between the [s]'s in the words seed, steed and speed . . . All such systematic variants of /s/, its allophones, comprise the phoneme /s/. Each phoneme designates a large class of sounds. For one, the phoneme /s/ consists of more than 100 allophones."[48]

2. "Every German who has not enjoyed a training in the physiology of sound is convinced that he writes as he speaks. . . . A word is not a united compound of a definite number of independent sounds, of which each can be expressed by an alphabetic sign; but it is essentially a continuous series of infinitely numerous sounds, and alphabetical symbols do no more than bring out certain characteristic points of this series in an imperfect way."[49]

This is to say that the premises of the *Musica enchiriadis* author and Hucbald's rationalizations for musical notation—"Just as letters are the elementary and indivisible parts of articulated speech . . ." and "As the sounds and differences of words are recognized by letters . . ."—are faulty descriptions of speech inasmuch as the individual letters do not sound as discrete units; we are taught to associate letters with speech sounds, but they contain no articulatory information. And by the same token the consequent parts of the analogy are faulty descriptions of music inasmuch as the individual notes do not for the most part function as discrete units in the music to which these treatises refer. It is, again, the doctrine itself, the ideal it expresses, that has priority.

I propose two simple exercises for the reader as a test of this doctrine of alphabetism:

1. Compare the following two word pairs with respect to the identification of their discrete sound units and the stability of the links between their component letters and those sound units: thorough, furrow; thorough, throughout. There is a temptation to regard such cases as anomalies or exceptions, but efforts to write out the rules for such exceptions in almost any language prove to be never-ending.

2. See if you can raed tihs txet wohtuit too mcuh dfitifcluy. I hvae smabrceld all the isdine ltetres but lfet the frsit and lsat ltetres in pcale [*sic*].

If you have been able to read these lines, the experiment favors the interpretation that we do not read simply by serially sounding out—even tacitly—the component letters of words, or merely by recognizing whole words, but rather that we do both. Reading in a language is a complex process involving the recognition or identification of individual letters and their conventional combinations in clusters, syllables, and words by aspects of their morphology and meaning, with the support of cues from syntax and semantics. I take this all-too-brief summary from the detailed review in Frank Smith's book *Understanding Reading: A Psycholinguistic Analysis of Reading and Learning to Read*.[50] That approach is most suggestive for understanding the reading of musical notation, which is not simply a matter of the identification of single notes, but of both the recognition and the identification of their configurations at every level.[51]

This brings me back around to Tanay's characterization of the premise of classical referential semantics "that words are pictures or images or imitations referring to prior objects in the world."[52] In a similar mode Carruthers identifies as a "governing model" of medieval epistemology the idea that every sort of sense perception is imprinted in memory as a "mental picture."[53] Other terms that she associates with this metaphor are "phantasm," "simulacrum," "imago," "eikon" (a Greek term which is translated in Lidell and Scott's *Greek-English Lexicon,* as "copy," "representation of a figure," "counterfeit," "image," "portrait," "description"). Borrowing from the philosopher Max Black an expression exactly adapted to these overlapping concepts, Carruthers calls this a "cognitive archetype."

In his book *Models and Metaphors* Black writes, "By an archetype I mean a systematic repertoire of ideas by means of which a given thinker describes, by analogical extension, some domain to which these ideas do not immediately and literally apply."[54] The *Oxford English Dictionary* (3rd edition, 1973) gives an emphasis to "archetype" that reinforces Black's definition and matches Carruthers's "governing model": "The original pattern from which copies are made; a prototype."

I believe the ideas that have so far been reviewed here come together in such a governing archetype, and I shall try to sketch its outlines. My sketch must be somewhat loose, as it must accommodate differences of formulation and conception in different sources. It must be something of a patchwork, but it will nevertheless be "systematic" in the sense that the ideas have tended essentially in a similar direction.[55]

The experience of reality (or shadows of reality) through the senses is received as though in a mirror, or as though impressed as images (pictures, phantasmas, affections of the soul) on the memory or the mind like an imprint in wax, recalled or summoned up by the eye of the mind, externalized and replicated as speech that may be represented, even replicated—through the medium of the alphabet—in writing that may be conceived as counterpart or "twin" of memory but that may function in collaboration with writing that calls up the sounds of speech, or of music. The core conceptions that show consistently through this review are those of mimesis, memory, and truth, the latter in the sense of a true copy, of Hucbald's "full and flawless indication of the truth," of Gombrich's "truth and stereotype," of Voltaire's "painting." In the sense of Carruthers's "governing model," these ideas have governed conceptions of language and its representations, of music and its representations, of the visual world and its representations. The effects of their governance are apparent in the dogmas of objectivism and of a fixed relationship between signs and what they signify, captured in the duality of "literal" and "figurative" or of "scientific" and "poetic" language (see chapter 2), the dogma of "playing like it is written down" (chapter 5), the "tyranny of the alphabet" (Harris), and the aesthetic of "representational accuracy" (Gombrich).

In my initial citation of Hucbald's phrase—"a full and flawless indication of the truth"—I allowed a degree of skepticism to show through about whether we should entirely understand his recommendation in the sense of a quaint slogan for the claims of a publisher about a critical edition, or of a CD-envelope boast about the authenticity of the early music performance contained inside. Barrett introduces another kind of motivation for, or significance of, the emphases we've encountered throughout this review—on likeness, imitation, copy, imprinting, completeness, correctness, truth; in a word, mimesis—with reference to the highly detailed and explicit notations in a book of chants for the mass, written for the abbey of St. Gall toward the end of the tenth century and still in its library (Antiphonary of Hartker of St. Gall, St. Gallen Stiftbibliothek 390–91) that seems to embody this ideal: meticulously drawn neumes, with alphabetic letters indicating nuances of pitch and duration. In its meticulousness the book seems to represent the chanting of the mass to the highest standard of the Augustinian ideal. A prologue enjoins users to "Devote careful attention to the right sounds" and concludes, "Whatever is celebrated in honour of God in these honest endeavours joins softened hearts to the heavenly choirs." Barrett finds a motivation for the first of the quoted lines in the second. Attention to the "right sounds," like Hucbald's method to achieve a "full and flawless indication of the truth," is one way to a "higher order" of musical being, higher realms of singing that lie beyond the senses," worthy of joining "the heavenly choirs."[56] He identifies the same aspiration in two further texts: another passage in the *Musica disciplina* of Aurelian of Réôme, who writes of "plainchant as a terrestrial copy of ongoing, unheard angelic praise"; and in an eleventh-century chronicle of St. Gall. A Roman cantor brought to the abbey "a copy of the authentic antiphoner," the authenticity of which the chronicler indicated by comparing the book with a mirror in which—we are to understand—are reflected images of the true—perhaps in Hucbald's sense—mass chants. In this book, writes the chronicler, "up to this day if anything in chant is contradicted, all error of such kind is corrected, as if in a mirror." The metaphor, writes Barrett, "which brings to mind Saint Paul's dictum that in this life 'we see in a glass darkly,' hints at a veiled presence in the antiphoner that mirrors a higher order of musical being," as in Plato's "epistemology of two worlds."[57]

Gombrich heads his chapter on "Truth and Stereotype" with an epigraph from Immanuel Kant's *Kritik der Reinen Vernunft*:

> The schematism by which our understanding deals with the phenomenal world . . . is a skill so deeply hidden in the human soul that we shall hardly guess the secret trick that Nature here employs.[58]

Among many images exemplifying this principle, Gombrich shows a "curiously stiff picture of a lion" drawn by Villard de Honnecourt in the twelfth century (Figure 6.2). He writes, "To us, it looks like an ornamental or heraldic image, but Villard's caption tells us he regarded it in a different light: '. . . and know well that it is drawn ['contrefais', recall 'eikon', more like 'copied,' like Voltaire's 'painting' (counterfeit; Plato take note)] from life.'" Gombrich continues, "These words obviously had a very different meaning for Villard than they have for us. He can have meant only that he had drawn his schema in the presence of a real lion. How much his visual observation was allowed into his formula is a different matter."[59]

But there is another possible emphasis that Gombrich mentions elsewhere in his discussion of "the medieval distinction between universals and particulars."[60] Here he suggests the interpretation that, through the instrumentality of the craftsman's schemata, it is the universal idea of Lion that the artist is rendering and that is intended to overrule the flawed visual observation of the imperfect, individual instance of the lion. Gombrich writes here, "It was on these grounds that Plato himself denied art its validity, for what value can there be in copying an imperfect copy of the Idea?"

As frontispiece of his book Gombrich reproduced a cartoon from *The New Yorker* magazine that parodies brilliantly the idea that image making is the imitation of the external form of an already existing object (Figure 6.3). Like a successful metaphor, its purport cannot be paraphrased in "literal" language. Take hold of it where you like: the model is accommodating enough to imitate the schema that the boys have been taught for such images; the art historians have been wrong all along—Egyptian women really looked and walked like that; the Egyptian canon is true to life; or Gombrich's question, "Is it possible that [the Egyptians] perceived nature in a different way [than students in a life class today do]"?[61]

FIGURE 6.2. Drawing of a lion and a porcupine from the sketchbook of Villard de Honnecourt, ca. 1235. Bibliothèque Nationale de France, manuscrits occidentaux-Fr. 19093, folio 24.

FIGURE 6.3. Cartoon by Daniel Alain, © 1955,
The New Yorker Magazine, Inc. Used by permission
of the Cartoon Bank/Condé Nast Publications, Inc.

2

The Musée Condé in the French city of Chantilly houses a manuscript volume collecting nearly 100 polyphonic songs of a type cultivated in the later fourteenth century in the courts of France, Aragon, and northern Italy. The manuscript was created in the last quarter of the century. The majority of its contents were likely composed approximately during that time span. Its notation is of a superb elegance and refinement of appearance and also, as we shall see, of technical achievement in the representation of the temporal dimension of music. It was the representation of time that posed the greatest challenge and opportunity for refinement in musical notation, the pitch dimension of Western music being relatively simple, not open to much differentiation and subtlety, and the means of its representation—to the extent that it was represented at all—having been essentially settled by around 1200.

Each of two leaves added to the beginning of the manuscript after its compilation records a rondeau by Baude Cordier, a composer known to have flourished from 1384 to 1398. These verses identify their subjects, translated from the French:

"Tout par compas" (Figure 6.4)
With a compass was I composed,
Properly as befits a roundelee,
To sing me more correctly.
Just see how I am disposed,
Good friend, I pray you kindly:
With a compass was I composed,
Properly, as befits a roundelee,
Three times around my lines you posed,
You can chase me around with glee
If in singing you're true to me.
With a compass was I composed . . .

"Belle, bonne, sage" (Figure 6.5)
Lovely, good, wise, gentle and noble one,
On this day that the year becomes new
I make you a gift of a new song
Within my heart, which presents itself to you.
Do not be reluctant to accept this gift,
I beg you, my sweet damsel;
(Lovely, good, wise . . .)
For I love you so well that I have no other purpose,
And know well that you alone are she
Who is famous for being called by all:
Flower of beauty, excellent above all others.
(Lovely, good, wise . . .)

Some immediate impressions:

1. Considering the two scores as totalities, they realize beyond his wildest aspirations Jehan de Murs's wish that "musicians ought to devise signs more appropriate to the things signified."

2. Referring to the distinction made in the first chapter between signs as denotation and as exemplification, that the denotation is transparent to the signified and the exemplification is not, these scores are exemplifications; they are emblems of the contents or

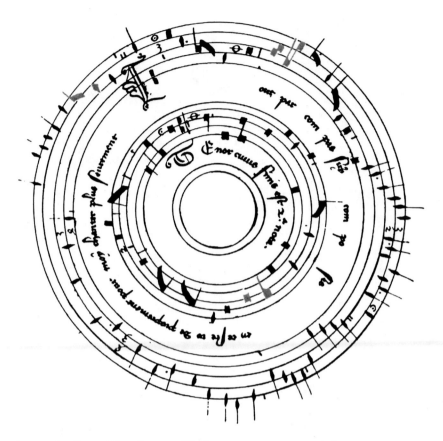

FIGURE 6.4. Excerpt from the score "Tout par compas suy composés," by Baude Cordier, ca. 1400. Chantilly Codex, Musée Condé, MS 564.

meanings of the poems that their music sets. Our interest in the graphic properties of the notation is not sublimated once we have assimilated the information it encodes about the musical contents.

This distinction has been expressed in terms of two properties of notation that can come to the fore in different measure: "utilitarian features," and "elements of choice in representational style and design." I am citing here James Haar's formulation in his essay "Music as Visual Language."[62]

Haar writes of fourteenth-century scores in "decorative shapes—circles, crosses, hearts, outlines of musical instruments (including the two added to the Chantilly manuscript)—aspects of design that carry meaning in themselves." But this heightened decorative interest partners in the music of this

FIGURE 6.5. Reproduction of the score for "Belle, bonne, et sage,"
by Baude Cordier, ca. 1400. Chantilly Codex, Musée Condé MS 564.

style with a notational system that refers in its smallest detail and large-scale
patterns to a subtle and complex rhythmic texture. This is a matter of fix-
ing time values to particular note shapes and colors, not individually but
as functions of their positions within temporal patterns and manipulating
such patterns through proportional shifts, indicated by signs that are part
of the notational system. Each voice in the polyphonic texture plays out or
sings out a layer in the sound. Each has a rhythmic life of its own, yet they
are coordinated with one another. It is as if one were to devise a notation

FIGURE 6.6. Reproduction of a score by Baude Cordier,
ca. 1400. Chantilly Codex, Musée Condé MS 564.

representing the simultaneous sound of three classical Indian tabla players, coordinated, but with each engaged in his own rhythmic program. The
notation is one of the most ingenious writing systems ever devised in any
domain.

Figure 6.6 shows another composition by Baude Cordier; twenty-three
such signs indicating proportional shifts are written. So refined and versatile
a sign system becomes itself an object of attention, overlapping the boundary
between denotation and exemplification. That happened in the music's own
time. The musical practice of the time, named after its notation, was called
"Ars nova," new practice or new technique. The label did not designate a style
period, as it does now. The notation itself was the unique identifier of the
style. As for the opaqueness of such scores, they may be compared to the
calligraphic traditions of the Orient, which are valued for their own beauty
independently of their utility as communication media.

Musical notation can communicate non-musical meaning in other ways.
Recently in observing the birthday of my granddaughter, Ella, it occurred to

EXAMPLE 6.4

me to accompany the gift I was sending her with a dedicatory message written in musical notation (Example 6.4, *Die Forelle*, "for Ella"; a musical rebus.)

Haar reports a case of the most ingenious and subtle use of musical notation conveying non-musical meaning. It is an emblematic intarsia in the

ceiling of Isabella d'Este's *grotta* in the Palazzo Ducale in Mantua (Figure 6.7). The elements are a staff, a clef, four mensuration signs, a repeat sign, and a series of signs for rests in a symmetrical arrangement. There are no signs for notes. Haar writes,

> This device ... was a favorite of Isabella's. She had it embroidered into clothing, wore a signet ring with its design, and included it among her emblems and those of her husband in a majolica service ...
>
> The device was surely meant to be read, then interpreted, as with all Renaissance emblems. How might a musically literate person of the time have read it? The staff and clef are givens [the musical frame]. The four mensuration signs mean, literally, the range of possibilities in measured musical time, figuratively the range of human circumstances. The repeat sign indicates just what it says, "start again," or "there is no limit to whatever the message may be" [recall the indication "Dal segno senza fine" at the end of the score of Chopin's Mazurka op. 7, no. 5, noted in chapter 5]. The rests, arranged symmetrically from large to small and back, are at first a pleasing design; next, they indicate the fullest extent of musical—or human—activity. Most important, and I think the reason rests were chosen rather than notes, is that in the notational system used in the sixteenth century, rests are perfect, subject neither to imperfection nor to alteration [triple value at each level, irreducible to duple], and hence immutable (the range of circumstances in human life). The message, redeemed from immodesty through its simplicity of presentation, is clear: the maker of the emblem is a rock of steadfast incorruptibility ... Representations of music as a liberal art and of music-making, celestial or mundane, in the visual arts have always been done chiefly through depiction of instruments, and of the act of singing or playing. The addition of notation to pictures centrally or peripherally concerned with music started slowly in the later fourteenth and early fifteenth centuries, becoming relatively frequent in the next century and almost commonplace from the mid-sixteenth century onward.[63]

But the focus of Haar's investigation is "the use of notation in painting and decorative art in contexts not illustrative of musical performance ... unheard music used as an important adjunct to iconographic schemes."[64]

There could not be a more striking instance than Isabella d'Este's emblem. That it would occur to someone of such station to encode this motto in musical notation shows something about the importance of music, and with it the prominence of music writing, in the attention of the culture.

FIGURE 6.7. Emblem of Isabella d'Este. James Haar,
"Music as Visual Language," Princeton, N.J.:
Institute for Advanced Study, 1995.

FIGURE 6.8. *The Union of Music and Comedy,* by Jean-Antoine Watteau.
Private collection, anonymous. Photograph courtesy of
Wildenstein & Co., Inc., New York. Used by permission.

Jean-Antoine Watteau's early eighteenth-century painting *L'alliance de la
musique et de la comédie* (The Union of Music and Comedy, Figure 6.8) is an
emblem of radical new social, political, and artistic conditions in France in
the late seventeenth and early eighteenth centuries. Comedy nudged tragedy
in theater and opera, an atmosphere of frivolity nudged the air of grandeur

Figure 6.9. The coat of arms of the House
of Bourbon, France, under Louis XIV.

and severity that radiated from the court of Louis XIV, class boundaries grew
fuzzy, parody and satire had free runs.[65]

Watteau's painting mocks the coat of arms of the House of Bourbon in
France, Louis XIV's dynasty during his reign (Figure 6.9). Up to a point the
parody is quite close, but the satirical imagination of the artist carried him
beyond that. The angels supporting the escutcheon on either side are replaced

by Thalia, the muse of comedy, on the left and Euterpe, the muse of music, on the right. Thalia holds a comic mask identified by Georgia Cowart as the face of Momon, the fool, traditionally carried about on a wand. Euterpe holds a lyre. The knight's head atop the escutcheon is replaced by a bust of Crispin, "the most famous comedian of the French stage and a symbol of French musical comedy." The theme of the painting is signified by the replacement of the wreath surrounding the escutcheon in the original with alternating fluttering leaves of musical scores and instruments with masks of the comic theater. And as if that were not enough, the triangular arrangement of three fleurs-de-lys of the original is replaced by a triangle of musical clefs surrounding a comic mask: F on the left, C on the right, G at the bottom. Cowart suggests that since the French *clef* means "key," "this emblem presents the key to the masked satire of the of the Parisian musical theater, the replacement of the king by the humble figures of the contemporary musical comedy as symbol of France." The object crossing the pastoral flute is Harlequin's bat, "evoking the 'Comédie Italienne' and fairground theaters, [confirming] the union of music/pastoral and comedy/satire . . . as symbol of an anti-absolutist France. Over the ensemble, a laurel wreath announces the victory of this new union."

If we want to get as inclusive an impression as we can of the kind of thing that musical notation has been, we should also take account of the reverse phenomenon: the introduction of painting and decorative art into what are primarily documents associated with musical performance, the genre of illuminated scores of liturgical and secular music.

A sublime example is the first page from a gradual approximately contemporary with the Chantilly codex of a representation of the opening chant—the introit "Puer natus est" (A child is born)—of the Christmas mass (Figure 6.10).[66] Here musical notation, calligraphy, and painting collaborate in an emblem, an exemplification, of the content and the spirit, meaning, significance—emotional and historical—of what is celebrated on Christmas day. The large size of the book of which this leaf was once the opening page (18" × 22") is itself emblematic of the performance situation—the cathedral choir gathered about the book—with enough space to accommodate the rich scenes depicted. Whether the singers needed the notation for their performance is a moot question. The book as focal point of the choir gathered about it was an aspect of the ritual.

Figure 6.10. A page from a 14th-century gradual. Used by permission of
the Pierpont Morgan Library, New York. Gift of J. P. Morgan (1867–1943),
1924. MS M 653.1. Photo credit: Photoservices, Morgan Library.

The European practice of accompanying musical notation with paintings that convey in their own medium the qualitative or affective aspects, the contents or meaning of the music, can suggest a way of thinking about the Chinese practice of representing the ways of producing sounds on the qin and the qualities of the resulting tones, as described in chapter 4. The landscape image and the poem embody in their own expressive media the feeling of the tone that is produced in engaging the string of the qin, as shown in the image of the hand.

These practices should alert us to the fact that musical notations together with their adjuncts have been written and read in numerous ways and for diverse purposes beyond the "utilitarian" purposes most familiar to us. But are there "elements of choice," notations of things unheard in the notations that we are accustomed to regarding as purely "utilitarian?"

The symmetrical hairpins in the piano part of this passage of Beethoven's *An die ferne Geliebte* comprise a performance direction that is in this case impossible to execute (Example 6.5; in case an editor's error or whimsey is suspected, the hairpins are in the autograph). In playing this accompaniment I know that I react to the sign, even though I cannot execute it. My response is always a kind of kinaesthetic movement, to match the suggestion of a sudden surge and fading of feeling. Two moments in the piano part of Schumann's *Fantasiestücke*, op. 73, for clarinet and piano, are similar (Examples 6.6a and b): in the first, a sustained dissonant E in the right hand (against B♭ in the left) must swell and subside, but can't; in the second, a crescendo from the first chord to the second can't be executed and a decrescendo after the second chord is unavoidable. Perhaps that can also be understood as a comment about the shape of this little gesture. Something like that seems more apparently to be the sense of a notation in two measures of Brahms's Sonata for Clarinet and Piano op. 120, no. 2 (Example 6.7). The decrescendo sign, considered as an instruction, cannot be executed by the pianist but is redundant, as it cannot be prevented from being carried out by the piano. The chord concludes the last statement of the movement's main theme, and what follows is an ending through the gradual mulling over and elimination of the thematic material. The decrescendo hairpin is a sign that the music that precedes it now fades away.

These enigmatic signs seem like notational counterparts of verbal "expression marks," conveying in their own language something of the "poetic

EXAMPLE 6.5

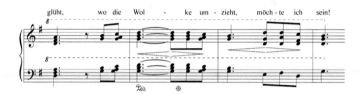

EXAMPLE 6.6 a

EXAMPLE 6.6 b

EXAMPLE 6.7

idea," as Schindler reports Beethoven to have said, or the "character" and
"spirit," as Beethoven himself wrote to von Mosel in 1817, of the music they
mark (see chapter 3).[67] It is no coincidence that this is a phenomenon of the
Romantic era. But it did not fade with the Romantic era. When Alban Berg
wrote *Tumultuoso* over the music that follows the moment in the first scene
of act 2 of *Lulu* when Alwa, on his knees, sings "Lulu, ich liebe dich," she replies, "Ich habe deine Mutter vergiftet," and the wind instruments fall away,
leaving the strings sustaining the Tristan chord (mm. 335–37; see chapter
8), it was surely a comment from the author rather more than a redundant
instruction to the orchestra about how to play that music. The word *tumultuoso*, thematic for this opera about tumultuous lives, occurs throughout
the score.

The first movement of Schumann's *Fantasiestücke* for clarinet and piano
is like his songs in respect to the roles of the *dramatis personae*. The piano
accompanies, but not only that. It has its own identity, spins its own yarn,
which tangles with that of the clarinet. If the clarinet is the protagonist and
the left hand of the piano provides the harmonic bass, the piano's right hand
is a split persona, providing a running triplet accompaniment and engaging
at the same time in melodic dialogue (in which the piano left-hand sometimes participates) with the clarinet. But since the clarinet speaks only in
duple time, the voice of the piano right-hand must speak the same dialect
in order to be understood, even as it must keep the triplet accompaniment
flowing. How does this diglossia square? It doesn't, really. What stands out
in this movement is the confident lyricism of the clarinet's song, supported
by the piano left-hand's bass, and in between the agitation of the piano right-
hand's uncertainty about its identity. This drama of conflict and indecision
is played out in the notation. Its emblem is the sort of invented notational
figure shown in m. 3 (Example 6.8a), a visual oxymoron that, when rendered
in performance (by rushing the attack of the second triplet note just enough
to make the duple isochronous without disrupting the effect of the triplet)
comes off as an audible oxymoron.

EXAMPLE 6.8 a

This is all set out, beat by beat, in the first measure: beat 1, a tonic bass in the left hand launches the triplet accompaniment; beats 2 and 3, the entry of the right-hand melody which, although it enters first, really comments on the center-stage solo of the clarinet, beginning on beat 4. For the first two measures there is no conflict. The first anomaly appears on the fourth beat of measure 3 with the upward stems beamed as a duple. This is not forced or suggested by what anyone else is doing, as will happen later. Looking ahead to the second movement, the motive that is identified by this enigmatic figure will become its principal theme (Example 6.8b).

EXAMPLE 6.8 b

The question about the duple or triple identity of the upper-right-hand piano voice begins to be urgent at m. 11, when the pianist must decide whether that voice should continue the unison relationship with the clarinet that had begun in m. 10 (Example 6.8c). The question becomes moot in m. 17, the moment when the clarinet's song reaches its expressive height, essentially forcing the piano right-hand's upper voice to drop out and ending the need for upward-stemmed notes.

The plurality of ways in which musical notations communicate and what they communicate about has implications for the question of the title of this chapter. Are the images and poems of the qin handbooks a species of musical

EXAMPLE 6.8 c

notation? Returning to the subject of chapter 3, are "expressive" and "performance" marks (there is no finite differentiation between them) musical notation? Leaping to say "of course not" would be to slip back to the "narrow focus" on musical notation that was queried at the beginning of this chapter. It would be to imply that writing down pitches and durations is encoding the whole of music. It is, finally, to ignore this fundamental insight of the *New Harvard Dictionary of Music*: "Musical notation is like any other text requiring realization by a reader who brings to bear on it an accumulation of habit and experience," and to reaffirm the semiotics of a fixed mind-free link between signifier and signified.

3

The *New Grove Dictionary of Music and Musicians* offers the following definition:

> Notation. A visual analogue of musical sound, either as a record of sound heard or imagined, or as a set of visual instructions for performers . . . A written musical notation requires further a spatial arrangement of the signs on the writing surface, which makes a system of the assemblage; it is this system that forms an analogue with the system of musical sound, thus empowering the signs to "signify" individual elements of it.[68]

The reference to "spatial arrangement of signs" points to our method of pitch notation, which is properly regarded as a system. It is as system that the pitch notation forms an analogue of the pitch system, and it is from its systemic properties that its signs derive their capacity to signify the individual elements of the pitch system, not the other way about. This can be underscored with a brief exercise in defamiliarization.

The staff, or any system of two or more staves, is a sign for the diatonic series. By writing a clef on the staff and/or writing sharps or flats at the left extreme of the staff, we fix where the semitones are and concretize the diatonic series as a structured key. When we write a note anywhere on the staff we pick out a position, which is to say a function, in the configuration of the key. This has the implication of conceiving a musical item not in terms of an array of pitches but as a configuration of functions. In almost all musical traditions that have a pitch dimension, if there is a notation that represents pitch, it does so by picking out configurations of functional positions in such a system.

There are other ways than writing round note-heads on the staff to represent sounds in functional positions. One such is the American shape-note system. A similar one is Guido's hexachord system. In the ancient Greek system there are names for the positions and the signs for them are based on the alphabet. Among the early medieval experiments in notating music the daseia system entails a notation in which each sign identifies a position in a system of tetrachords. In the system of the Byzantine chant tradition of the twelfth century the notation of each chant begins with a signature that indicates its mode and starting tone. Subsequent signs indicate the interval size within the modal structure of successive moves upward or downward. In short, in none of these notations is the representation a matter of serial, one-to-one fixed links between signs and tones. In Western practice the structures or systems represented by notations are clearly not limited to tonal ones. They may be the constituent segments and formulas of modes, or the motives and configurations of serial sets.

At the bottom of the menu for July 14 some years ago the proprietors of La Duchesse Anne, a French restaurant in Woodstock, New York, had printed the following: "la laa la laaa laaa laaa laaa laaaaa la laa la laa la laaa laaaaaa laa la laaaaaaa." They had counted on their patrons, francophile enough to opt for a French meal in observance of the French national holiday, to recognize this as a notation of the French national anthem. What are the cues? The syllables "La laa la laaa . . ." are representations of singing; the line represents a song, of which these syllables represent the notes. The different number of a's in the syllables make for different horizontal distances between them, and the key to the recognition of the song is the intuitive conversion of spatial distance to distance in time, just as vertical distance in the system of pitch notation came to represent distance in the pitch system, and with that the exact temporal distances come naturally from both the presence of the anthem in our memories and our innate proclivity for recognizing temporal patterns. That gives us the rhythm, which is sufficient to give us the tune's pitch content. We do not need to count and compare the number of a's in the syllables to make that happen. Nor would someone who does not know the song be able to arrive at the rhythm by means of such counting and comparing. The process entails both recognition and identification. But I suggest that our ability to achieve this recognition is at once a function of our internalized knowledge of "La Marseillaise" and of an aspect of our musical nature, a competence that allows us to lay out time spans mentally and articulate them in proportionally ordered patterns. It is striking that the mind's ability to hold exact spans of time, on which the kinds of performances that I have been describing depend, was recognized and described on the analogy of the parallel ability with respect to the dimensions of space by both Aristotle and Augustine.[69]

In his insightful article "Rhythm" in the *New Harvard Dictionary of Music,* Harold Powers writes,

> In modern English musical usage, the word rhythm appears on two semantic levels. In the widest sense it appears beside the terms melody and harmony, and in that very general sense, rhythm covers all aspects of musical movement as ordered in time. In the narrower and more specific sense . . . rhythm denotes a patterned configuration of *attacks* . . . A perceivable pattern of *temporal space* between attacks constitutes a rhythm [my emphases].[70]

This formulation has the advantage of inclusiveness over more common-place descriptions that privilege duration and accent as principal factors in provoking rhythmic experience. A member of the performance group called The Flying Karamazov Brothers, four virtuoso jugglers with a musical consciousness about their skill, put it most simply during a performance: "Rhythm is things happening in time." As Powers writes,

> A succession of attacks can be articulated in many ways: by striking or blowing an instrument; by articulating a consonant in singing; by change of density in a multilayered texture; by change of harmony or timbre; even by mere change of pitch in an otherwise unarticulated melodic line.[71]

The sensation of rhythm as patterns of attack points—most literally—and the temporal spaces between them, playing off one another in a multilayered texture, is produced in the purest way by Steve Reich's "Music for Pieces of Wood." In each section of the piece each of three to five players, using two claves, one as striker, the other as resonator, articulates the time span of some number of $\frac{6}{4}$ measures through a different pattern of attack points, resulting in a counterpoint of attack-point structures that is heard against the steady pulse of the highest-pitched resonator (see Example 6.9, the first page of the score). Alban Berg, in the first scene of act 2 of *Lulu*, suggests a rhythm of attack points literally, with precisely timed gunshots directed by Lulu at Dr. Schön. As background to the pistol's solo the orchestra plays a ubiquitous, obsessive, sinister rhythmic motive that bears the label "RH"—*Hauptrhythmus* (Example 6.10 shows it in its first appearance, as the conclusion of act 1, a role it plays in all three acts). In every appearance throughout the opera it is always a pitch repetition in that rhythmic pattern; see chapter 8. The more the motive forces itself on the audience's attention in all of its versions—shifting positions with respect to the measure, canon, retrograde form, and combinations of these, the more clearly it foregrounds its attack-point pattern as its rhythmic essence. Berg's intention about this is most evident in the version at m. 559 and following in act 2. The cellos and horns play the motive in canon, the cellos in a retrograde version, the horns in the prime order (Example 6.11). Now a strict retrograde version—the durational values played in reverse order—would not be recognizable as a version of the motive at all (Example 6.12). The last thing we hear in the motive is two attacks in quick succession. So to make a recognizable backward version Berg puts that event at the beginning, followed by two attacks at the ends of longer silences (Example 6.13, two

EXAMPLE 6.9

music for pieces of wood

Steve Reich

EXAMPLE 6.10

Ende des I. Aktes

EXAMPLE 6.11

EXAMPLE 6.12

EXAMPLE 6.13

versions, both of which come off as retrograde). The retrograde form that is experienced as running in reverse is the retrograde of attack-point patterns, not the retrograde of durations.

The early history of Western efforts toward rhythmic notation is a story of trials at conceptualizing the rhythmic competence that I have sought to identify as it was exercised in performance practice and at finding a way to represent the practice with graphic signs. I shall try to summarize that story from this point of view, because it provides the most convincing kind of demonstration of the way that a notation can serve to trigger a deep-seated ability, and in that way play the role of mnemonic in a more fundamental way than is commonly thought. But first I want to probe this competence as it is manifested in a kind of extemporaneous rhythmic performance of poetry of which we are all capable.

> Ride a cock horse to Banbury Cross
> To see a fine lady upon a white horse.
> (With) Rings on her fingers and bells on her toes
> (And) She shall have music wherever she goes.

Reading this nursery rhyme aloud, most of us will intuitively distribute the syllables and stresses as shown in Example 6.14a. The words in parentheses are mutually exclusive variants: if one appears the other is omitted.

EXAMPLE 6.14a

A word about my notation: it is an "ideal" representation in the sense that no actual performance would render it strictly as shown, there would always be some degree of rubato—something like the ontological status of jazz transcriptions, which sound horribly stiff if played "as written."

Eighth notes represent syllables. I do not mark syllables followed by an interval with quarter notes or dotted quarters because the syllables are not sustained. The rhythm of this rhyme is a matter of patterns of attack points and temporal spaces between them, stresses, and rhymes. Halle and Keyser use the term "stress group"—a fixed group of equidistant pulse positions, of which the first is stressed and in which each position may or may not be occupied by a syllable.[72] This rhyme proceeds in stress groups of three positions each. Stress or its absence is not an inherent property of syllables. Whether a syllable is stressed or not depends on its position in a stress group. Such spontaneous recognition, write Halle and Keyser, belongs to our competence as speakers of English.

The figures in Example 6.14a in parentheses represent the variants shown in the text. If we read, "With rings on her fingers . . ." we will begin the last line, "She shall have music . . ." That is governed by our sense of syntax. Similarly, if we read, "Rings on her fingers . . ." we will read, "And she shall have music . . ." The way we accommodate such variants can give us an inkling of what is involved in such intuitive readings. To preserve the temporal pattern we tuck the added syllable in at the end of the preceding line, reducing the two-beat interval between lines by one beat.

With the same intuitive ease we know how to recite this nursery rhyme (see Example 6.14b):

Jack and Jill went up a hill
To fetch a pail of water.
Jack fell down and broke his crown
And Jill came tumbling after.

EXAMPLE 6.14 b

The essential difference in our enactment of this rhyme is that the stress groups comprise two syllables, two attacks. In the performance of both rhymes the words serve us as a notation that activates a competence that we have with respect to its rhythmic performance.

The earliest Western systematic rhythmic practice of which we know in detail was an exercise of this kind of competence. The earliest efforts to explain the practice and to put it under the control of a system of notation were made around 1200. The notation was a major part of the enterprise and there was great pride in its achievement. What musicians of that time codified in the practices of performing and writing music can be understood as the roots of our rhythmic practice today.[73]

Two tendencies in modes of explanation of the time, and one evolution of musical style, are visible as background to these efforts:

1. A tendency to model explanations about musical matters on doctrines about language.

2. A convention for formulating comparisons of quantity in terms of proportion, regardless of the accuracy of such formulations. For descriptions of the performance of music, this meant that in quantifying the time element differences were expressed in terms of proportions.

3. The emergence of a melodic practice out of the melismatic elaboration of chant melody in organum, which raised the possibility of the rhythmic patterning of melody without the control of language. This development is documented in books with notation referring to the singing practice, and texts witnessing the exertions of learned musicians of the time to explain and normalize the practice and the notation from what had no doubt been an oral tradition.

The control of a temporal parameter in the performance of melody was accomplished by means of the firming up of a set of standardized patterns called "modes" (modus: measure by size or quantity). The temporal spacing of notes in performance was not fixed to the shape or color of their notational representation, as in our notation, but was contingent on the patterning of written figures representing one to four notes ("simple" notes and "ligatures"—two or more notes "tied" together) and by the position of each note in the pattern. One read not individual notes but configurations. That entailed a radical move: positing a measurable time dimension of sounds and bestowing on the notational figures that represent them the attribute of quantity. This was first pronounced by John of Garland, around 1200:

"All simple figures are valued according to their names," and "A figure is a representation of a sound according to its mode."[74] The radical nature of this is proclaimed in the title of the treatise in which these assertions appear, *De mensurabili musica.*

The writers agreed in describing six modal patterns. (One, Franco of Cologne, counted five, recognizing the sixth as a version of the first. This is one indication of his understanding of the essential nature of the system. That will become clear below.) They differed in their explanations of the system and in their time conceptions, with differences that have consequences for commonplace conceptions today. The earliest description by John of Garland is founded on an elemental unit of time, the note called the "brevis" (B). The "longa" (L) normally has a value of two B's. The conception adopted the a priori principle that the patterns of the modes comprise successions of L's and B's, and the patterning of the notational figures represents the exact ordering of those units.

Two of the modal patterns produced in the practice entailed notes with a value equal to three B's. As a purely nominalist device to preserve the principle of B–L alternation, John's explanation posited two varieties each of B's and L's: "correct" (we could say "default") and "beyond measure."[75] The B of one unit (or beat) and the L of two beats are "correct." "Beyond measure" describes a B of two beats and an L of three. Through these definitions John rationalized the representation of the modal patterns by the figures shown in Example 6.15 (note that the figures indicate something about rhythmic configuration for which the writers found no language).

EXAMPLE 6.15

1. LBL . . .
2. BLB . . .
3. LBBL . . .
4. BBLBBL . . .
5. LLL . . .
6. BBB BBB . . .

Whether a note is "correct" or "beyond measure" depends on where it falls in the pattern of one of the six modes. But how is the singer to determine which of the modes is represented by a notational pattern? A good question, especially as there are circumstances that can break down the ligatures of a normal pattern—the introduction of a new text syllable or the repetition of a pitch on an internal element of a ligature. The singer had to project a modal pattern and make corrections if it did not work out—a straightforward case of the hermeneutic circle. All told, in this conception the time of a musical passage is built up by a succession of B and L notes.

The other, later conception, is first represented in the *Ars cantus mensurabilis* (The Theory of Measured Song) by Franco of Cologne, around 1280. Franco begins by appearing to reverse the condition described by Garland, that the position of a note in a modal pattern determines its value. He writes, "A figure is a representation of a sound arranged in one of the modes. From this it follows that the figures ought to indicate the modes and not, as some have maintained, the contrary."[76] But he soon shows that this is an unfulfilled ideal, seemingly without noting the inconsistency. First, however, he states an axiom, gives a definition, and proclaims a rule. And these together should be entered in an imaginary register of "Great Moments in Music History." The axiom: "Of simple figures there are three species: long, breve, and semibreve, the first of which has three varieties—perfect, imperfect, and duplex. The definition: "The perfect long is said to be the first and principal, for in it all the others are included and all the others are reducible to it. It is called perfect because it is measured by three 'tempora'"; a "tempus," he writes, "is a minimum in fullness of voice". Franco's theological justification of "perfection" with reference to the Holy Trinity notwithstanding, "perfectus" carries the sense of completeness, which is the operative principle in his explication of the system. A perfection is a full three-beat time span. The rule: "Be it also understood that in all the modes concords are always to be used at the beginning of a perfection, whether this beginning be a long, a breve, or a semibreve."[77] Taken together with the earlier remark that "immediately before a concord any imperfect discord concords well,"[78] the implication is that dissonances are resolved here—that is, on the attack point that we call "downbeat"—with the further implication of directed motion toward that goal. With this understanding we can see that the whole conception is inherent in the way the notes are configured in the notation from the beginning, and it was Franco's achievement to give a clear exposition of it. The consonant rule, in its second clause ("whether it is long or breve") distinguishes between accent and duration. That is made possible for music by Franco's concept of the perfection. Garland's explication, lacking such a concept, is not subject to that distinction. Given the distinction, under the concept of the perfection, the first mode moves from an upbeat B to a downbeat L. This is really shown by the notation, which begins with L and continues BL, BL, BL, and so forth. I illustrate with a rendering of a familiar melody in modal notation, "Pop Goes the Weasel" (Example 6.16). The second mode begins with an accented B and unaccented long, and continues BL BL BL, and so forth, as in the Scotch Snap (Example 6.17).

EXAMPLE 6.16

EXAMPLE 6.17

Although Franco begins his exposition by positing a note value, it is soon clear that his conception is founded on a time span, the three-beat measure oriented to the downbeat as goal. He makes explicit that the value of notes is indicated by their configurations, not by their graphic shape: "The imperfect long has the same figure as the perfect but signifies only two 'tempora.' It is called imperfect because it is never found except in combination with a following or imperfect breve";[79] that is, the two together fill the measure. Then "the breve, although it has two varieties, proper and altered, is represented in each case by a quadrangular figure without a tail." Later, "of two successive breves, the first is proper, one 'tempus,' the second altered, two 'tempora,' to fill out the perfection." All this is summarized: "The valuation of simple figures is dependent on their arrangement with respect to one another," not with respect to the mode, as in Garland's explanation, but with respect to the perfection, or the three-beat measure.

I suggested that the ability to recognize "The Marseillaise" from the verbal notation on the menu of La Duchesse Anne was enabled in part by a deep-rooted competence. I did not, and cannot, speculate whether it is inborn or a product of early learning. I suggest now that our intuitive ability to perform the two nursery rhymes and the ability of thirteenth-century singers to sing in modal rhythm and to read its notation are and were enabled by a similar competence, and I suggest that the invention of the notation system and Franco's explanation of it entailed a tacit and stunning exercise of it.

In an article "Rhythm in Music: What Is It, Who Has It, and Why," John Bispham, of the Leverhulme Centre for Evolutionary Studies/Centre for Music and Science, University of Cambridge, writes: "Crucially, musical rhythmic production implies reference to an internal time-keeper and/or to an internally created and volitionally controlled pulse." He adds to that the resources of "period production" and "phase correction," which he characterizes as "mechanisms [that] can be supposed to be operational in all activities involving future-directed attending where expectations are constantly updated."[80] I suggest that these characterizations speak very closely to the kinds of rhythmic performances that I have described.

Sometimes while reading chamber music, stumbling over a difficult passage, and dropping out as the others go on, we project ahead to the moment when we can get back in to rejoin them. Leibniz is credited with a way of characterizing this ability that we have: "Music is the pleasure the human mind experiences from counting without being aware that it is counting."[81] Irish traditional musicians gather in pubs for *caeili* sessions. These may be likened to the jam sessions of jazz musicians for their informality, their spontaneity, and often the technical and improvisatory virtuosity of their participants. There is one striking difference, however. Jazz musicians agree about tune and key before beginning, more or less together, and they end together. In an Irish session there may be agreement about the tune, but it may be that one player begins without a word and the others join in, in any order. It can also be that a new tune is taken up by one of the players without any break from the conclusion of the preceding one, the others jumping in at will, like sprinters jumping onto a moving train. When the tempo is very rapid the experience can be breathtaking.

But not as breathtaking—or heart-stopping—as the circus flying trapeze act in its climactic moment. The flyer, hanging by his hands from his trapeze bar, reaches the far end of his second swing as the catcher, hanging by his knees, swings toward him. At precisely the right instance, the flyer lets go of his trapeze and is propelled by his momentum toward the catcher, who grasps his wrists, and they swing together to a platform. There can be no more precise a coordination of the movements of two humans. We have a word for what makes these performance acts possible: timing, a word we use easily without being conscious of the capacity it evokes.

Pianists performing Chopin's Prelude in D minor, op. 28, no. 24, must execute with the right hand eight spectacular upward or downward plunges, always paced against a driving ostinato in the left hand that produces a pulse of two beats per ⅜ measure. These runs are of different lengths, comprising from twelve to twenty-eight notes, to be executed within the time span of one-third, one-half, or a full measure. The tempo indication is *allegro,* and pianists typically take it at about sixty quarter notes per minute, hence the time span of a measure is two seconds. All runs end on the downbeat of the following measure, which the performer projects as the figure's goal. The time span between its initial attack—which the performer locates with reference to the pulsing ostinato figure—and the next downbeat must be felt or projected in the performer's mind, for she sets the speed of the run so that it exactly fills that time span and finishes on the following downbeat, ideally without any variation of internal tempo.

Example 6.18a shows the first of these swoops. It spans two octaves and a fourth and runs through twenty-eight notes (not counting the downbeat of the following measure) in the two seconds allotted it. Example 6.18b shows an identical figure at a different pitch level. Example 6.18c. shows the same figure at yet another pitch level which is, however, allotted only two-thirds of a measure, one and one-third seconds. The performer must set her tempo for this a tiny bit faster. That she knows instinctively how much faster is a manifestation of the faculty that I have been calling "timing."

The extensive bibliographies at the end of Bispham's article, along with Tomlinson's references, provide a glimpse of a widespread turn toward biological explanation in which a number of interrelated fields have participated: music perception, music psychology, evolution studies, inter-species comparative studies regarding the "music faculty" or proto–music faculties, brain studies, paleoanthropology, and an emerging field that may be called "paleomusicology," in which new kinds of historical questions are asked—about the nature and origins and evolution of human faculties that have come

EXAMPLE 6.18 a, b, c

together as musicality—as a new way of paraphrasing Schenker's question, "Wie war ein Beethoven musikalisch?".[82] "Wie ist, wie war, und wie wurde der Mensch musikalisch?"

From this vantage point, questions about the evolution of musical behavior are being seriously raised and pursued with scientific investigative procedures and on the grounds of hard evidence. That was my motive for identifying Bispham's institutional affiliation. It is against this background that cues delivered through music notation can be understood to trigger the engagement of deep-seated faculties. With that understanding we may ask again, more broadly, What kind of thing is musical notation?

SKETCHING MUSIC,
WRITING MUSIC

This chapter originated as a contribution to an interdisciplinary conference organized by the Princeton Institute for Advanced Study and the Center for Advanced Study in the Visual Arts at the National Gallery of Art, under the title "Creativity: The Sketch in the Arts and Sciences." My assigned topic was the earliest recognizable practice of sketching in Western music. The assignment implies a mutual understanding of what kind of a practice in the creation and writing down of music at any time would be readily identified as "sketching." But the conference was called by two art historians, and such understanding is not to be taken for granted. It is not clear that when an art historian says "sketch," the music historian hears what the art historian has in mind, or that the art historian means to be asking about whatever practices that word brings to the music historian's mind.

"Sketch" is a loanword from the language of the visual arts in discourse about music. It continues to be associated in dictionaries first with painting or drawing, then with literary or theatrical production; scarcely at all with music. Dictionary definitions use such language as this: simply or hastily executed, short, fragmentary, slight, brief outlines, roughed out, delineations, ephemeral, lacking finish. Although such characterizations *can* be found in studies of musical sketches, they stand for qualities that have not been in the main responsible for the interest that music historians have taken in what they call sketching, nor have music historians usually valorized music sketches for just those qualities in the way that art critics and historians, especially, have done.

Before turning to what it is that has been of greater interest to music historians, I want to take note of how closely these modern definitions capture the way in which the word and the conception to which it refers were first understood, and the purpose for which they were brought into modern languages and critical discourse. The term entered the discourse about drawing and painting first, around 1500, in the service of a constellation of aesthetic values and modalities for those arts, newly promoted principally by Leonardo da Vinci. The word itself (*schizzo*) has been traced to the Greek word for two of those associated values, *skhedios*, meaning "extempore,"[1] and "temporary."[2] David Rosand takes the etymology from *schizzare*, "splash." He writes, "*Schizzare* implies a sudden spurt or splash of liquid."[3] Under this conception the purpose of the sketch is to stimulate the imagination of the artist and the viewer with an open work, in which the viewer imagines more than he sees. Openness would be a consequence of rapidity and roughness in the drawing, with little detail and without finish (*diligenza*). In the following generation Giorgio Vasari speaks of the artist working in a "creative fury" (*furor dello artifice*),[4] a notion that descended from the Greek concept of "poetic madness," as expounded in Plato's *Phaedrus* and that resonates with our conception of "brain storm," both touching from opposite directions on the Romantic notion of artistic "genius." Working in such a state, writes Vasari, the artist makes sketches that are "a sort of first drawing . . . as a rough draft made in the form of a blot."[5] Leonardo advises looking at stains on walls, ashes, clouds, or mud as an aid to reflection, "obscure things" to stimulate the mind to various discoveries. The resulting "rough composition" in turn stimulates the same faculty, inspiring variations on itself. Picking up on this conception, Goethe wrote of "Good sketches by great masters, those enchanting hieroglyphs . . ."

I'm drawn to this metaphor, for Goethe's choice of the word "hieroglyphs." Why that word? Goethe had explained just before:

> A good, half-defined idea, sketched out as it were symbolically, does not detain the eye, but excites the mind, the wit, the imagination, and the am-

ateur is taken by surprise and sees what is not really there ... Mind speaks to mind, and the means by which this should happen is done away with.[6]

It is worth reading these lines of Goethe and thinking that the subject might be music writing.

It is the speed of the act of sketching that led commentators like Vasari and Albrecht Dürer[7] to move their focus to the mind or imagination of the artist, rich with images or figures that may be expressed, or deposited repeatedly, as ever more variations. Much like this, I suggest, was the production—orally and in writing—of traditional music, what Ritva Jacobsson and I have called sketching archetypes in reference to early medieval Western compositional practice (both poetry and music).[8] The writing down of music—inseparable from its creation—was from the beginning in the ninth century a matter of sketching. A clear and consistent distinction between the categories "sketching" and the "writing" of "finished works"—whether or not on the model of the visual arts—is not to be *found* in music-writing practice before 1600[9] and is, in a sense, as much a product of the much later interest in studying it as it is a fact of composers' practice.

The weight of scholarly interest in musical sketching, which was kindled in the nineteenth century, has fallen on studies of notational representations or schemata of plans or ideas for works that have been deposited in finished scores, or passages of such works, written down at varying levels of detail, or representations of the actual working out of some part of a composition. To be sure, such a relationship between sketch and finished work has played a role in the history of painting, as we see in a statement from the artist posted in the exhibition Pierre Bonnard: The Late Interiors:

> I always make a quick, directly observed water color and without which
> any subsequent work would be impossible. I set down my impression
> of the colors. I refer to this sketch constantly to avoid going off track when
> executing the work itself.[10]

The principal objective of modern studies of musical sketches has been to gain access to compositional process in general and particular cases, and to a lesser and more controversial extent, to use sketches explicitly as clues for the analysis of the corresponding works.[11]

There is an implicit and scarcely avoidable reversal of such interpretive practice when the finished work, always a backdrop in the study of the sketches, becomes a guide for their interpretation, just as the outcome of a historical development is a backdrop and a guide for the study of the history under a teleological conception. It is asking quite a lot of the interpreter to contemplate the sketches for a work with a mind emptied of familiarity with the work itself. Given the devotion to a musical canon and to the work concept, there has been less attention to sketches not associated with finished work and scarcely any interest at all in musical sketches for their aesthetic qualities or the glimpse they afford of the mind at work, in contrast to the interest in sketches of visual artists.[12] These orientations to the reciprocal relationships between musical sketches and finished works can be manifestations of a complicated ideology about the compositional process, featuring the composer as original genius and the musical work as organic and teleological creation. It is hardly a coincidence that the paradigmatic subjects of musical sketch studies under the influence of this ideology have been the sketches of Beethoven, the paradigmatic genius figure of the nineteenth century. Lewis Lockwood, in his essay "On Beethoven's Sketches and Autographs: Some Problems of Definition and Interpretation," has spelled out the expectations under such an ideology (his tone betrays a skepticism inspired by his long experience with the material and its study according to that ideology:

> [A]s a work progresses from first inklings to final realization it should pass through successive phases of growth and clarification of structure, and of complication of detail in relation to that structure, becoming progressively more definite en route to its goal. Following the historian's bent for discerning genetic patterns, we suppose too that the relevant sources should articulate this progress, that they should ideally reveal a sequence passing from many and far-reaching revisions to fewer and less significant ones, affecting only minor details. In the case of Beethoven, a century-old tradition made up of a certain amount of close study and considerably more popularization of that study has led us not only to regard the progressive refinement of ideas as being his most basic and characteristic trait, but to look for evidence of it in the sketches, and to seek the final product in the autograph. The concluding stage should be the autograph as "fair copy" containing the work in final form, ready to be transmitted to the copyist or printer, with no further corrections required.
>
> But a close look at even a handful of Beethoven autographs so far brought out in complete facsimile shows that they more often frustrate these expectations than fulfill them.[13]

Lockwood illustrates with reference to scores that have been regarded as autographs in the sense of final copies, but that show substantial revisions. One of these is the autograph of the Violoncello Sonata in A Major, op. 69. His focus is on the pages representing the development section of the first movement, which he characterizes as "a battlefield of conflicting ideas." He writes,

> From the tangled threads of these pages one can unravel two full-length versions of the entire development section, of which the second version . . . represents a total recasting and exchange of the roles of the violoncello and piano that had been set down in the first version. . . . Apparently, only when he [Beethoven] had written down one version of the development in this autograph did he see how he really wanted the two instruments to be fitted together.[14]

This passage is profound and revealing in two ways. First, it shows one of the principal complications of the ideologies underlying the tradition of musical sketch studies. On one hand, given the emphasis on the teleological character of the process of creation under the organicist doctrine and the Romantic "genius" concept (the artist under the power of his genius), the final state of a work is predetermined. On the other hand, the mode set for the interpretation of the Beethoven autograph materials—principally by Gustav Nottebohm—portrays them as sites of "Beethoven's struggle with his demon, the wrestling with his own genius,"[15] regarded in the later nineteenth century as a struggle with ethical and moral dimensions that reflected on the character of Beethoven himself. Second, and more broadly suggestive, the final sentence of the passage reveals a consequence of the writing down—whether intended or not—that had not been noted before in such studies. It allowed Beethoven to see—in both a literal and metaphorical sense—an intention or necessity that he could not grasp, a decision he could not make while the music was confined to his mind. This sort of role for writing down—quite distinct from the transactions between composers and performers—was both an impulse for and a consequence of the launch of a practice of music writing in ninth-century Europe, the radical move of depositing onto a writing surface through the use of arbitrary graphic signs referring to the movement of a voice through a tonal space the musical part of a centuries-old oral tradition of song that had been conceived as a unity of words and melody. As a consequence of the very act of writing down, participants in the tradition were forced to recognize properties and problems of the tradition that they could not have conceived and would not have confronted in the oral tradition.[16]

Just as motives for making visible something conceptual in the domain of the visual arts have produced sketches associated with texts since the beginning of that practice—think of Leonardo's sketch of 1485 for a parachute, or the sketches accompanying the texts in art historian Meyer Schapiro's book *Meyer Schapiro Abroad: Letters to Lillian and Travel Notebooks*, so among the oldest surviving specimens of European music writing are musical sketches illustrating explanations in theoretical and pedagogical tracts. It may be that the systems of notation were invented for that purpose. In any case, a more pressing need for them than for the systems used first in representing the enormous repertories of ritual song in the oral tradition is suggested by the circumstance that the music writing used for such purposes is significantly more precise in its denotations of pitch than the earliest notations in the chant books. The utilitarian function of such sketches is frequently signaled by the writing of the formula *ut hic* (as here) following a verbal explanation.

Before turning to the other task for which musical notation was called into service in the beginning for a different kind of sketching—the depositing of the prolix tradition of chanting in books by way of the sketching of archetypes—I want to describe an unexpected parallel in a modern practice in the visual arts that can help me to convey a sense of the practice in medieval music.

In 2001 the Reina Sofía Museum of Modern Art in Madrid mounted an exhibition called Picasso: The Great Series. The exhibit encompassed four constellations of paintings, each a series of variations on an original image: Delacroix's painting *Les femmes d'Alger*, Manet's *Le déjeuner sur l'herbe*, Velasquez's *Las Meninas*, and Picasso's studio in his house in Cannes, *Le Californie*. In a fine study featuring the first three of these series, Susan Grace Galassi has called the practice, which Picasso pursued intensively from 1954 until the end of his life in 1973, interpretive copying, variation, and improvisation.[17] She cites as legitimation for the "new generation" of such practices a letter written by Van Gogh to his brother in 1889: "in music and more especially in singing the composer's work is performed, and it is not a hard and fast rule that only the composer should play his own composition." In copying, he wrote, "my brush goes between my fingers as a bow would on the violin, and absolutely for my own pleasure."[18]

Even if the paintings hadn't been dated, showing that each was made within a single day, and sometimes two within a day, one could have seen the haste with which they were made, the absence of any sign of editing. The urgency of capturing on canvas the mental image of the moment obviously had priority over any aim for finish. Galassi writes, "Picasso once told John Richardson that it was often the first or the penultimate version in a series of paintings that he considered the best; the final was often too finished,"[19] but of course only in some of his work. That quality of instantaneity and continuous transformation was the commanding impression given by the exhibition, more than the thought of the virtuosity that made such speed possible. And beyond the figurative elements of the model that one recognizes in the paintings of each series, one recognizes in all of them the gestures and transformations that are Picasso's own.

While each of the paintings in a series clearly takes its point of departure from the model, they all make references to other works across a broad spectrum wherever Picasso saw a connection elsewhere to some aspect of the model that he was developing.

The record of musical creativity that began to produce notated books in the ninth century displays a practice with a basic similarity to the "variation and improvisation" practice of Picasso that has just been described. To begin the comparison it is important to see that both document performance practices. That is what Galassi has caught with her emphasis on the transformations in the Picasso series. And it is evident from the following representations of a line from a chant for Easter, taken from four Italian books of the eleventh century (Example 7.1).

What is represented is a constellation embodying an aggregate of essential musical ideas, themes, motives, and relationships that mark the melody's identity. These ever-present elements reveal an archetype that is given concrete formulaic expression in the notations. But the archetype is tacit and formless. I mean "archetype" to refer to knowledge that we have by virtue of its embedding as a condition of mental life—in a sense a Jungian conception of archetype. Access to it is gained through some kind of transformation in an ongoing productive process, resulting through different associations and intersections and stylistic emphases in different local, or individual, variations, which I call

EXAMPLE 7.1

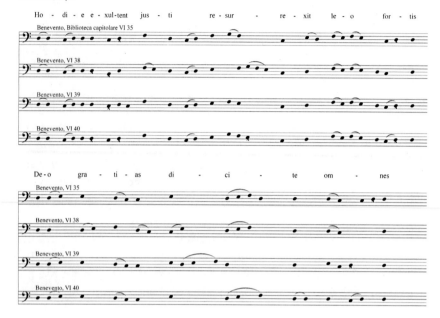

sketches. I intend the connotation of the ephemeral in that word, because it emphasizes the continuity of the process, and because in its very ephemeralness the sketch comes nearest to the mental images that are held tacitly and whose embodiment is the unfolding of the song. The sketch catches those ideas in the instance of their entry into the world outside the mind, before they have accommodated themselves to the objectified forms that are the medium of worldly discourse. That is its aim, in contrast to the autonomous and closed work. Hence to ask of the five notations in the example which is the original, or the final, or the authentic version would make no sense at all.

Just as the sketch is ephemeral, so the archetype has a timelessness about it. That is an aspect of their relationship. It means that in that tradition the constellation is always being produced, always being practiced. Each text is a documentation of the continuing practice, but such sketches could emerge, could be improvised at moments in which they were called for by the ritual or social occasion, whether or not they were deposited in books. The creative process could be productive, whether or not the products were written down. That is a point of fundamental importance for our understanding of musical creativity during this central era of the Middle Ages.

As it happens, musicians of this time did have reasons to try to make textual representations of the archetypes that underlay their productions, in compilations they called *tonaria*. In this time the ritual music of the church was classified into eight modes for a number of practical reasons, and the *tonaria* were in effect the catalogues in which the chants were listed according to their modal-class assignments. But as one way of distinguishing the classes according to the melodic properties that were proper to them, model melodies were written out for each mode. Musicians wrote out two such melodies for each mode, one with nonsense syllables that are vowel-rich and thus especially singable, the other with words from biblical texts that include the number of the particular mode. Example 7.2 shows the two model melodies for the mode of the tunes in Example 7.1 (mode 2) from five different *tonaria*. The resemblance among them and between them and the melodies in Example 7.1 should be apparent.

EXAMPLE 7.2

These written models must have been in the service of the composition and the singing of chants from memory or from books or both. They represent what musicians knew by ear, as we would now put it. This small example can give us an inkling of the struggle to interject visible form and a kind of authority into an age-old practice that took place between the mind and the singing voice.

For the composer and pianist Ferruccio Busoni, the success of music writing in this struggle was neither so clear nor altogether a gain, as we saw in the passage from his *Entwurf einer neuen Ästhetik der Tonkunst* in chapter 5. The ideal expressed in that passage is apparent in a letter that Schiller wrote to Goethe in 1801:

> The poet must think himself fortunate if through the clearest consciousness of his operations he comes only so far that he still finds the first dark total idea of his work unweakened in the complete work. Without such a dark but powerful total idea that precedes everything technical, no poetic work can arise.[20]

One last demonstration to thicken the mix.

Frederick Chopin, once settled in Paris (1831), published his music with houses there, in Germany, and in England. His usual practice was to send autographs to all three. For the Nocturne in A♭, op. 62, no. 1, he sent off three autograph scores on the same day in August of 1846. Example 7.3 shows measures 53–55 of that piece, a harmonically enriched reprise of the kind that Chopin usually turned out as purple passages, in six versions that we can compare: a sketch (Example 7.3a); the autograph material prepared for the edition of Brandus, the Paris publisher, which includes three versions of the passage (Example 7.3b); and the autograph prepared for the German Breitkopf edition, which has one variant from the edition as well as from the Brandus autograph, and the three first editions (Examples 7.3c and d).[21]

EXAMPLE 7.3 a

EXAMPLE 7.3 b

Brandus MS

EXAMPLE 7.3 c

Breitkopf MS
Breitkopf Edition
Wessel Edition

EXAMPLE 7.3 d

Brandus Edition

The English (Wessel) edition, for which Chopin's autograph has not survived, is identical to the German edition of these measures. Pianists looking for guidance to *the* authentic version will not find it here, any more than singers would find guidance to the original or authentic version of the song represented in Example 7.1 in its sources. But if I play all the versions of Chopin's passage, I hear them all as unfoldings of the same underlying harmonic and melodic sweep, a relationship like that among the versions of the chant in Example 7.1 and their underlying archetype. Is there not, then, a temptation to regard all the versions of the three measures as sketches? Or perhaps to think that the sharp divide between between sketch and finished score breaks down here too?

For Chopin, the score seems not to have been the ultimate touchstone for the work. He did not always copy it faithfully when he needed copies. He seems not to have minded having different versions of pieces in circulation; he did not act as though the process of composition had a terminal point. This is evident from such comparisons as the one I've shown here, as well as from presentation copies that he made after the publication of the works and from alterations that he made in the published scores of his music being used by his piano pupils. The fluid character of the music's ontological condition carried over into the performance tradition, for which there is abundant evidence in recordings of Chopin's music made from the beginning of the twentieth century into the 1930s, as we saw in chapter 5.

The appreciation of musical sketches in the sense in which their study has been a sub-discipline of musicology is obviously much more private, autonomous, and arcane an occupation than the appreciation of the sketches of visual artists can be. But if we are to gain an understanding of the phenomenon of sketching and sketches in a broader sense as an aspect of artistic creativity, then we should not fail to take cognizance of musical economies that favor effects like those of visual sketches—for example the taste in the Romantic era for music given names like "impromptu," "caprice" or "capriccio," "moment musicale," "fantasy," "Kinderszenen," flourishing around the very time that the musical masterwork was held up as the highest achievement of the composer's art. And in view of the hieroglyphic character of musical notation, we should, I think, keep open the question, What is it that sketches represent?

PART FOUR

Interpretative Frames

THE LULU CHARACTER AND
THE CHARACTER OF *LULU*

The wordplay in the title of this chapter is directed toward a way of thinking that inquires about the stage character Lulu, conceived as an artifice, even as a puppet executing its lines and actions in the time and space represented on the stage, but at the same time about that character as it informs and is informed by the character of the drama. That is a different sort of question than is asked in discussions about the character and motivations of the persons of a drama, as though they might be persons that one would encounter off the stage.

I shall take my perspective from two points of view: the style of the Lulu plays (Frank Wedekind's *Earth Spirit* and *Pandora's Box*) and their adaptation by Alban Berg, and the backgrounds of the several personae that the character presents under its rich array of signs—snake, Pierrot, dancer, whore, prostitute, and all the names by which the male characters address her, which are like tokens (Lulu, Eva, Nelly, Mignon).

The difference that I have begun to indicate here has immediate consequences for the critic's choice of moral categories for judging the character's behavior and fate. Consider first Pierre Boulez's commentary provided with the recording of the Paris performance of the opera: "*Lulu* is definitely a morality play, a sort of *Rake's Progress*. The protagonist moves up in society until the murder of her rich protector Dr. Schön. Then she undergoes a progressive degradation down to the wretched state of a London prostitute."[1]

Strong moral judgments are entailed here—in the word "murder," to which I shall return later, and in the phrase "degradation to the wretched state of a prostitute." "Degradation" and "wretched" ride along as natural attributes of "prostitute," as though "fallen woman" were a redundant synonym of "prostitute." That reflects a widely socialized view, which may indeed be on the whole the most sociologically accurate view that one could take. But sociological accuracy in the portrayal of character is not the only sort of truth to which the theater can aspire, especially the sort of theater that Wedekind was developing. We shall only cloud our view of the Lulu character and of the meanings in the drama if we treat the character as though she had just walked onstage off the street, enveloped in such conventionalized attitudes.

What is striking about the attitude embodied in Boulez's comment is that no one asks the woman herself. In the artistic milieu of the Lulu plays and Berg's opera, the position of the prostitute could be seen quite differently, and in a way that claimed to take into account her own interests. An early instance is the prostitute Marie of Nygränd, in Strindberg's novel *The Red Room* (1879). She says that she is not a victim; she has chosen her profession voluntarily because it gives her more freedom than any of the other alternatives open to her. A much more recent instance is Luis Buñuel's film *Belle de jour* (1968), about a middle-class housewife who makes an independent life for herself, free of her ambitious medical-student husband, through daytime prostitution.

During the long love scene between Lulu and Alwa in act 2, scene 2, Alwa says, "If it were not for your great childlike eyes I would have to take you for the most cunning whore that ever drove a man to his ruination." Lulu replies, "I wish to God I were that!" As she sings those words, the orchestra intones music that is associated with her throughout the opera (Example 8.1). It is heard first in the prologue, as the stagehand carries "the performer who is to play Lulu in front of the curtain" (Berg's direction), dressed as Pierrot but identified by the Animal Trainer as a snake. It accompanies her major entrances throughout the opera, in particular the entrance, dressed in an "elegant ball-dress, very décolleté," in act 2, scene 1, in the midst of her strange masculine coterie of Schigolch, the Athlete, and the Student (Example 8.2); and the entrance in act 2, scene 2, following her escape from prison. Because of these associations, this radiantly gorgeous music has been called "Lulu's entrance music." But it is not just a sign of her entrances, it is a sign of her identity. Through it she says, "This is me." It fills the air, as her presence fills the stage. This music, which sings her identity, accompanies Lulu as she says to Alwa that she wishes she were the cunning whore that he almost takes her for. The great climax of the entrance in act 2, scene 2 (just after her escape from prison) is the moment when, dropping her sickly demeanor, she sings, "O Freiheit! Herr Gott im Himmel!!" On the first syllable of "Freiheit" (freedom) she sounds the highest note of this music, B, a note rich with meaning as well as resonance, as we shall see (Example 8.3). To Lulu as a sexual person, freedom of choice and the fulfillment of her identity are one and the same. In act 2, scene 1, when the Marquis attempts to blackmail her into letting herself be sold to a brothel in Cairo, she says, "I can't sell the only thing I've ever owned." She adds that she can tell "in the dead of night and at a thousand paces whether a man and I are made for each other. And if I find I've sinned against my judgment . . . it takes weeks to overcome my loathing for myself."

EXAMPLE 8.1

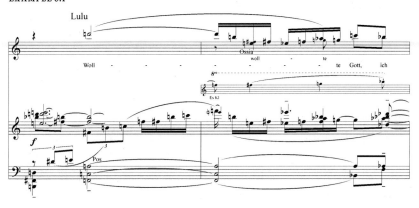

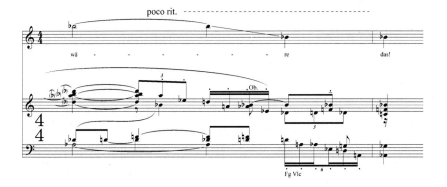

EXAMPLE 8.2

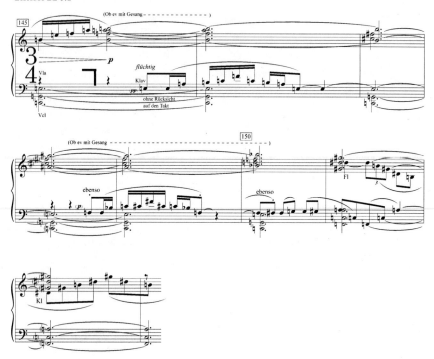

Naturalist artists and writers portrayed the prostitute as a fallen woman, all right, albeit with compassion—Dostoevsky's Sonya, Zola's Nana. But at the same time they endowed her with an ultimately superior morality in order to show up the counterfeit righteousness of the bourgeois world of the men for whose pleasure she exists (Figure 8.1). By contrast, Expressionist artists and writers turned a cool and cynical eye on the scene: the woman, neither fallen nor merely submissive, delights in the active play of her sexuality; the man of the world is spellbound, perched on the edge of disaster (Figure 8.2). The aggressive uncovering of the woman's body in the second image exposes as well the brutal dynamic of the whole situation. But some things remain unchanged: the central placement and full view of the woman on display (interestingly enough, our view of the male observer is in both images partially occluded); the intensity of the man's gaze, and the precise way it is targeted on the woman's anatomy; and the lie that these details give to the costume he wears as symbol of his worldly respectability and power. Therein lies the social commentary that both images render up.

EXAMPLE 8.3

In Luis Buñuel's film *Belle de jour,* the woman carries on her daylight activities in a brothel that has the appearance of an idealized setting for her bourgeois life with her husband. That cinematic *trompe-l'oeil* concretizes a favorite topos of Expressionist dramatists: the bourgeois household as brothel (and vice versa), the woman suspended between the roles of wife (or sweetheart or mistress) and whore. (Polly Peachum, in Brecht's *Dreigroschenoper,* is the classic case.) In Alwa's remark quoted above, it is only Lulu's "great childlike eyes" that keep her from slipping into the second role. This thematic idea is evident even in the progression of domestic stage sets in the opera: act 1, scene 2, "A very elegant drawing room"; act 2, scene 1, "A magnificent room in German Renaissance style"; act 3, scene 2, "An attic room without windows [furnished with] tattered mattress, doors which close badly, rickety flower stand, smoking oil lamp . . ." In each of these scenes Lulu is surrounded by what Schön sarcastically calls his "family circle," but what really is Lulu's family circle. The last scene, in which Lulu has become the family provider through open prostitution, comes off as a kind of distillation of what was

FIGURE 8.1. *Nana*, 1877, by Edouard Manet (1832–83). Oil on canvas,
154 × 115cm. Inv. 2376. Photo: Elke Walford. Photo credit:
Bildarchiv reussischer Kulturbesitz/Art Resource, N.Y.

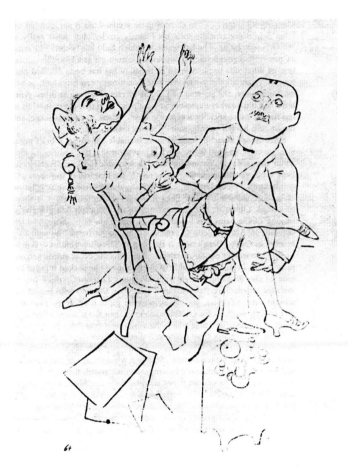

FIGURE 8.2. *Near the Limit,* by George Grosz. Used by
permission of the Estate of George Grosz, Prinecton, N.J.

implicit in all of them. What has been distilled out, ironically, are all the
material things that money can buy, and, at her own insistence, the portrait
of herself as Pierrot. Nothing is more symbolic of the earlier exploitation
of Lulu for a price than that portrait—but in less direct, more socially ac-
ceptable ways. When, in the last scene, she finally sells herself openly, money
means little to her.

Since Berg's sketches have become available for study, a brief notation
has come to light from which it is evident that this ambivalent idea about the
conjugal relationship lived in his mind, too.[2] In several cases Berg assigned to

a single singer one role in the first half of the opera and another in the second half. Special meaning derives from the association of each of those pairs, and Berg made cryptic notes hinting at those meanings. One instance is the pairing of the Prince in act 1, scene 3, singing of the happiness he anticipates with Lulu as his wife, and the Marquis in act 3, scene 1, pressuring her to let herself be sold to a brothel in Cairo. Berg's note is the slogan *Treulich geführt* (opening words of the Wedding March from Wagner's *Lohengrin*)—*Bordel ist Ehe* (bordello is marriage). And into the dense music accompanying the Prince in the earlier of the two scenes he packs most of the tune of the Wedding March (Example 8.4; the solo cello begins the tune in mm. 1143–44, the solo violin picks it up in m. 1146 and carries it through its four notes in m. 1147. But those are the first four notes of Schön's twelve-tone row, through which the violin now continues.)

Susan Seidelman's film *Desperately Seeking Susan* (1985) embroiders this idea into a slick fable of contemporary pop culture, thereby highlighting its archetypal nature. Susan, a whorish drifter portrayed to perfection by the rock star Madonna early in her career, communicates through the personal columns of a tabloid paper with her boyfriend Jim, a pop musician. (That an actress named Madonna is so perfectly typecast in this role is a rich coincidence.) The ads are followed with wonder and longing by Roberta, the pretty, sweet, and quintessentially innocent wife of Gary, a mindless salesman of hot tubs. After four years of marriage in their modishly luxurious suburban house in Fort Lee, New Jersey, they have no erotic life together—Roberta sublimates through rich desserts and fantasy, Gary through the hot tub business and a mistress.

Susan and Jim arrange a rendezvous through their ads, and Roberta turns up to watch from a distance. The encounter is brief, as Jim is about to go on tour. Now sinister gangster elements are after Susan in connection with an earlier liaison; they place another ad with Jim's signature in an effort to trap her. She knows that Jim is out of town but Roberta does not, and it is Roberta who turns up for the fake rendezvous. Jim, seeing the ad while on tour, recognizes the trap and calls his friend Des, asking him to be on hand in order to protect Susan.

Roberta, Des, and a gangster all arrive at the same time. The gangster grabs Roberta, Des plows into the gangster with his motor scooter, Roberta is flung against a lamppost and knocked unconscious. She wakes up with amnesia, and with Des standing over her. The amnesia makes her even dumber and

EXAMPLE 8.4

more puppetlike. Des takes her to his loft and takes care of her. They fall in love. She gets a job as a magician's assistant in a cheap nightclub, scooped into a minimal costume that she seems at any moment about to overflow; in that role she is a parody of innocent allure. On her first night, the gangster is in the audience and after the show he follows her home through a dark alley (she is still in costume). He grabs her, they scuffle, a police car pulls up with lights flashing, he flees, and the cops pick her up, book her on charges of streetwalking and fling her into a cell filled with real ladies of the night.

Through a well-designed coincidence, Gary, looking for Roberta, follows a lead that gets him Susan's telephone number. He calls, they meet, one thing leads to another, and Susan happily installs herself for awhile in the Fort Lee house. Gary is confused—things have gone out of his control. He learns that Roberta is in jail and arranges for her release. But she chooses to stay with Des. The switch is complete.

It is not really a reversal. Rather, the two female characters, who are presented at the beginning as diametrically opposite types, are developed until each displays the attributes of both types. It is really only the bourgeois male character, Gary, who is thrown off balance by this. He, and the morality that he represents, are the real target of the film's social criticism.

In this brief description I have said virtually all that one could say about the main characters in the film. They will strike most viewers as pretty hollow, even two-dimensional, and that can well be a point of criticism. But in the tradition of theater that essentially began with Wedekind, characters are created hollow as a way of keeping them at arm's length from the audience. I mentioned puppets at the outset. In the *Lulu* prologue, the Animal Trainer invites the audience "into the menagerie," to see the "soulless creatures" that inhabit it. We are not meant to suffer with such characters, to judge them, to wonder what they did before the drama began, or what will be their fates after it ends. We do not care whether Gary and Susan could live happily together in Fort Lee or if Roberta and Des will make a lasting life together in Manhattan. The story, so far as it concerns us, is complete within the boundaries of the play.

The prologue of *Lulu* establishes the separateness of actors and characters. It sets up in the viewer's mind a perception of the characters as creatures of the stage. In Berg's setting that is reinforced by the device of the double roles. The curtain that is the backdrop for the prologue concretizes the separation of realms—the stage and the world of daily life. (To set the prologue in a circus ring on the stage, as is sometimes done, obscures that essential separation.) Ultimately there is a connection to be made between the two, but that will be in the mind of the viewers, as they contemplate the meaning of what has been played out before them.

The stage is a showplace—part theater, part music hall, part cabaret, part circus—and the drama is a showpiece. Alwa objectifies the action from within, saying one could write an interesting piece about Lulu. For a moment he assumes the voice of the Animal Trainer, even taking up the imagery of the menagerie from the prologue: as Lulu steps onto the music hall stage in act 1, scene 3, he says of the applause and shouts of the audience, "That racket is like the noise in the zoo, when the food is brought in front of the cages." In the opera the effect is still more vivid: the orchestra anticipates Alwa's thought about writing an opera by striking up the beginning of *Wozzeck* (Example 8.5).

EXAMPLE 8.5

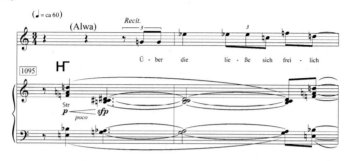

Such games of hopscotch between the stage and the world outside are characteristic features of Expressionistic theater and cinema; think of the plays of Pirandello, *The Cabinet of Dr. Caligari,* moments in Marx Brothers films when Groucho turns his face straight to the camera and addresses the audience. That is precisely what Berg's device does. For a moment the music leaps across the proscenium to make a wisecrack to the audience. The citation of Wagner's Wedding March is another such device, but more subtle. Wagner's tune breaks off after the first four notes of the second phrase. But in fact those are the first four notes of Dr. Schön's row in one of its prime transpositions, and the violin simply wanders off into that and plays it out (with an assist from the A♭ of the vibraphone's bell) instead of finishing the *Lohengrin* tune (Example 8.4). The message is direct, though obscure: Lulu's marriage to the Prince is really Schön's project. It pleases him to have Lulu set up in respectable marriages, from which she can join him in occasional liaisons. Still another instance occurs in the scene between Alwa and Lulu in act 2, scene 1 (Example 8.6). Alwa says, "Mignon, ich liebe dich." At the word "liebe" the strings are exposed playing the Tristan chord in its original position. Lulu's reply is, "Ich habe deine Mutter vergiftet" (I have poisoned your mother). That calls up the symbolism of the Tristan chord as love potion, for which we should now read "poison" in Berg's language of motives and references.

EXAMPLE 8.6

But I meant to return to the moral judgment entailed in Boulez's use of the word "murder" in reference to the death of Dr. Schön. That judgment, even more than the one on Lulu's prostitution, violates the separation of realms that I have been talking about. It distorts the sense of the drama in a fundamental way, and on more than one level. There are three main points to be made.

First, consider it in terms of the criminal code in the world of our experience. A husband, a powerful man of the world, is in a jealous rage at his wife/mistress because of the circle of associates and, presumably, lovers she keeps around the house. He presses a gun on her and tries to intimidate her into shooting herself. Protesting that he made her what she is and has every reason to expect such behavior from her, she shoots him instead. A good lawyer would plead self-defense.

It certainly is not premeditated murder. That the action in the second half of the drama has as its premise Lulu's identification as a murderess (she is imprisoned and escapes, the Marquis blackmails her with the threat of turning her over to the police, and so on) is not to be taken as the author's intention that we should see her as a murderess, but as an instance of the hyprocrisy and the double standards on which that world functions. (The Viennese writer Karl Kraus, in a talk introducing the first performance, in 1905, of *Pandora's Box*, the second of the Lulu plays, said, "One of the dramatic conflicts between female nature and some male blockhead placed Lulu in the hands of terrestrial justice, and she would have had nine years in prison during which to reflect that beauty is a punishment from God, had not her devoted slaves of love hatched a romantic plan for her liberation."[3]) This becomes the more apparent, the more we understand that Schön's hatred is based not only on his suspicions of Lulu's infidelity but more deeply on his recognition that he has lost control of his life—something for which he projects blame onto Lulu. But, as she insists during their long exchange before his death, the choices were his; he could have known what he was getting himself into.

The point here is not to take issue with Boulez. His remark was not made as an assertion about Lulu's guilt; it takes Schön's death as the midpoint of the opera—something that is indisputable—and characterizes it as it is characterized inside the drama. However, the acceptance of it as murder is central to much of the prevailing criticism, and that brings me to my second point.

It is a commonplace in much of that criticism that Lulu's death at the hands of Jack the Ripper brings revenge for the deaths of her husbands. That interpretation has seemed especially to be confirmed by the fact that each of the actors in Berg's setting who plays the role of a husband—"victims," they are sometimes called—in the first half is cast as a client in the final scene.

The earliest source for the revenge theme is that introductory talk by Kraus on the occasion of the first performance of *Pandora's Box.* He spoke of the "revenge of the world of men," but then continued, "who strove to revenge their own guilt."[4] In focusing on the first phrase, the subsequent criticism has reversed the meaning of the comment; now the clients of the second half—especially Jack the Ripper—are avenging their alter egos for their deaths at Lulu's hands. In the sketches to which I have referred, Berg wrote just "revenge of the world of men" in explaining the double roles of husbands and clients. He heard and was deeply impressed by Kraus's lecture, and his note may have been an abbreviation. Or he may have transformed Kraus's meaning in his own mind. His attitudes about these matters were complicated, as we have begun to see. However that may be, the omission and consequent change of meaning shed light on the attitudes that underlie the criticism, and on aspects of the meaning of the drama itself. I shall return to that as my third point.

The deaths of the men in the drama are brought off with the quick dispatch and matter-of-factness of a comic book or a penny dreadful: the *Medizinalrat* falling dead on the spot with a thud, Alwa felled with one whack of a blackjack, the melodrama of the painter's suicide with a razor at the throat; and—

talk about melodrama—Schön's histrionics before he expires. The succession of these deaths is grisly, all right, but no one of them evokes compassion or mourning. It is the succession itself, the rhythm of it, that works its effect. One by one these figures become lifeless. That point is even stronger in Berg's setting, where each death is orchestrated in a precise way. The extreme case is the death of Schön, which Berg took as occasion for a bit of his obsessive numerology: five shots, fired at the climax of an aria with five strophes, which is determined by the number five in various other ways.[5] All the men have already been destroyed in and through their lives; their physical deaths are theatrical events with the emotional charge of the deflation of a dummy.

There is an ineluctability about events presented in such a clinically objective way. It is not the inevitability of actions whose motivations have been carefully provided by the author, as in Dostoyevsky's *Crime and Punishment*. It is rather more like the inevitability of events in a Greek tragedy, because the world is that way, and that is what the author means to show. Lulu's death has the greatest sense of inevitability, coming as it does as the endpoint of a process that informs the whole drama. Lulu dreams her death, and she expects it. She speaks of a recurrent dream in which she falls into the hands of a sex maniac. Of the painter she says that if he had really understood her he would have tied a stone to her neck and thrown her into the sea. To Schön she says, "Strike me! where is your whip? Strike me across the legs!" One critic has called Lulu's movement toward her own death a *Totentanz*.[6] Lulu's persona as dancer, whether in the foreground (act 1, scene 3) or in the background, has that sense about it. Over and above the signs for this interpretation in the contents of words and actions, Berg lends an inevitability to Lulu's death as well as to those of Schön and Alwa through the formal determinisms of the opera. The three deaths span a harmonic process at the highest level. Each of the opera's three acts ends with a four-note chord, and in the third-act ending the final chords of the first two acts, respectively, precede the very last chord, so that the final ending is a kind of summation (Example 8.7). The chords have three common tones, while the upper voice descends chromatically, $C\sharp$–C–B. It is in effect a progression that settles into the final chord. Now in the context of these chords, the tones $C\sharp$ and $C\natural$ are associated—through row derivations and associations—with Schön and Alwa, respectively.[7] $B\natural$ is associated with Lulu.[8] At the end of act 1 Schön has just finished writing the letter to his fiancée—dictated by Lulu—in which he breaks off his engagement to her. His will is broken, his future consigned to Lulu, and he sings "Now comes the execution." Act 2 ends with the great love scene between Lulu and Alwa, who sings, "You've robbed me of my reason," to which Lulu responds, "Is this the same sofa on which your father bled to death?" In both cases it is not the death of the male protagonist but his capitulation to lust for Lulu that is the climax of his plotline. But then, capitulation is death in this drama.

EXAMPLE 8.7 a

EXAMPLE 8.7 b

EXAMPLE 8.7 c

EXAMPLE 8.7 d

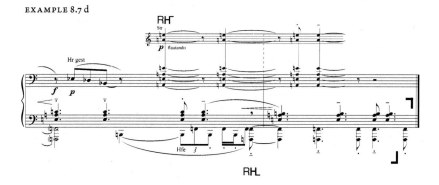

The third act ends with the Countess Geschwitz's dying farewell to the dead Lulu—"Lulu, my angel . . ." Lulu's death is a kind of apotheosis. It is hard to escape the inference that the poet has presented it as her ultimate, and wished-for, liberation, given the way she has walked into it in the last scene, and in reality through the whole second half of the drama. That is a major point of inconsistency between the two halves.

In a way this sort of determinism is external to the dramatic structure; one could say that it is in the music alone. It certainly must be understood on one level as a manifestation of Berg's general proclivities for tight formalisms, particularly symmetrical ones. But at the same time this determinism conveys exactly the feeling of imposed necessity about events that Wedekind sought, too; but the music conveys it in a more palpable way. We cannot help feeling the heavy hand of fate in the progression of endings to the three acts. So in this sense Berg's formalisms are not external to the drama, with only their own musical interest. They are perfectly suited to a dramatic style, which we may identify as Expressionist, that depends on the acceptance of actions and events without the expectation that they should be motivated from within. It is hard to square these reflections about the deaths of Lulu's husbands and about intentionality and causality in this drama with the tabloid newspaper concepts of "murder" and "revenge." Lulu is no Don Giovanni being sent to hell for her wanton promiscuity, as one critic has suggested in a comparison that is still further off the mark than the analogy with *The Rake's Progress.*[9]

When it comes to intentionality and morality as against determinism, *Lulu* is, not surprisingly, more akin to *Wozzeck*. For there, too, the action is an ineluctable process, driven by inescapable human conditions and historical forces. And the sense that events follow a pre-determined pattern is immensely enhanced by musical associations and formalisms.[10] One could well get the impression from these operas alone that Berg's well-known leaning to symmetrically closed forms and tight motivic networks is not a matter of musical inclination alone but a fatalism about life.

The deaths in the opera—and now I mean all of them—are the ravages of socio- and psychosexual struggle. Their formal inevitability on the stage is an objective reflection of the inevitable struggle between Eros and society, and of the implication of death in that struggle. If there is authorial comment it is at that level, not at the level of moral judgment on individual acts. The characteristic paradox of this kind of drama is that we cannot take the characters on the stage seriously as real people. But we are meant to take very seriously the reality of what they have been put on the stage to show us.

Wedekind concretized the paradox. What the Animal Trainer promises to show in the prologue is characterized not only as "soulless creatures" but also as "das wahre Tier," "the true beast, the wild and beautiful beast, not the house pets that inhabit ordinary comedies and tragedies." It belongs to the paradox that Wedekind, who declared himself an antinaturalist, claimed to show his characters in their true and natural state. The Animal Trainer says to Lulu, "You should speak naturally and not unnaturally, for the basic element of every art is that it be self-evident." Lulu says of herself that she is "a product of nature."

These "natural" creatures Wedekind placed in the grotesquely artificial circumstances he designed in order to allow them to act out their natures. They do so without any awareness of the seriousness of what they are in— something that only the audience can see. In a way Schön's long harangue to the Painter, which leads to the latter's suicide, has that as its message: you have been acting without an awareness of the realities of your situation. That is essentially what Lulu tells Schön before shooting him, when she says, "You knew as well why you took me for your wife, as I knew why I took you for my husband. You fooled your best friends about me; you should have known better than to be fooled yourself."

But this "prodigy of nature," as Lulu calls herself, plays a counterpoint on the stage with a Lulu character that is a complex of roles projected onto it by the men in the drama, out of their own needs, fantasies, and fears about Woman. One of the plotlines of the drama is Lulu's struggle to establish her own authenticity in the face of that burden. If one is looking for parallels, there is a close one in this respect with Petrouchka: the Pierrot character, through a painful exertion of will, coming into possession of its soul.

The consequences of this struggle are catastrophic and, in a way, tragic. But there is too much irony, too much of the grotesque and the sardonic, too much droll play with the very materials of the drama to identify it as tragedy. It belongs to the Expressionist style that Wedekind, more than anyone else, invented: what Jan Kott, following Eliot, has called "tragic farce."[11] Compared to Strindberg's plays about the ferociousness of sexual conflict (both Wedekind and Berg admired Strindberg very much), Lulu is a burlesque. Despite the similarities in their subject matter and their equal seriousness in the end, there is a very great stylistic distance, something like the distance from Edvard Munch to George Grosz. (The closer parallel is really between Munch and Grosz, on one side, and Strindberg and Brecht—by way of Wedekind—on the other.)

Berg entered into Wedekind's sardonic spirit and provided plenty of drollery of his own, playing in all the semiotic registers that he established for himself through the density of motivic and serial associations in which the work is enmeshed, and which could hook into virtually any music outside. The citations from *Lohengrin,* and especially from *Tristan,* are examples. Even without the Tristan chord, Lulu's line about the couch makes one shudder, then smile. But with it the irony is sharpened truly to the point of farce.

The perspective on the Lulu character as a compound of male projections provides one key to the inconsistencies in the character that have been the subject of some discussion. Absolute consistency is not to be expected when Lulu is construed to meet the different needs of her husbands at the same time as she poses the threats that constitute the grounds of their different fears. This will prove to be a central matter for the interpretation of *Lulu,* one that will therefore have to be pursued more fully. But first I want to develop a different sort of interpretation of the inconsistency, at which I have already hinted. It is that the inconsistency in character reflects an inconsistency in the style of the two Lulu plays. The characterizations that I have given thus far really pertain more to the first of them, *Earth Spirit,* than to the second, *Pandora's Box. Earth Spirit* is an unflawed masterpiece of Expressionist theater. Its effect is diluted by *Pandora's Box,* which returns part of the way to the manner of the naturalists. One feels this especially in the heavily sentimental treatment of Alwa and of Geschwitz, whom Wedekind identified as the real heroine of the second play. As early as 1920, the critic Paul Fechter called attention to this contrast:

> Compared to *Earth Spirit,* the second part of the tragedy is a step backward. It lacks the tight concentration, the sharpness of dialogue . . . *Earth Spirit* is unsentimental, pathos-free to the point of blasphemy . . . It is pure objectivity. An unmoved onlooker, in consciousness of his indifference . . . only points . . . , he does not speak. In *Pandora's Box* his need to become visible shows. The mere setting down of how things are no longer suffices. The poet begins to speak, along with the others[12]

Early journalistic reviews of the plays are interesting in this regard, for the critics almost unanimously preferred productions of the two parts separately.

The contrast survives and is magnified in Berg's setting. The sentimentality in his treatment of Alwa and Geschwitz in the second and third acts borders on the maudlin. But most striking of all in this regard is the musical treatment of Lulu's death. It is of a savagery that overreaches all preparation for it in the opera, and all expectation that one would have from a reading of the second play. The impact is all the greater in a live performance, particularly if one sits close enough to the orchestra to see the ferociousness with which the percussion players must attack their instruments. The violence of the act, as an act done by Jack the Ripper to Lulu, focuses attention on his rage and her agony. Wedekind, having brought the play to the point where her death is required, found a brilliant solution to the problem of how to accomplish it: bring in a famous principal in the sexual warfare of which Lulu is finally a casualty. Everyone knows enough about him to sense the appropriateness of his choice as executioner. There is no curiosity about the mind that has become so twisted as to perform such acts, or about the personal history that resulted in that condition. Wedekind locates the deed offstage. He reports it as Alwa reports that a revolution has broken out in Paris, or as the value of *Jungfrau* stocks is reported in act 3, scene 1. With a well-known historical figure as its instrument, Lulu's death is given the aspect of another event in the world on the other side of the proscenium.

But in the musical moment of Lulu's murder, the feelings that Wedekind held off with that device are poured onto the stage in abundance. The musical setting demands a direct participation in the horror that is at most implied in the play. And in the aftermath of the horror, the pathos of Geschwitz's final cantilena ("Lulu, my angel") seems as much an authorial commentary on the tragedy of Lulu's death—a signal to feel that tragedy—as a final statement of Geschwitz's undying devotion.

And the confusion is only compounded by Berg's transformation of Jack into a reincarnation of Schön, for it loads that neutral, almost mechanical agent of Lulu's death with all the feelings we have about the despicable and tortured Schön. Lulu's death is in the air throughout the opera as both fated and self-willed. Jack is only the instrument of its execution. To be sure, he is a monster, but his monstrousness has not been provoked by the Lulu character.

By making him a Schön persona Berg implicates him in all of her history. Lulu's death becomes a crime of passion, and we are asked to respond to it as the tragedy of the drama—as though Berg had determined to repeat in it the death of Marie in *Wozzeck*.

The musical setting of Marie's murder is of an equal savagery, and it is similarly followed by a musical expression of pathos (the D-minor interlude, which Berg himself identified as an authorial comment).[13] Marie's death, too, is presented as an ineluctable outcome. But the necessity of it develops before us, in the mind of the male protagonist. The motivation is part jealous rage over Marie's infidelity, part paranoid construction in which Marie comes to stand for all the sinfulness—particularly the sexual debauchery—of the world. In identifying Jack the Ripper with Schön, Berg shaped the outcome of *Lulu* in a way very like that of *Wozzeck*: the female protagonist is brutally murdered by a man whose homicidal urge toward her arises at one level out of his very specific sexual rage at her, and at another out of his hatred for some generalized idea of Woman that she symbolizes in his mind. I cannot help associating this striking parallel with Berg's note *Bordel ist Ehe* and with the extreme brutality in his musical depiction of both murders. What comes through are archetypal attitudes toward women that are in tension with dramatic judgment.[14]

How could it be otherwise for anyone—poet, composer, or critic—working on this subject? In particular, how could critics—especially male critics—fail to be influenced in their interpretations by masculine images of Woman and the relationship between the sexes in view of those images, since these are central themes of the *Lulu* drama? My third point about the judgment on Lulu as a murderess is that it reflects such attitudes as they are held both within and outside of the drama.

In the prologue, the Animal Trainer lures the members of the audience into the menagerie in order to reflect back to them a true image of themselves. Alwa, hearing the shouts and applause of the audience backstage in act 1, scene 3, tells the "real" audience, "It sounds like the menagerie at feeding time." Douglas Jarman catches the sense of it: "[T]he listener in the opera house is forced to realize that he is as much a part of that menagerie as the characters he has come to watch . . . he is forced to recognize the hypocrisy and the capacity for self-deception of both the characters on the stage and himself."[15] Wedekind and Berg address their audience with the ironic attitude of Baudelaire beckoning his readers into *Les fleurs du mal* (1857). The resonance is sufficient to think of that work as a source:

> If rape and arson, poison and the knife
> have not yet stitched their ludicrous designs
> onto the banal buckram of our fates,
> it is because our souls lack enterprise!
>
> But here among the scorpions and the hounds,
> the jackals, apes and vultures, snakes and wolves,
> monsters that howl and growl and squeal and crawl,
> in all the squalid menagerie of vices, one
> is even uglier and fouler than the rest,
> although the least flamboyant of the lot;
> this beast would gladly undermine the earth
> and swallow all creation in a yawn;
>
> I speak of boredom which with ready tears
> dreams of hangings as it puffs its pipe.
> Reader, you know this squeamish monster well,
> —hypocrite reader,—my alias—my twin![16]

How truly the spectator is reflected in the drama can be read out of the critical literature. Patrice Chereau, the director of the 1979 Paris production of *Lulu*, goes right to the nub in his commentary provided with the recording. To judge from the criticism with which the work is surrounded, he writes, it would seem that

> Berg and Wedekind had well and truly held up to the audience an exact, unflattering mirror. Like Schön they would like Lulu to be an incarnation of Evil ["You beast, dragging me through the mud to an agonized death! . . . You dark angel! . . . You hangman's noose! You inescapable tormentor! . . . Monster! . . . Murderess! . . . Do you see your bed, with its slaughter victims?"] Like Schön, they see in her only a devourer of men and would, in the last analysis, prefer her to take on the seductive, perverse guise of a star from some imaginary pantheon of the cinema in order to carry out her work of destruction.[17]

Chereau is right in his choice of the expressions "would like" and "prefer," because the characterizations of the "daemonic" Lulu that commentators have in effect accepted from Schön show not what Lulu is, but one side of what she, as quintessential Woman, is held to be by men on both sides of the curtain. The Animal Trainer virtually anticipates Schön's words: "She was created to make trouble, to tempt, to seduce, to poison, and to murder."

Wedekind put on the stage an ambivalent vision of Woman that is probably as old as humankind and that seems endemic in all societies. Schön's daemonic Lulu is one side of that vision. The other is represented by Alwa's panegyric in act 2, scene 1, "A soul that will rub the sleep from its eyes in the next world": the passive, innocent, submissive love object, childlike, alluring, and seductive . . . and terrifying; the woman dreamed of, and dreaded. A billboard description of the female protagonist in a 1962 film by Joseph Losey suggests she might be the imagined film goddess in Chereau's comment: "Mysterious, tantalizing, alluring, wanton, but deep within her burning the violent fires that destroy a man."[18] The character (and the film) are called Eve—the first woman, but hardly in her original innocence. Eve is one of the Painter's names for Lulu. That has to be read as ironic sign for his complex perception of her.

Tilly Wedekind, the playwright's wife, was the first stage Lulu. In her memoir about the role, she reports her husband's impression about the critical commentaries, and it is strikingly similar to Chereau's:

> He apparently wanted Lulu played like a madonna. But the critics who wrote about the production were of a different opinion, and to this day [1969] many of them cling to the conception that Lulu must be portrayed as a wild animal who has already devoured a couple of men for breakfast. "It is no longer possible to take the play seriously if the part is played like that," Wedekind used to say. And men get out of the way of that sort of woman.[19]

The association of Lulu and Madonna can seem ironic, like the name Madonna for an aggressively sexy pop singer. But it is more profound than that. Edvard Munch created several images entitled *Madonna* that make plausible a persona that can be voluptuous in its innocence. The face in one of them (Figure 8.3, a lithograph) is virtually repeated in another lithograph, which Munch entitled *Salome* (Figure 8.4); the face of John the Baptist is a self-portrait; the two women's faces in Figures 8.3 and 8.4 have the same model, the artist's lover since 1903, Eva Mudocci.[20]

Mystery—the first attribute in the characterization of the Eve in the Losey film—is of the essence in this conception of Woman. Lulu is a shadowy char-

FIGURE 8.3. *Madonna*, 1903, by Edvard Munch (1863–1944).
Lithograph on thin Japan paper, 608 × 470mm (image),
782 × 565mm (sheet). John H. Wrenn Memorial Collection,
1947.689, The Art Institute of Chicago. Used by permission
the Artists Rights Society (ARS), New York. Photography
© The Art Institute of Chicago.

FIGURE 8.4. *Salome*, 1894, by Edvard Munch.
The Epstein Family Collection, Washington, D.C.
© 2010 The Munch Museum / The Munch-Ellingsen
Group/Artists Rights Society (ARS), New York.

acter. There is vagueness about her age, her parentage, her name. Schön and Alwa call her Mignon, and they have presumably called her that since Schön picked her up, a child of twelve, in front of the Alhambra Cafe. The name derives from the character Mignon, the twelve-year-old dancer in Goethe's *Wilhelm Meister.* Thomas Carlyle described her in the preface of his English translation of 1826 in a way that might almost have inspired the title of Wedekind's first Lulu play: "The daughter of enthusiasm, rapture, passion and despair, she is of the earth, but not earthly . . . When she glides before us through the light images of her dances we could almost fancy her an ethereal spirit."[21] Goethe's Mignon dances herself to death; so, in a way, does the Wedekind/Berg Mignon.

The names Lulu and Eve must be understood in terms of one another. Schigolch says he has always called her Lulu, and he is the person who has known her longest (there are even intimations from Schön that Schigolch is her father). "Lulu" is a thinly veiled transformation of "Lilith," the mythological demon-woman whom we encounter first in an apocalpytic poem in the Book of Isaiah, which describes the end of the kingdom of Edom and the return of the earth to the chaos of the beginning. Probably Wedekind's direct source was Goethe's *Faust,* where Lilith is mentioned in the *Walpurgisnacht* of part 1. Mephistopheles points her out to Faust.

> Lilith, the first wife of Adam;
> Beware of her fair hair, for she excels all women in the magic of her locks
> And when she winds them around a young man's neck
> She will not ever set him free again

That she is the first wife of Adam derives from Jewish biblical commentaries, where she is also identified as the incarnation of the dark side of Eve, and that is the key to the relationship between the names Eve and Lulu. There is an important difference in the origins of the personae they identify, according to these sources: Lilith was made of the same dust as Adam and considered herself his equal. She fled from the Garden of Eden when Adam ordered her to lie beneath him. He begged God for another partner and God gave him Eve, made this time from Adam's rib. In Christian commentaries Lilith is the daughter of Satan, and is identified with the serpent in the Garden of Eden. As a snake with a woman's head she is a common nineteenth-century image—hence Lulu's presentation as a serpent in the prologue.[22]

The identification of Lilith as Satan's daughter illuminates the hints that Schigolch is Lulu's father. He, too, is a shadowy figure who seems to have no beginning to his life history, and he is the only one of the main characters whose life has no end within the drama; he slips out for a drink just before the final slaughter. There is something primeval about him, which Berg magnified. Among the animals mentioned by the Animal Trainer in the prologue is the *Molch* (lizard). Berg picked up on the sound association between *Molch* and Schigolch, and he accompanied the Animal Trainer as he speaks of reptiles and lizards with music that becomes associated with Schigolch—slithery, chromatic music (Example 8.8). The way he drags his feet, the way he acts the man of the world who has seen better days, his cynicism, his agelessness, his ugliness all suggest a Mephistopheles figure. In *Wilhelm Meister,* the first master of Mignon is a showman known as "The Great Devil." Recognizing this aspect of Schigolch, we can appreciate a wonderfully ironic touch in act 3, scene 2. Lulu is desperate to get the Athlete off her back, and she promises Schigolch her favors (not for the first time, we gather) if he will throw the pest out the window. He agrees, she insists he swear; he says, "by all that's holy," and Berg has him punctuate with an asthmatic gasp.

EXAMPLE 8.8

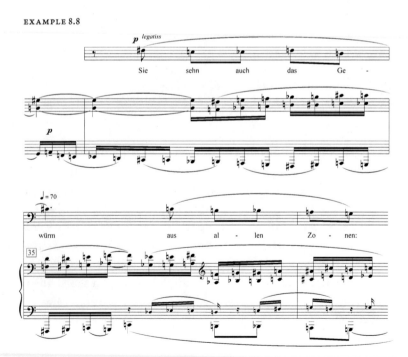

It is in the first scene that the Painter, enraptured by Lulu, calls her Eve. The exchange goes like this:

HE: No pity . . . (sits down by Lulu's side and covers her hands with kisses). How do you feel?
SHE: (with closed eyes) My husband will be coming soon.
HE: I love you!
SHE: (still with closed eyes) Once I loved a student with 175 dueling scars . . .
HE: (calling her) Nelly . . .
SHE: (as if awakening) My name isn't Nelly, it's Lulu.
HE: I'll call you Eve—Give me a kiss, Eve!

Why Nelly? Three associations converge on the name. The first is the opera *Maschinist Hopkins* by the Austrian composer Max Brand, which received its first performance during the music festival of the *Allgemeine Deutsche Musikverein* in Duisburg in 1929. Berg was a member of the jury for selecting the program, and he owned an autographed copy of the score. Similarities of plot and character between Brand's opera and Wedekind's Lulu plays suggest the possibility of reading Brand as a gloss of Wedekind. In both, the heroine moves from being a working-class girl of few morals to a rich industrialist's lover and at her apogee, a nightclub singer. In both she is blackmailed by someone with designs on her and also a grudge toward her and she resorts to prostitution, only to be murdered by the man she loved but betrayed. Brand's heroine is named Nelly. It also happens that Hopkins is the name Wedekind gave in the first edition of the Lulu plays (1895) to the character he later renamed Dr. Hunidei, and who survives in the opera as the Professor (whom Berg associated in a double role with the *Medizinalrat*).[23] Second, Nelly was a name often taken by showgirls and prostitutes. That the painter calls Lulu Nelly first, and then Eve, focuses exactly the ambivalence that I have been talking about. Then we should carry our understanding of that ambivalence into the second scene, where the Painter has set Lulu up in a sort of *Doll's House* scenario, and set himself up for disillusionment and suicide. Third, in a letter to his wife Helene (June 17, 1928), Berg characterized John Erskine's novel *The Private Life of Helen of Troy* as "a delightful book: the only possible interpretation of Helen, as Lulu."[24] Now, Nelly is a common nickname for Helen, but it was of course already in Wedekind's text—yet another odd coincidence.

The universal female pantheon is everywhere bipolar, showing protective and nourishing figures on one side, and threatening and destroying ones on

FIGURE 8.5. *Vampire,* 1894, by Edvard Munch. © 2010
The Munch Museum/The Munch-Ellingsen Group/
Artists Rights Society (ARS), New York.

the other. Individual figures may combine these antithetical properties. Mary
is the unambiguous opposite of the demon goddesses through virtually the
whole tradition of Marian images, but in Munch's representations, as we saw,
she shows that seductive quality that is the beginning of what is threatening
about those godesses. Eve, whom Mary resembles, embodies an antithesis
of the spiritual and the carnal. And Eve herself has her double, who is Lilith.
These images represent ambivalent masculine conceptions about Woman: as
lover and whore, as nourisher and devourer, as seductress and destroyer.

The type of figure that embodies these opposite attributes was widely
known in the Romantic era as the femme fatale, but it is recognizable in the
art, literature, and mythology of virtually all times and places. The Salome
we see in Munch's lithograph exemplifies the continuing preoccupation with
the type. Next to her in Munch's gallery of female images is his Vampire, who
gave us our word "vamp" (Figure 8.5).

The Eurydice of the Orpheus legend is a character of this type—especially in Jean Cocteau's film *Orphée*. The Lorelei and Rusalka of German and Russian mythology, respectively, are such figures, as is the Queen of the Night—especially in Ingmar Bergman's film *The Magic Flute*; Lola Lola, of Josef von Sternberg's film *The Blue Angel*; Medea. That is the sisterhood among which Lulu is portrayed.[25]

There can be something misleading about the recognition that a character, in this instance Lulu, belongs to a certain archetype—the femme fatale—that is represented over a broad range of literature and mythology. It tends to imply an explanation. Showing that the author has created a character that follows a certain tradition can seem to ascribe to tradition the author's particular way of displaying psychological states that arise from the intersection of the universal human condition and the social and economic conditions of the culture that he reflects and comments upon in his work. The robustness of the archetype in mythology and literature is a reflection of the constancy and urgency of the conditions that generate it. To be sure, in a culture with an active and self-conscious literary tradition, such as the European culture of Romanticism, genres and types are perpetuated for their own sake, and that was surely the case with the type of the femme fatale. But this is not a purely literary phenomenon; it reflects a preoccupation with psychological conditions, and the particular role of the femme fatale in the social ecology of the literature in which she is situated demands understanding in terms of the social dynamics of the time.

As a clue to the nature of those conditions, it is worth thinking about the fact that we do not identify a corresponding type of the "homme fatal" in literature, and wonder why that is the case. A possible contender is the Don Juan figure. But the virile, aggressive, and restless seducer is hardly the counterpart of the alluring, passive beauty for whose possession men are led to their destruction. Accordingly it is the femme fatale who is despised as the "Death Angel" (Schön's epithet for Lulu). If women are ruined by a Don Juan, they usually suffer sexual use and abandonment. But the ruination of men by the femme fatale means their death (why else is she called that?); men are not thought to be ruined by being sexually used and abandoned. The fatal woman is not satisfied to love them and leave them. She craves the destruction of men, like the female spider or praying mantis. Not so the Don Juan. The killer of women—Jack the Ripper, the Boston Strangler—is a different type altogether. He acts, ultimately, in rage against an idea of Woman that may be represented by the femme fatale. He has no female counterpart in literature or myth, or for that matter, in life. These differences are symptoms of the alignment of sexual roles and identities, not only in the Romantic European culture that identified and was obsessed with the femme fatale, but in all cultures whose iconologies feature such an ambivalent image of Woman. That image must constitute a background for reading *Lulu*.

The femme fatale has only to be, she does not have to act, in order to activate men's fear of women in a male-dominated society. What is at risk is the loss of control in the one domain in which male control is most vulnerable. The cliché of wife or lover as whore is not, then, just a display of cynicism or ambivalence, but an amelioration, for it is a way of regaining control; but it has its threatening side as well. Loss of control in that one domain can mean loss of control in the world altogether, and even loss of life. In the type of drama of which *Lulu* is an instance, that threat reveals the masochist in Man, and the corresponding androgynous aspect of Woman. In *Lulu* the male protagonists invest in Lulu the attribute of unrestrained sexuality—an attribute they cannot allow for themselves because of its inconsistency with the conduct of a responsible life in the masculine world of power. Having done that, they then try to invent a tamed persona for her. But Lulu senses the duplicity in this as an animal senses a trap, and she refuses to cooperate. The failure of the illusion results in their destruction. It shows how irrelevant the "revenge" motif is, and how much more to the point it is to see Lulu as a scapegoat. Wedekind showed great depth of insight in producing, as the final match for Lulu, a figure whose madness put him beyond vulnerability.

In *Lulu* the tragedy inherent in these configurations is forced to the surface by Lulu's own resistance to all such role manipulations. The issue is focused in the pitched battle between Lulu and Schön—between the snake and the tiger—in act 2, scene 1, a battle so ferocious that it makes the political revolution in Paris reported by Alwa seem trivial. Lulu's death at the hands of Jack is another battle in the same war. She plays with death in her effort to break free. The stakes are that high, higher than those in the various money transactions that are always in the background of the drama. Jack is himself a casualty of the same war. If we associate him with Schön, it should be not as avenger but as mindless parody.

Jungian psychology interprets the femme fatale figure as the projection of an inner image, the anima, which is the female personification of the masculine unconscious. This image is always a product of the childhood relationship with the mother; the femme fatale reflects the case where that relationship is a threatening and fearful one, and the widespread appearance of that image in literature is a measure of the prevalence of that condition in the culture.[26] Before Jung described it, Strindberg exemplified it in his play *The Father*. The Captain, who is the play's male protagonist, first enters into the relationship with the woman he is to marry almost as child to mother. As she becomes his lover and wife, the relationship becomes increasingly threatening to him because of its implicitly incestuous character, and he reacts defensively with growing hostility toward her.

The most palpable sign for the Lulu character as a creation of male desires is the Pierrot portrait. Berg made quite a point of showing the Pierrot persona as a source for the character. His directions (not Wedekind's) have Lulu appear in the prologue in her Pierrot costume; and in that arcane semiotic register in which he seems to address musical analysts, or perhaps himself, he derives Lulu's characteristic tone row from the series of chords that he associates initially with the portrait. Like the Eve-Lilith symbolism, the Pierrot portrait connects to a shatteringly ambivalent attitude about Woman. But it is at the same time a symbolism that allows the poet and composer to show the Lulu character struggling against that attitude to gain her own authenticity, a struggle that reflects the struggle of sex roles from another side.

In the last scene of the opera Geschwitz brings in the portrait, which she has salvaged. Lulu screams, "My portrait! Out of my sight! Throw it out the window!" Alwa interrupts, "But why not? In the face of this portrait I can regain my self-respect. It makes my fate understandable. Whoever can feel secure in his bourgeois position in the face of these blossoming, swelling lips, these great, innocent eyes—let him cast the first stone." But by this time Lulu wants no more of that sort of responsibility. She wants love without entanglements. Berg makes that audibly clear in his setting of the encounter with Jack. As Jack is admiring her, the orchestra intones the music that had been associated with Schön's entrapment in the relationship with Lulu. But as she puts her arms about him and says, "I like you so; don't let me beg any longer," that music gives way to the music that has become familiar as the sign of her identity, and that has been associated with her aspiration to freedom (Example 8.9). One dimension of this drama is the story of Lulu's fatal progression from character to person (think, again, of Petrouchka). But that is the symbolism of Pierrot.[27]

In the portrait, as in the music hall scene, Lulu is presented as the essential actress, the role player, the person on display, passively at the disposition

EXAMPLE 8.9

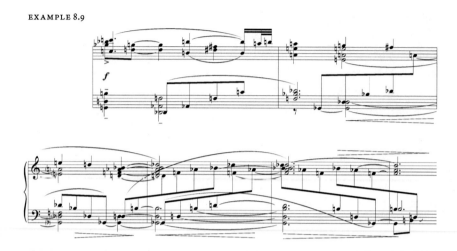

of the paying onlooker. In her Pierrot costume she conveys the ironic conceit that had become so enormously important in the art and literature of the turn of the century—that essential and ultimate truth is to be found in the illusions of such otherworldly and artificial settings as the popular theater, circus, or cabaret. That is in effect what Alwa says in his reaction to the portrait in the final scene of the opera.

But there is often a darker penumbra about such images, an elusive edge of the melancholy and even the macabre that gives them a threatening quality on which Wedekind and Berg played. They represent illusion and play, but at the same time disillusion, dejection. They are soulful but soulless. The double aspect of their appealing character and otherworldliness can be deadly, for they cannot safely mix with ordinary creatures of the daily world. This double aspect reflects the androgynous character of the images. They unite the passive beauty that draws the spectator to their subject (think again of Alwa's lyric about the portrait near the end) with the active and threatening persona (think of Lulu as Pierrot in the beginning, provoking the Painter, evading him, ensnaring him, and leading him straight to his self-destruction). This bipolar creature of the masculine imagination is a different, highly specialized expression of what is embodied in the femme fatale.

FIGURE 8.6. *Facing. The Alley (Carmen),* by Edvard Munch. The Epstein Family Collection, Washington, D.C. © 2010 The Munch Museum/The Munch-Ellingsen Group/Artists Rights Society (ARS), New York.

It is on this point that a rather more meaningful parallel with *The Rake's Progress* comes into view. The attributes of the bipolar, androgynous Pierrot figure are invested separately in the characters of Anne Truelove and Baba the Turk. Baba is a parody, of course, and her appeal for Tom Rakewell lies precisely in her lack of appeal. But his coupling with her is the fullest expression of his ruination. The sharpness of the separation and the palpably symbolic nature of the two figures are of the essence in this opera; Boulez is right that it is a morality play. The female characters are matched in that respect by the two main male characters, Rakewell and his (Nick) Shadow, whose identity as the trickster in the Jungian picture of the unconscious is hardly disguised.

Tilly Wedekind remarked about the Lulu portrait: "It is painted during the first act of *Earth Spirit* and, as a result, the painter becomes infatuated with his model. In the following act and in the last act, the picture is on stage, and each time a man is ruined by his passion for Lulu."[28] In this brief remark Tilly Wedekind displayed her deep understanding of the sinister symbolism of the Pierrot portrait: not only as sign of seduction and doom for each of those men, but as reminder that it is not Lulu but their own desire that brings them down.

Exit through the gallery of Munch, with wordless reflection on two other lithographs: his rendering of Carmen, the one relevant figure we have neglected so far (Figure 8.6) and one entitled *Hands* (Figure 8.7).

FIGURE 8.7. *Facing. Hands*, 1895, by Edvard Munch. Lithograph in black ink on cream card, 485 × 292mm (image), 514 × 389mm (primary support), 595 × 497mm (secondary support). Clarence Buckingham Collection, 1963.284, The Art Institute of Chicago. Used by permission of Artists Rights Society, New York. Photography © The Art Institute of Chicago.

9

HISTORY AND
ARCHETYPES

If you were fortunate enough to have access to the household of Dorothy and Dick Swift in the mid-1950s you didn't need Prozac. You could cheer up, instead, on wit and delight and laughter, and on an appreciation of the ridiculous that helped to ward off any danger of pomposity.

In this latter task one member of the household was particularly active. Her name was Lulu, and that she bore the same name as the lead character in the opera about which Dick was writing a master's thesis was no mere coincidence. In my mind's representation of them each one reflects something of the other's aura—perhaps because I came to know them together. But I am absolutely convinced that their sharing of one another's qualities is essential, not coincidental.

She was a brown dachshund who lived in the family, high sheen, perky, bright-eyed, "bien dans sa peau," as the French say, one of those "Haustiere, die so wohlgesittet," as the Animal Trainer says, sharing in the household's pleasure in the world and in her in particular. The operatic Lulu, "Das wilde, schöne Tier," partook of those qualities and in return lent to her canine sister something of her ravishing nature. As the dog wore that quality in a kind of self-contradiction, it was reflected back on the human (or serpentine) Lulu, but it came back just a little off, like a cocked hat. If I indulge in the wild fantasy of directing the opera, I see the actress playing the Lulu character display that skewed lushness as a component of her complex make-up. With characteristic wit Dick hit upon the expression "Lulu's interchangeable parts" to label some ingenious compositional operation of Berg's. By the simple orthographic device of moving the apostrophe one space to the right I can underscore my sense of the relation between the two ladies—the Lulus' interchangeable parts. In the following, in talking about the operatic character, I will always have the spirit of the dog tacitly in the background as a way of keeping in mind the aspect of farce that undeniably flavors *Lulu*.

The path leading to the front door of the Swift house was bounded by fences (the word dignifies them; "wire strung on one-by-twos" is more apt) separating it from a perfunctory lawn. Lulu's daily forays into the world entailed a short trot the length of that path, then a ninety-degree turn in one direction or the other, still following a fence. One day the fences were gone. But here Lulu parted ways with her namesake. Did she exit the house, look around her, and belt out, "O Freiheit! Herr Gott in Himmel!" as she frisked diagonally over the lawn? No, she trotted silently down the now-unfenced path, remaining to the end of her days always obedient to the constraints that were the lasting power of the phantom fences over her.

And the operatic Lulu? Tied up in a web of constraints that are steel cables to the dachshund's flimsy wires, her act of slipping out of every one of them like some female Houdini gives one dimension to the opera. Her bonds are the personae—all fantasies and fears through which the male characters project their hopes and dreads vis-à-vis woman—of which this character is patched together: the femme fatale—embodiment of feminine evil and instinctive seductress and destroyer of men; Helen of Troy; the first woman and wife of Adam—now the uppity, serpentine Lillith, now the pure and obedient Eve; the innocent child; the Pierrot and dancer, both objects of the male's voyeuristic gaze; bourgeois domesticity, embodied in madonna on one side and whore on the other; playgirl (and daughter) of the devil; Narcissa toying with lesbianism; the creature of nature; the frail dependent; the oppressed woman seeking freedom and self-realization in prostitution. It is not only the men in the opera who are driven by these images, they are somehow in the minds of the author (playwright and composer) and of the critics, who reflect them to and from the public. These images define, in other words, an aspect of the habitus of the culture of and about *Lulu*. When they are displayed, therefore, there is always the question, to whom should they be attributed? Whose attitudes are betrayed by their display? It is Schön and the Animal Trainer of the prologue, for example, who most explicitly see in Lulu the femme fatale. She is introduced in the opera's prologue when the Animal Trainer says, "Bring out our snake," and as she is brought on by the ravishing music that identifies her he sings, "She was created to incite disaster, to attract, to seduce, to poison, to murder, without letting the victim feel a thing."[1] In his life-and-death struggle with her, Schön calls Lulu "death's angel." Much of the critical literature, however, betrays the belief that this is the standpoint of the opera and—hence—of the author. A nice symptom of this easy belief can be found in the English translation of the libretto that you get with the 1979 Boulez recording,[2] where the phrase "the root of all evil," which corresponds to nothing in Berg's text, accompanies the other epithet in Schön's outburst. It is as though one would believe that the artist George Grosz meant to celebrate the attitude toward women that is displayed by the porcine cigar-smoking industrialists he portrayed.

In the preceding chapter I suggested that the critics' representation of that standpoint as the assertion of the work itself, voiced especially through the topos of the revenge of the victims as theme and temporal extension of the opera, must come forth out of their own internalized construction of sexual character and conflict, and that altogether this circle of work, author, critic, and public manifests deep-set attitudes about these matters that are to be seen everywhere in art, literature, and theater of the period. Accordingly I labeled them archetypal and located the images they conjure up in "the universal female pantheon." But I did not see, then, the weakness of that interpretation when it stands alone.

In emphasizing the universal and enduring nature of these archetypal components of the Lulu character I elevated them to a transcendental, atemporal realm (atemporal in the senses of being of no or all time and of having its ontology unaffected by the passage of time), where they are inaccessible to history and where the work and its author are protected in an aesthetically autonomous zone in which the work is aesthetically static. I may have managed to enrich what had been a simplistically stereotyped interpretation of the opera's meaning, but I nevertheless represented it as an instantiation of a universal structure. The explanatory value of such an interpretation is limited precisely in its failure to offer understanding of why just such a structure is evoked in particular circumstances. Those images define an aspect of the habitus of the culture surrounding Lulu, all right.[3] But a habitus is a system of dispositions functioning as a matrix of perceptions and apprecia- tions and as a generative principle of action, which responds and adjusts to the particular conditions under which it functions. Bourdieu captured the sense precisely with the image of "a train bringing along its own rails."[4] To be sure, the temptation to frame interpretations in terms of archetypes is especially great in a work so strongly Expressionist, a style that favors arche- types to deliver its meaning—puppet-like characters with whom one does not identify, for whom one does not feel compassion, and who, unlike the characters of Naturalist drama, are not expected to be apprehended as his- torically real. But such a drama does not depend for its historical character on the historical realism of its characters, setting, and actions; the many refer- ences to historical specifics inside the work are all stereotypes in the service of a general tone of mockery.

It is in the meaning that the work takes on as it passes through the light of the history in which it is generated that its historical character lies. The prominence of such archetypal female images as are so densely packed into the Lulu character in *fin de siècle* theater, art, and literature in general—Elaine Showalter speaks of "*fin de siècle* misogyny"[5]—becomes better understand- able in the light of the intersection of several historical and cultural force fields of the time: the pressures on the traditional polarity of masculine-femi- nine roles manifested in the advances of suffrage movements and movements for the liberation of women in general, the class structure of European soci- ety, the development of mercantile capitalism.

Such *fin de siècle* misogyny as is displayed right at the beginning of the opera is interpreted by Showalter in the context of rising antifeminism as the expression of a fear of women's aspirations for and achievement of sexual and economic emancipation, and of their unwillingness to conform to the roles that had been set out for them during the course of the nineteenth century.

But it is only the climax, and perhaps the enduring end state, of a progres- sion of male attitudes toward women traced through images of women in the visual arts from the mid-nineteenth century into the first two decades or so of the twentieth, in one of the most comprehensive works of iconology I have ever seen.[6] Every one of the personae through which Lulu is presented in the opera can be identified in Dijkstra's display of the procession of iconographic traditions.

I can summarize this only very briefly. The middle-class male engaged in mercantile capitalism is dependent upon credit. In order to demonstrate his credit worthiness he must engage in conspicuous consumption and in the display of conspicuous leisure. In this his wife must play a major role, must show no signs of engaging in productive labor, must instead be a showpiece. The male, since he must engage in the business world in competitive, aggressive, rapacious behavior (think of Dr. Schön, represented in the prologue as a tiger), is dependent upon his wife to be guardian and savior of his soul. She must therefore be the embodiment of moral purity and virtue—the household nun, as Dijkstra puts it. This role implies chastity, and raises the dilemma over the perpetuation of the species. Auguste Comte, the nineteenth-century French progenitor of positivism, is cited for his suggestions about artificial insemination. The woman, shut in, comes to behave as an invalid. In these stifling circumstances women become dissatisfied and seek escape in a succession of directions: into nature, into the mirror (symbolizing narcissism and homoeroticism), into prostitution, and ultimately into the open and seductive display of their sexuality and into economic self-sufficiency.

Reinforcement of the precepts about woman's role come from evolutionary, biological, and sexological science, which claim to reveal women to be intellectually inferior (and more intuitive), both innately (in terms of the consistency and weight of the brain, for example) and in consequence of their exhaustion from child-bearing and rearing (Eduard Hanslick attributed the scarcity of women composers to this factor). This attitude manifests itself in pictorial representations of childlike women and women with vacant stares (for Alwa, who speaks of the innocent look in her eyes, Lulu is childlike). At the same time, nineteenth-century scientific research and reasoning claim to reveal the tendency of women toward nymphomania—manifesting again the femme fatale imagery and through it, the expression of masculine anger over and fear of women's independence and sexuality.

This general description will suffice to show the nature of Dijkstra's iconology. Now I want to look more closely at two of his specific interpretations in order to identify further the two general problems that I am aiming to put out for consideration here: the problem of attribution—whose attitudes are being displayed in an interpretation?—and the interplay of history and archetype in the interpretation of art.

In the course of his discussion of what he calls "extinguished eyes and the call of the child" (the vacant look and the woman as child), Dijkstra reveals how much his interpretations are based on his own biases, guided, in fact, by universal archetypes that *he* has internalized, and perhaps not as much so as he would claim, on nineteenth-century culture-directed investigation. He reproduces a work from around 1895 by the Swedish painter Carl Larsson entitled *The Little Girls' Room*. A blonde girl, perhaps six years old, naked except for her stockings, facing the viewer and holding her nighty behind her, stands on one side of the bedroom that she shares with an older girl who stands fully dressed on the other side of the room, facing away.

Dijkstra writes that Larsson "chose to straddle the line between sentimentalism and obscenity in his certainly not entirely innocent portrayal of *The Little Girls' Room*. Not even the world of the smallest toddlers, in fact, could escape the eroticized imagination of the turn-of-the-century painters, who, having been told by the highest scientific authority that woman remained a child all her life, inevitably came to recognize traces of woman in all stages of childhood."[7] I was stopped by this because, as it happens, I have lived for several years in Sweden, long enough to know that Carl Larsson occupies a place in that country roughly comparable to that occupied in the United States by Norman Rockwell as a painter of solid bourgeois home values, but with Larsson turned more than Rockwell toward the snug, secure world of the child in the home. I have even visited, with my own small children, Larsson's house in the Swedish countryside, which is a kind of pilgrimage place for young children and their parents. I am not fully persuaded that this child should be viewed as a little woman. I also know of the normality of child nakedness in Swedish life. Dijkstra's interpretation violates the very principle on which his book is ostensibly founded—the interpretation of art in the light of the conditions and attitudes of the culture in and for which it is produced. He has failed to inquire whether members of the culture in and for which this painting was made would have seen erotic content—obscene or otherwise—in it, nor has he shown evidence of an effort to familiarize himself with Carl Larsson's oevre and to inform himself about the role that it plays in the culture. So I cannot help wondering whose "eroticized imagination" is at play here, the painter's or the critic's, and whether it is not really an archetypal idea of nakedness as obscenity—an idea held by the interpreter—that is driving the interpretation here. This is a question that I often have as I read this book, for the author regularly interprets images without inquiring how they were interpreted by the culture for which they were intended.[8] The problem generalizes as a problem of interpretation on a broad front—including the interpretation of music—that is particularly troubling just now.

What is at stake here is more than a quibble about a particular interpretation. It is a question about how the interpretation of art will proceed, now that it has executed its turn toward anthropological and sociological knowledge. The failure of the one-time ambition for scientific historical and aesthetic knowledge about art—especially music—can be understood in retrospect as the consequence of a misassessment of the proper grain of knowability in this enterprise. The wish to have that kind of knowledge led scholars to look the other way when it came to an honest assessment of the value of the knowledge they generated. The faith in the importance of the questions stood in as a criterion for the weight of the answers. I fear one has to say the same about Dijkstra's interpretations, however much more congenial the kind of knowledge he aims to generate may seem to the temper of our time. The principal symptom is the absence of any inquiry about how the images that are his objects actually functioned, and how they were actually perceived, in the culture in which they were produced and circulated. This is a common omission in recent interpretative literature. Despite frequent appeals to the dialogic nature of the historian's enterprise, the participants in the past cultures that are the objects of investigation too often fail to be asked their opinions of the ingenious exegetical work of today's interpreters.

The other interpretation at which I want to look more closely concerns the iconography of images—often produced during this period—of the woman gazing at her reflection in a mirror. In Dijkstra's decoding, the fascination of a woman with her mirror image is a symbol of her independence from men. I do not question this interpretation in the same way. Indeed, the author finds the interpretation quite explicit in Lulu's remark, "When I looked at myself in the mirror I wished I were a man . . . my own husband!" Dijkstra quotes a couplet from a poem of 1929, "Laus virginitatis" by Arthur Symmons: "The mirror of men's eyes delights me less, O mirror, than the friend I find in thee."[9] This poem is cited also in Lawrence Kramer's essay, "*Carnaval*, Cross Dressing, and the Woman in the Mirror," in which the author, through a lengthy hermeneutic exercise, finds "meanings that challenge established forms of social, intellectual, and sexual authority."[10] What interests me in particular here is Kramer's identification, after showing signs of Schumann's feminine side in other connections, of what he considers a mirror relationship between a harmonic progression "from a subdominant F Minor to a tonic C Minor [in

Chiarina] and a dominant C Major to a tonic F Minor [in *Estrella*]." This he interprets in the following way:

> In the nineteenth century the mirror increasingly becomes the space re-
> served for women's subjectivity rather than, as was traditional, the sign
> of their vanity. By gazing into the depths of the mirror a woman can enjoy,
> explore, and to some degree construct her own identity. . . . The mirror pre-
> serves rather than resists male control unless the reflected image becomes
> too absorbing, in which case the mirror arouses male hostility—and desire
> —by making the woman psychologically and sexually impenetrable.[11]

This interpretation is psychologically more subtle and differentiated than Dijkstra's, and it is an engaging account of the iconography of the woman-in-the-mirror theme. But think of the interpretative moves that must be sup-posed in order to find that meaning in the music: the listener apprehends the structural relationship—the symmetry in the harmonic movement of the two pieces—as a salient property; the symmetry registers as a juxtaposition of mirror images (this is to say that the listener executes cognitively the meta-phor entailed in denoting that symmetrical relation with the word "mirror," rather than "crab," for example, a metaphor that would not entail transform-ing a moving process into a frozen image); and the listener, aware from the titles that the pieces are meant to characterize women, makes the leap from a musical "mirror" relationship to the associations of the woman in the mir-ror that are described in the preceding paragraph. The harmonic symmetry is interpreted as a symbol of the mirror imagery and as the linchpin for the connection. There is no inquiry aimed at learning whether the apprehension of the meaning of this, or of any piece of that time, would have entailed such recognitions and thought processes, no search for reports on listening as an exercise of this sort.

Does that matter? It depends on what claims the interpreter makes for the status and purpose of the interpretation. It was a practice of music critics in the nineteenth century to render accounts of instrumental music in terms of well-known mythological and literary subjects—the *Iliad, Faust,* the *Ae-neid*. It was a way of guiding listeners to the expressive or dramatic character and through the narrative course of the music as the critic apprehended them. No claim was made for the status of those accounts as giving the true mean-ing or contents or subject matter of the music. They were means of conveying something that could be conveyed directly through descriptive language with only the greatest difficulty, and without precision, if at all; they represented one solution, in other words, to the problem posed for the critic by the ostensible ineffability of music, something that was much worried over at that time. We can take such associations as evidence of the cultural currency of those themes, but not of a belief that those themes were in the music—that the *Aeneid,* for example, is enacted by the first movement of Mozart's String Quartet in D Minor, K. 421.[12]

But where the critic takes such pains to link the musical structure to contemporaneous psychological themes and ideological issues and social structures in the sense that it expresses, represents, or embodies them, there is not only an implication that the music itself, through its musical properties, participates in the practice of this cultural expression, there is a positivistic implication that such meaning is imprinted on the musical structure, and can be read off from it. We are therefore entitled to look for that claim to be made explicit, and also the claim that the music actually functioned in that way, and then for evidence adduced in support of such claims. In the absence of that, the gesture toward historicalization, the notion that understanding music depends on understanding it in its social and cultural situation, while intuitively appealing after the failure of the opposite doctrine, remains unconsumated.

More apparent and striking musically is the mirror aspect of the whole of *Lulu.* This is not one of those secret structures of Berg's whose meanings lie in some not-quite-audible register; the close listener will recognize the reflection in the middle of the film music, which begins audibly to reverse itself. We might be tempted to regard this form, too, as a symbol of Lulu's "psychological impenetrability," especially in view of what she herself says about her image in the mirror. But if so, what shall we say about "mirror" forms in Berg's instrumental works?[13] When I hear that moment in the film music at which it begins to retrace its steps, I experience it directly with an awful feeling of entrapment in an unbendable process, like a recurrent nightmare in which I know everything that is going to happen and every quality that is going to be displayed, yet I can't stop it or alter its course. And of course that purely musical experience feeds the experience of the drama as a whole. But I have to face up to the fact that the experience is not historically specific. It is a broadly human experience.

Elaine Showalter writes, "Women have traditionally been perceived as figures of disorder, 'potential disrupters of masculine boundary systems of all sorts.' Women's social or cultural marginality seems to place them on the borderlines of symbolic order, both the 'frontier between men and chaos,' and dangerously part of chaos itself, inhabitants of a mysterious and frightening wild zone outside of patriarchal culture."[14] That is the sense of the word "anarchy" in the title of her book.

The theme of women as symbols of chaos and the disruption of order (that is exactly the charge made by Schön to Lulu) is embodied in expressions found throughout Western history of an anxiety or an anger over the threatened or actual decline of music, in which often the aspect of decadence is identified with a loss of discipline or order, and with lasciviousness and effeminacy—those two properties often being treated as synonymous. It may be particularly melody that is identified as the feminine element. Order would be represented in any case by "masculine" elements—words (Wagner wrote of opera as the creature of an act of procreation—the union of female music with "man-creative" form-giving word[15]), harmony, rhythm, and, above all, form. Schön's five-strophe aria, at the conclusion of which he is shot by Lulu, is a last desperate attempt to maintain musical order, and as he dies he falls into musical disorder: his twelve-tone row dissolves into the primal set of the opera.

10

GENDER AND OTHER DUALITIES
OF MUSIC HISTORY

Western music history is among the discourses of myth through which our culture contemplates and represents itself in its desire to affirm its identity and values. From early on it has been guided by gender duality in its description, evaluation, and narrative form. Boethius, a principal conduit of ideas about music from antiquity to the Middle Ages, sounded a theme in the sixth century that would become typical in evaluations of the state of music:

> A lascivious mind takes pleasure in the more lascivious modes, and is often softened and corrupted by listening to them. Contrariwise, a sterner mind finds joy in the more stirring modes and is braced by them. This is why the musical modes are named after certain peoples, such as the Lydian and Phrygian; the mode takes the name of the nation that delights in it ... Ruder peoples delight in the harsher modes of the Thracians, civilized peoples in more restrained modes; though in these days this almost never occurs. Since humanity is now soft and fickle, it is wholly captivated by the modes of the theater. ... Hence Plato holds that music which is carefully and modestly composed, so that it is chaste, simple, and masculine, not effeminate, savage and inconsistent, is a great guardian of the commonwealth.[1]

Typical in this passage is the linking of gender with a duality of ethnicity, or it may be nationality or race, and with the duality of the chaste and the lascivious, in dichotomies of Self and Other that function as markers in the pathways and panoramas of understanding in our culture. The wording of my title is intended to identify gender as the archetypal duality. I came to this interpretation by way of the pursuit of certain canonical beliefs that run through a particular discourse of Western music history—the story of medieval chant. I shall try to give an account of them and their broader associations. These beliefs are sustained by an ancient mythology that explains human consciousness as divided in two permanently antagonistic parts, a mythology in which reason and sensuality are mutually opposed, and that opposition is characterized as the duality of the masculine and the feminine.[2]

But the functioning of that duality as a structure of music interpretation has in turn depended since antiquity on the unreflected identification of gender attributes in music. There is a question whether music can have an immanently masculine or feminine character that transcends history and culture, which has been posed anew—with highly specific ideological motifs and motives—along with much-debated issues of aesthetic theory concerning what music conveys, expresses, and represents, and how one can know about such things, in the context of postmodern and particularly feminist music criticism. The question is whether, in this new context, claims regarding these issues merit the privileged status to which they seem to have been raised and whether their newly explicit ideological dimension exempts them from critical reflection.

Finally, the idea of essentialism that is entailed in the practice of gender identification in music points to a parallel conception with respect to race. The two modes of essentialist thinking have the same culture-historical background, they have played parallel and linked roles in the criticism and historical narrative of the arts, they have functioned under the same ideological tenets, and by the very nature of essentialism they are both given to dogmatism.

The story that serves as my gateway may seem out of the way, to say the least: the modern reception history of the liturgical chant of the medieval Western church. I shall refer to it simply as "plainchant," following Jean-Jacques Rousseau, the writer with whom that history begins.[3]

Example 10.1 shows two stylistically different versions of an Introit antiphon, a chant that accompanied the entrance of the celebrant into the church and his procession to the altar to begin the mass. The two versions belong to different medieval traditions. One, the Old Roman tradition, was sung only in Rome, and then only until it began to be superseded by the other in the twelfth century. We have the Old Roman chant in manuscripts written in Rome in the eleventh and twelfth centuries. Until at least that time the tradition was an oral one. The other version belongs to a Frankish tradition that was transmitted in writing rather uniformly throughout most of Western Europe and the British Isles from the ninth century on; it has come down to us as "Gregorian" chant, a label deriving from the tradition's myth of origin that attributes its creation to Pope Gregory the Great, circa 600 (the myth, an invention of the ninth century, is not substantiated by any evidence). This Frankish tradition was not sung in Rome before the arrival there of Frankish chant books in the twelfth century. The judgment that the two chants are versions of the "same" item is based on what they have in common: their ritual function in the mass on the fourth Sunday of Advent, their biblical text, their underlying melodic outline despite differing surface details. These constants—which describe the relationship between the two traditions in general—point to a common origin, and there are different theories about their pathways to the versions that have come down in writing.

Melodies from the two traditions have been compared from a different vantage point in chapter 4. The Old Roman melody is marked by a persistent recursiveness. It turns on itself repeatedly in numerous circular figures that create a florid texture. The melodic line shows an overall direction, but it is highly decorated. The outlines of the Gregorian version are more direct. It, too, is ornamented, but not as uniformly so. This difference of style is characteristic of the two traditions, a product and sign of their divergence in the early history of plainchant in the Middle Ages. And since plainchant is the earliest European music known to us, the efforts to interpret the difference open out to nothing less than theories about the origins and nature of European music. I shall sample some of the interpretations that have been offered and consider what they portend for vital matters of cultural identity that are at the center of my subject.[4]

Here is Bruno Stäblein, a preeminent German medievalist-musicologist, writing about Old Roman chant: "Endless streams of melody that overflow the boundaries of textual divisions. . . . melodies that spread over their texts

EXAMPLE 10.1.

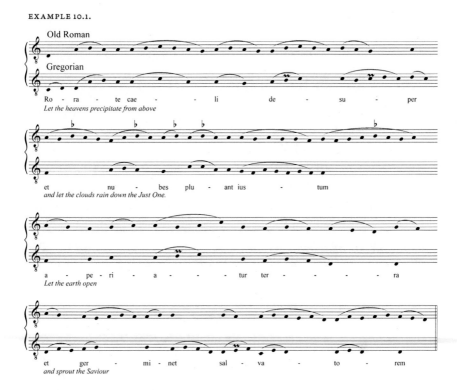

Old Roman

Gregorian

Ro - ra - te cae - - li de - su - per
Let the heavens precipitate from above

et nu - bes plu - ant ius - tum
and let the clouds rain down the Just One.

a - pe - ri - a - - tur ter - - - - ra
Let the earth open

et ger - mi - net sal - va - to - rem
and sprout the Saviour

like a chain of pearls or a voluptuous gown . . . soft, elegant, charming and graceful, without sharp edges or corners."[5] Their style is "naive, youthfully fresh, blossom-like, the expression of a general Italic, folk-like feeling."[6] The Gregorian melodies, by contrast, are "disciplined and ordered, a product of rational thinking." They are "clear, sculpted configurations, systematically chiseled; a system of musical rhetoric reigns in them." They display a "more complete knowledge—*perfectior scientia*—a wonderful expression that carries with it the thought of the thoroughly systematic working-through of the musical language, accomplished with the highest intelligence."[7] Stäblein appends a list of attributes that medieval writers had themselves found in Gregorian chant: *vis* (strength), *virtus* (manliness), *vigor, potestas* (power), *ratio* (reason).[8]

Stäblein held the Old Roman tradition to be the older one, from which the Gregorian tradition was achieved by "stripping down and reshaping the unrestrained coloratura of the originals." This happened in Rome, whence the new melodies were carried, as the *cantus Romanus,* to the major ecclesiastical and political centers of the Frankish North during the reigns of King Pepin and the Emperor Charlemagne. Through this transformation, writes Stäblein, the provincial Roman melodies were raised to a higher, super-regional level as "melodies for a world power."[9] "Rome" is presented as two kinds of place: the provincial Italic home of a luxuriant Mediterranean singing practice, and the place where an efficient and economical model was fashioned for a European melodic style. What is played out in this discourse that may seem to be simply a matter of style history is (Western) world-defining ecclesiastical, nationalist, and imperial politics.[10]

Clarity, system, understandability, strength, vigor, power, reason, manliness, on one side; on the other, softness, roundedness, elegance, charm, grace. It does not require much exegesis to recognize here, as the underlying principle, gender duality and its association with the duality of the rational and the sensual and with the concept of power, at the root of European music history.

Jean-Jacques Rousseau knew nothing of Old Roman chant, but he nevertheless managed to embed what he called "plainchant" in a gender duality. In the *Dictionnaire de musique* he wrote of plainchant as "a noble relic, very much disfigured, but very precious, of [ancient] Greek music, which having passed through the hands of barbarians has not, however, been able to lose its natural beauties. There remains yet enough of it to render it much preferable . . . to those effeminate and theatrical pieces which in some churches are substituted in its place."[11]

The plainchant is, by implication, masculine, and the word with which Rousseau labels its opposite—*effeminée*—carries a sense of deterioration from what is by nature manly. This "dread of corruption," as E. H. Gombrich has called it, was an obsession with writers of the Enlightenment, and a fear they implanted deeply in the modern unconscious.[12] As for the Old Roman-Gregorian question, we might well wonder why, of all possible interpretations, it would enter anyone's mind to differentiate these two singing traditions as *masculine* and *feminine*. The answer is surely that it was already in his mind, as a primary form of cognition and therefore as "the very stuff" of a historical narrative that transcends its apparent content.[13] What is displayed here is an archetypal mythic story that is told and retold with changing material. My purpose is to expose it the more starkly in this story in which the very idea of medieval chant traditions contrasted as masculine and feminine must strike us as strange, if not bizarre, on the face of it. But the narrative of a cultural ascendance from a feminine condition to a masculine one is readily transformed, in the same mythology, into the parameters of other dualities.

In 1921 Peter Wagner, possibly the most influential German writer on this subject to date, used language similar to that of Stäblein when he characterized Gregorian Alleluia chants as "models of clear formal structure and symmetrical organization, the work of aesthetic deliberation."[14] Thirteen years later Dom Paolo Ferretti, a writer equally influential for readers of Italian and French, characterized the composers of Gregorian chant as "artists," creating under the inspiration of their "personal genius" and the "logic" of musical principles. Their chants are "organic," "harmonious," "homogeneous," and "logical."[15] Wagner's language aimed at a contrast with an older layer of chants whose melodies were "unregulated and without plan." The difference is like that between a "skillfully laid-out flower bed" and a "luxuriantly proliferating growth." Those older melodies remind him of the "unregulated undulation of the melismatics of the Orient," whereas the later ones display "Latin, Roman traits."[16]

That these traits, which come down to matters of formal order and unity, are seen as epitomizing European music altogether comes out in one of the most extravagant bits of encomium in the whole story, a passage in Willi Apel's 1958 survey of Gregorian chant. Concluding an analysis of a group of mass Gradual chants, Apel wrote that "the perception of their structural properties greatly enhances their significance as unified works of art, no less so than in the case of a sonata by Beethoven."[17] This remark makes explicit what was implicit in the project all along: its task of qualifying Gregorian chants for their position at the headwaters of the main stream of European— as against Oriental—music by finding in them just those qualities that count as value and greatness in the culture that validated them in this way. At the same time the chants, by virtue of their historical authority as the beginning of European music, validated those qualities as *the* quintessential qualities of European music.[18]

Given the role of this aesthetic doctrine in casting the story of "European music," it is hardly surprising to find it displayed in almost identical form in a passage in Anton Webern's book legitimating "the new music." Webern, recall, was a historical musicologist as well as a composer. At the conclusion of a formal analysis of a Gregorian Alleluia melody he exclaims that it is "already the full structure of the large symphonic forms, expressed exactly as in the symphonies of Beethoven."[19] This time the reasoning drives in the opposite direction: the formal principles inherited by the new music from Beethoven are still more deeply rooted, lying in the most ancient European tradition. But there is a difference between these accounts. Apel's version is embedded in the duality of the European and the Oriental, which is not really an issue for Webern.

No one has contributed more to our understanding of that duality as a structure of history than Edward Said in his book *Orientalism*. "Orientalism," writes Said, is

> a way of coming to terms with the Orient [the Near East] that is based on the Orient's special place in European Western experience. The Orient is not only adjacent to Europe; it is also the place of Europe's greatest and richest and oldest colonies, the source of its civilizations and languages, its cultural contestant, and one of its deepest and most recurring images of the Other. In addition, the Orient has helped to define Europe (or the West) as its contrasting image, idea, personality, experience [and as] a surrogate, underground self for the West.[20]

Later, in "Orientalism Reconsidered," Said wrote directly about the parallelism of the male-female and Europe-Orient dualities:

> Orientalism is a praxis of the same sort . . . as male gender dominance, or patriarchy, in metropolitan societies: the Orient was routinely described as feminine, its riches as fertile, its main symbols the sensual woman, the harem, and the despotic—but curiously attractive—ruler.[21]

I would take that one step further: the two are not only of the same sort, they are the same myth, differently peopled.

The similarity implies a psychological factor operating together with the ideological, political, and sociological factors that function to define our historical fields. It is the tendency to build an identity—individual or cultural—by positioning the Self against a sharply defined Other that is contrasted with the Self in essential ways. But what are regarded as the opposite traits of the Other are interpretable as the traits of a surrogate, underground—we might as well say unconscious—Self. The Other, in effect, is a projection of a suppressed and feared aspect of the Self and consequently inspires deeply ambivalent attitudes in the acknowledged Self.

Recall that Rousseau's influential article on plainchant in the *Dictionnaire de musique* begins by characterizing the chant as "a noble relic, very much disfigured, but very precious, of [ancient] Greek music, which, having passed through the hands of Barbarians, has not, however, been able to lose all its natural beauties." Two related themes are set out here that are essential elements in the cultural self-portrait that was being drawn: the theme of the ancient Greek heritage of this founding tradition of European music—whence it derives its purity and perfection—and the "dread of corruption" (the dark side of the expectation of perfection in Enlightenment historiography) at the hands of barbarians: Graecophilia and barbarophobia.[22]

Rousseau wrote as a participant in a major project in the forging of a European identity, which has been described by Martin Bernal in his *Black Athena*:

> [There are] two models of Greek history: one viewing Greece as essentially European or Aryan, the other seeing it as Levantine, on the periphery of the Egyptian and Semitic cultural area. I call them the "Aryan" and the "Ancient" models. The "Ancient Model" was the conventional view among Greeks in the Classical and Hellenistic ages. According to it, Greek culture had arisen as the result of colonization, around 1500 BC, by Egyptians and Phoenicians who had civilized the native inhabitants[23]

But under the paradigm of "races" that was applied to all human studies at the end of the eighteenth century,

> it became increasingly intolerable for Greece, which was seen not only as the epitome of Europe but also its pure childhood, to have been the result of the mixture of native Europeans and colonizing Africans and Semites.[24]

Bernal calls this conception "European chauvinism." The European-Oriental duality is itself entwined with the theme of Greek patrilineage. The two ideas reinforce one another. The Aryan Model, which most of us have been brought up to believe, developed only during the first half of the nineteenth century. In its earlier or "broad" form, the new model denied the truth of the Egyptian settlements and questioned those of the Phoenicians. According to the Aryan Model, there had been an invasion from the north—unreported in ancient tradition—which had overwhelmed the local "Aegean" or "Pre-Hellenic" culture. Greek civilization is seen as the result of the mixture of the Indo-European-speaking Hellenes and their indigenous subjects. "It is from the construction of this Aryan Model that I call this [first of three] volume[s] *The Fabrication of Ancient Greece 1785–1985.*"[25]

A rash alternative to this reconstruction of Grecian history—but out of the same racialist motive—was to throw out Greece altogether as the bedrock of European history. This was done for European music by R. G. Kiesewetter, a Viennese nobleman, civil servant, amateur music historian and musical man-about-town (he turns up repeatedly between 1820 and 1826 in Beethoven's conversation books) who rejected Rousseau's idea of chant as a Greek patrimony in his *Geschichte der europäisch-abendländischen oder unsrer heutigen Musik* (History of European-Occidental or Our Contemporary Music), published in 1834. In this first specimen of the genre "Histories of Western Music" he wrote,

> It is a preconceived opinion as widely spread as it is deeply rooted, that modern music was modelled on that of ancient Greece, of which it is in fact merely a continuation. Modern music flourished only in proportion as it began to separate and withdraw itself from the system laid down and enforced by the Greeks . . . it reached . . . perfection only when it succeeded in completely emancipating itself from the last remnant of the ancient Grecian. . . . That Grecian or Hebrew melodies should have found their way into the assemblies of Christians seems altogether incredible. . . . Their natural horror of everything connected with the heathens . . . was too great for the admission among them of such melodies as had been common to the pagan temples or theatres; whilst they evinced an equal anxiety also to separate themselves from the Jews.[26]

Nevertheless Rousseau's doctrine prevailed, but under the reconstruction of the Aryan Model. There is nothing unusual in this legitimation of a conception and evaluation of the present through reference to the authority of origins. Nor is it a coincidence that the Greece that emerged through this process became at once the epitome of what counted as Western Civilization, the transcendent and timeless context for all our cultural achievements; that was the role for which it was created.

Figure 10.1 is a vivid embodiment of that quality of timeless transcendence. When Willi Apel emerged from his analytical labors over Gregorian chants and proclaimed them to be as unified as a sonata by Beethoven, he was rescuing them from slipping into the Orient and assuring their place in this Graeco-European musical order presided over by Beethoven (notice the "classical" details of the setting). The invention of Ancient Greece provided both a patrimony for European culture and a model to contrast against the cultural Other. The two aspects work hand in hand.

Figure 10.1. *Musical Hall of Fame.* Reproduced
from *The Etude* magazine, December 1911.

The chauvinist/racist and sexist undertones of the historical and critical
categories that underlie the modern reception of medieval chant were turned
up to full volume in the culture-historical ideology published in the Germany
of the 1920s and '30s. I refer first of all to work that was presented, not yet as
National Socialist propaganda but as "scientific" research of a kind called
Rassenforschung (Race Research), heritage of a Romantic preoccupation with
roots in the late eighteenth century[27] and productive of books with titles such
as *Kunst and Rasse, Rasse and Stil, Rasse und Seele, Rassenkunde Europas, Die
Rasse in den Geisteswissenschaften, Rassengeschichte des Hellenischen and des
Römischen Volkes, Rassenkunde des Jüdischen Volkes, Musik and Rasse.* My interest here is in the last of these, by Richard Eichenauer.[28] Eichenauer displays
exactly what Bernal describes as the racist dimension of the Aryan Model
of Greek history: "Race research has demonstrated that Greek behavioral
patterns as a whole show the picture of a great ascent under Nordic influence
followed by a decline brought about by *Entnordung*" (de-Nordification, we
might say; he also speaks of *Semitisierung*—Semitization).[29] Greek musical
styles he characterizes with yet another duality that has its own background

of identification with the duality of the rational and the sensual: that of the Apollonian, which is Nordic, and the Dionysian, which is Near Eastern, that is, Oriental/Semitic.[30] The history of Gregorian chant begins in the latter cultural domain, with the Jewish chant of the Near East. But with the spread of Christianity it "wandered into the heartland of the Nordic race," where "the Germanic musical feeling expressed itself ever more strongly." Peter Wagner is criticized for having had all the facts in his *Einführung,* yet failing to draw this clear conclusion. But Eichenauer did not fail to pick up the passage in Wagner that I have already cited:

> We recall that one of the strongest Orientally flavored characteristics of ecclesiastical chant were the long melismas. Wagner thus distinguishes an older, still purely Oriental group from a younger group with Roman traits. He finds the difference in the turn from unregulated up-and-down meandering [of the former] to the clear structure [of the latter].[31]

Thus Eichenauer citing Peter Wagner.

This prompts his confrontation of the difficult question: What is meant by "Roman?" He turns again to Wagner: "Systematic and design-wise melodic process was ever the spiritual task of a strong side of the Roman genius"; and to Heinrich Besseler, author of the influential *Musik des Mittelalters und der Renaissance:* "In [the Gregorian Alleluia chants] rational control [Besseler's word is the more violent *Bewältigung*] and the establishment of musical form are felt most strongly as against the voluptuously proliferating [the German *wüchernd* carries the pejorative sense of a decadent fleshiness] Oriental melismatic style." According to Eichenauer, Besseler attributes to the Roman cantors "a certain ideal of melodic cogency, terseness, and clarity."[32] In all this Eichenauer sees a "racial influence." He writes, "If it was really 'Roman genius' that was at work here, then it was surely the ancient Roman-Nordic, still showing through in individual creative spirits" (this is Wagner's "Latin-Roman," as opposed to Stäblein's "old-Italic"). Eichenauer continues: "But for the period in question it is not impossible that a 'new-Roman' = Germanic genius ['Holy Roman'] is also speaking. In either case it would be the Nordically strict constructive spirit that strives for the clear working-through of form."[33]

Insofar as the virtue of rational form has been held to be a defining character of European music, no music has been more closely identified with that character than the work of Beethoven, the Apollo in the Parnassus depicted in *The Musical Hall of Fame* (Figure 10.1). The arrangement of that scene around his figure models the construction of European music history about his work. Not far behind the scene, however, is the implication that Beethoven epitomizes the consolidation in European music of this formal aesthetic with masculinity, and specifically with male sexuality.

It was unexpected that this consolidation, which has always had a misogynist aura, would be made most explicit as a facet of the emerging domain of feminist music criticism—to be sure in pejorative voice. First this:

> The tonality that underlies Western concert music is strongly informed by a specific sort of erotic imagery. . . . [M]usic after the Renaissance most frequently appeals to libidinal appetites: at the historical moment at which the legitimation of culture moved from the sacred to the secular realm, the "truth" that authorized musical culture became expressly tied to male defined models of sexuality. . . . For most of the history of post-Renaissance Western music and in virtually all of its critical literature, the sexual dimensions of its mechanisms have been shamelessly exploited and yet consistently denied. The principle of building to climax three-quarters of the way through a piece is discussed in metaphors that almost always betray their underlying erotic assumptions, while at the same time the climax principle (like the phallus of the classical Greek column) has been transcendentalized to the status of a value-free universal form.

Then this:

> As if the thrusting impulse characteristic of tonality and the aggression characteristic of first themes were not enough, Beethoven's symphonies add two other dimensions to the history of style: assaultive pelvic pounding (for instance in the last movement of the Fifth Symphony and in all but the "passive" third movement of the Ninth) and sexual violence. The point of recapitulation in the first movement of the Ninth is one of the most horrifying moments in music, as the carefully prepared cadence is frustrated, damming up energy which finally explodes in the throttling, murderous rage of a rapist incapable of attaining release.[34]

So much is an aspect of McClary's staging of European music history. The consolidation calls for the knack of finding gender and sexuality inscribed in music with the ease that enabled the historians of medieval chant to construct the panorama that I have reviewed here, and that likewise enabled nineteenth-century music theorists to narrativize sonata form in similarly stereotyped gender terms.[35] No less surprising is the same critic's adoption of the dualities of that narrative in her own account of the first movement

232 · *Interpretative Frames*

of Brahms's Third Symphony in the same essay—seduction and resistance, heroic and lyrical, aggressiveness and Oriental exoticism, and, taking a cue from Hermann Kretzschmar (whom we encounter in the next chapter), posing Saint-Saëns's opera *Samson and Delilah* as a narrative model for the Symphony.[36] By way of corroboration, the story of Samson and Delilah is reported to have been "especially popular in the late nineteenth century, when this symphony was written," and Brahms is reported to have attended twenty performances of Bizet's *Carmen*.

Introducing the enterprise of his book, Eichenauer comments how limited music's representation is; it is never concrete but is confined to stirrings of the human soul and to moods and changes of mood. We can certainly agree with him about this important condition that sets music apart from the figurative and literary arts. But then he asks: "Are there nevertheless ways and means to read out of the disembodied lines of a musical work the face of a particular racial character [*Rassenseele*]?"[37] Of course he thinks there are, and the body of his book is given over to thumbnail racial characterizations of musical traditions and of the works of individual composers—an essentialism of race in music—framed in apposite historical narratives.

The historical links between the essentialisms of race and gender are un-mistakable.[38] By virtue of their common roots in antiquity and their ratio-nalization in eighteenth- and nineteenth-century social, cultural, and bio-logical thought, the essentialist doctrines of race, ethnicity, and gender each constitute an aspect of the historical context of the others. They developed simultaneously as scientific concepts with explanatory force and as ideologi-cal precepts supporting political will. But as scientific concepts they have, on the whole, been discredited. We cannot read passages like the following, from one of the most influential treatises on music aesthetics of the nineteenth century, and think that anyone would say such things today:

> The cause [of the fact that] women . . . have not amounted to much as com-posers lies . . . in the plastic aspect of musical composing, which demands renunciation of subjectivity . . . while women are by nature preeminently dependent upon feeling . . . it is not feeling which composes music, but the specifically musical, artistically trained talent.

Or

> The tyranny of the upper vocal part among the Italians has one main cause in the mental indolence of those people for whom the sustained penetra-

tion with which the northerner likes to follow an ingenious work of harmonic contrapuntal activity [is impossible].[39]

The essentialism of gender, race, and ethnicity that we have encountered here has the meaning that music and its history are ineluctably determined by a nature to which its mediators are born and from which they cannot escape. It is the critic's and historian's task, accordingly, to enunciate the principles of that nature and to write exegetical works of criticism and history based on them. But what is evident from this study is that such supposed natures are not natural at all; they are constructions that have been responsive to philosophical, political, cultural, or personal needs or ideologies. Criticism and history under these constraints become autonomous, alienated from their objects, which are reduced to occasions for such enunciations. We cannot hope to hear the contrast between chants that are "soft, elegant, charming and graceful" and those that are "clear, sculpted configurations, systematically chiseled" in the melodies themselves, but we can see what the author of those lines had in mind when we come to his conclusion that the latter are "melodies for a world power." We must wonder whether Susan McClary's language about Beethoven's Ninth Symphony could really be about the same piece as Hermann Kretzschmar's language— "The development unrolls the Faustian portrait still further: seeking and not attaining, rosy fantasies of future and past, . . . the fulfilled reality of a pain that now suddenly makes itself felt"[40]—until we take account of the political-cultural contexts in which the two critics wrote.

Such archetypes work against criticism's subordination to its objects, tend to liberate it from its texts, to make it autonomous. They challenge not only the authority of the idea of "the music itself," as they have lately been meant to do, but even the authority of music and of composers, which (who) become demystified and reduced to occasions for criticism. It is imaginable as a next step that criticism will reduce composers and music to occasions for criticism. Perhaps there will be talk of the death of the composer as there has been about the death of the author, while the critic rises to a newly privileged position from which to make arbitrary statements about music with which one can neither agree nor disagree—statements that provoke the question: "What are the rules for playing this game?" Whatever the answer, such criticism is not about music.

11

HERMENEUTICS,
EXEGETICS, OR WHAT?

The label "musical hermeneutics" has been coming at us from many directions. But the air, or more precisely, the airways, are saturated with implications of hermeneutics in all endeavors. The word's etymology—out of Hermes, the messenger—has come home to roost. It seems every act and every episode sends a message that is hidden beneath its surface. As long ago as 1961 Susan Sontag published an essay that became instantly famous and has by now been pretty much forgotten, "Against Interpretation," in which she points to the destructive aims of interpretation.[1] The challenge is always taken up by someone. We are all the time reading out a meaning that isn't spoken, or listening to the professional hermeneuts we employ as "pundits." The message channels are clogged. The traffic in meanings has become a traffic jam. A poet friend in Woodstock, New York, where I spend my summers, has proposed the establishing of a *Popular Hermeneutics* magazine (on the model of such old, established magazines as *Popular Photography* or *Popular Mechanics*).

Sontag, whose prophetic resistance is timely now, wrote,

> Directed to art, interpretation means plucking a set of elements (the X, the Y, the Z, and so forth) from the whole work. The task of interpretation

is virtually one of translation. The interpreter says, Look, don't you see that X is really—or really means—A? That Y is really B? That Z is really C? What situation could prompt this curious project for transforming a text?[2]

Is the spread of the words "hermeneutic" and its derivatives through the professional literature of musical studies in recent years a manifestation in our profession of this cultural fashion? It can seem so. In chapter 1 we engaged with the concept of "music as language," a subject that no longer receives much attention. The spotlight in recent years has moved to the concept of "music as text." A sign of that: the original of this chapter was a keynote address delivered to the 13th Nordic Musicological Congress meeting in Aarhus, Denmark, in 2000, and the programmers had placed it at the beginning of a session labeled "Music as Text."

We might look for a clear idea about what, beside fashion, is behind this attention from Lawrence Kramer's *plaidoyer* for a musical hermeneutics in the first chapter of his book *Music as Cultural Practice,* "Tropes and Windows: An Outline of Musical Hermeneutics."[3] There Kramer develops four beliefs:

1) that works of music have discursive meanings;

2) that these meanings are definite enough to support critical interpretations comparable in depth, exactness, and density of connection to interpretations of literary texts and cultural practices;

3) that these meanings are not "extramusical" but on the contrary are inextricably bound up with the formal processes and stylistic articulations of musical works;

4) that these meanings are produced as a part of the continuous production and reproduction of culture.

The first three have been central beliefs of musical hermeneutics from the beginning, but the fragility of faith in the third even among some of its leading champions threatens to undermine it and turn it into something else, as we shall see. They are articulated in Edward T. Cone's essay "Schubert's Promissory Note: An Essay in Musical Hermeneutics,"[4] where they are identified as the grounds of Hermann Kretzschmar's practice of "musical hermeneutics" in the early 1900s, the first practice to be so called. Cone's essay will be a subject of these ruminations further on.

Kramer writes, "musical hermeneutics . . . like psychoanalysis, seeks meanings where meaning is often said not to be found."[5] This parallel between the interpretation of art and psychoanalysis was drawn by Sontag in the essay cited, where she notes the influence of the interpretive systems of both Marx and Freud in planting in the modern consciousness the theme that "things are seldom what they seem."

Who is it that says meaning is not to be found where musical hermeneutics seeks it out? "Formalists," is Kramer's answer. Indeed, "musical hermeneutics" was launched as half of a dichotomy, the other half being "formalism." One cannot understand the originating "musical hermeneutics" except in the context of that opposition. It made a certain polemical sense in the beginning, but a hermeneutics that depends on an opposition to formalism is like a three-legged race in which the partners impede each other's progress. To be freed of such a dichotomy is one of the hopes we can have for musical hermeneutics. As for psychoanalysis, it has indeed often been held up as a hermeneutic practice from which there are things to be learned about hermeneutics in general. One of those things is that psychoanalysis is provoked by behaviors that are inscrutable. One seeks out the psychoanalyst when one needs urgently to be brought to understanding about distressing feelings, experiences, behaviors. Kramer's analogy has us instead imagining psychoanalysts on the prowl, looking for strange behaviors to explain. To generalize, hermeneutic practice is a response to a need. It is a struggle against misunderstanding, occasioned by cultural or temporal or conceptual or linguistic gulfs. It is alienation that provokes hermeneutics. In the plain language of anthropologist Clifford Geertz, it answers to the need "to figure out what the devil [people] think they are up to,"[6] a need of which the urgency seems never to be well enough understood in the present world.

Hermann Kretzschmar justified his practice as response to a very concrete need created by a difficulty of understanding between subcultures—those of common people and of the elite—and when he polemicized against formalism it was precisely because of his belief that it stood in the way of the mediation that he sought. Clearly, in such urgent situations hermeneutics seeks meanings that are not on the surface, that are hidden. What is the need that drives the search for hidden meanings? Kramer's answer lies in his fourth claim about musical hermeneutics, that "musical meanings are produced as a part . . . of the continuous production and reproduction of culture." That is the need that motivates the rest of his book.

In his 1990 book *The Limits of Interpretation,* Umberto Eco writes about the difference between interpreting a text critically—reading it in order to discover, along with our reactions to it, something of its nature—and using it, starting from it in order to get something else, "even accepting the risk of misrepresenting it from the semantic point of view." Eco illustrates with this striking pair of examples: "If I get sexual enjoyment from a pornographic book, I am not using it, because in order to elaborate my sexual fantasies I had to semantically interpret its sentences. On the contrary if . . . I look into the *Elements* of Euclid to infer that their author was a scotophiliac, obsessed with abstract images, then I am using it because I renounce interpreting its definitions and theorems semantically."[7] Interpretations of both kinds have recently been offered as exemplifications of musical hermeneutics. Lawrence Kramer, in a subsequent essay, has identified a specific musical act that demands explanation as to its motive and effect, and that affords us an opportunity to reflect about what it is we expect and demand of musical hermeneutics. It is Beethoven's choice of a march (marked *Alla Marcia*) following the words, "And the Cherub stands before God" at m. 331 of the Finale of the Ninth Symphony. Kramer begins, "Everyone knows that there is a Turkish march in the finale of Beethoven's Ninth Symphony, but no one seems to think the fact is worthy of much remark."[8] The consequent part of this antecedent-consequent sentence is a bit exaggerated, but never mind. It is the antecedent part of the sentence that provokes the first question that arises in considering this essay as an exercise in hermeneutics. Just what is it that everyone knows when we know that "there is a Turkish march" at that moment in the finale? Unpacking the question: In what sense do we know it as a *Turkish* march? Are we able to say with confidence on the basis of musical features alone that some other march—say, the march in the third scene of *Wozzeck*—is *not* Turkish? A corollary of the same question: Is our knowledge linked to a kind of memory bank of musical types—such as "Turkish march"—so that we would say the march in *Wozzeck* is not of that type? And another: Is the identification linked to the particular time and place of the Ninth Symphony, so that identifying the march in *Wozzeck* as Turkish would be nonsense? Do these questions matter? I think they do, because Kramer's continuation presupposes answers to them. His second sentence: "Perhaps this [neglect by everyone of the presence of the Turkish march in the finale] is because the *alla turca* [note the *en passant* change of Beethoven's marking] is a sufficiently well-established *topic* in the idiom of Viennese classicism that it seems to need no explanation" [my emphasis, to be explained shortly]. But the matter is more mysterious than that, implies Kramer. The theme that will be developed in the essay, then, is intended to supply the neglected explanation, an account of what it is that Beethoven intended to convey with his reference to Turkey at that moment. There is even a link with psychoanalysis, following on the exposition in *Music as Cultural Practice*. By way of explaining the avoidance of the question by everyone, Kramer writes in his third sentence, "Or perhaps the Turkish topic creates a certain uneasiness when it comes knocking at the gates of the definitive Viennese masterwork." Repression and denial, traced back through Tovey to the first review by Friedrich Kanne in 1824, which "seeks to normalize the passage."[9] With these three sentences the motivation is in place and the stage is set for an exercise in what Kramer has described as musical hermeneutics.

The core of Kramer's continuation so far as the meaning of the appearance of the Turkish march at that moment in the Ninth Symphony is the confident assertion that the music "is a representation of what, when the symphony was composed, stood as a non-European, indeed an anti-European militancy." The assertion has the form "A (the music in mm. 331ff.) represents B (Turkish march), which is a sign of C (anti-European militancy)." Two quick observations: (1) This gives a preliminary sense that we may have here an exercise more in semiotics than in hermeneutics; and (2) An expression of such confidence about such a system of signs and signifieds presupposes the clear definition and stability of both, and of the connections between them.

To the question of the definition and stability of the signs Kramer has given an implicit answer with his identification of "Turkish march" as a "topic." The word, of course, has been adapted from the Latin *loci topici* (subject areas), of the classical principles of rhetoric for formal discourse— conventional formulations of language with rules for their disposition. Following the efforts of musical theorists of the Baroque era to adapt this idea to musical composition, some music scholars since the nineteenth century have offered accounts of the expression or meaning of music of the Baroque and Classic eras on the basis of a phantom *Affektenlehre* that comes down from these principles of rhetoric—"phantom" because "[n]o one systematic theory of musical figures for Baroque and later music has been demonstrated . . . Recent research has clearly shown that a concept of stereotyped musical figures with specific affective connotation never existed in composers' minds or in theoretical explanations."[10] Nevertheless we can read that "Mozart was in possession of something we can call an expressive vocabulary, a collection in music of what in the theory of rhetoric are called *topoi* . . . He held it in common with his audience, and used it in his operas with the skill of a master craftsman. This vocabulary, when captured and categorized [by the modern critic] provides a tool for analysis." This passage is followed by a parsing of the first-movement exposition of Mozart's Piano Sonata in F Major, K. 332, in terms of the "topics" of "singing style, "learned counterpoint," "*Sturm und Drang*," "tragic style."[11] Although the classification of these *topoi* is modern, the author's characterization of the effect of these quick shifts of gesture as "theater" does identify a musical quality, a character, that one can recognize upon hearing it.

With Kramer's identification of the "*alla turca*" as a topic, the situation is somewhat the reverse. On one side, "Turkish march" is the ideal type of the idea of "topic," a genre that was recognized, talked about, widely used in musical composition in the eighteenth and nineteenth centuries, with defined musical features and defined associations.[12] It is probably unique. Mozart wrote to his father on August 1, 1781, "The day before yesterday Stephanie Junior gave me a libretto to compose . . . The libretto is quite good. The subject is Turkish . . . I shall employ a Turkish style of music for the symphony, the chorus in the first act, and the closing chorus."[13] The following year, on July 22, he wrote to his father of the success of the resulting opera: "I hope that you have by now safely received my previous letter informing you of the good reception of my opera . . . I send you herewith the original, and two libretti. . . . It was given just as you have it there, except that the parts for trumpets, kettle drums, flutes, clarinets, and *Turkish music* are occasionally lacking, as I could not get paper ruled with so many lines [my emphasis].[14] Here Mozart uses the expression in a sense that was commonplace in his time and into the nineteenth century, to designate a group of instruments. An acquaintance has told me about a recent concert in Berlin with the title *Alla Turca*. One can think of other styles to which composers referred in a self-conscious way— Spanish gestures for nineteenth-century French composers, Japanese references in *Madame Butterfly*, yet none other with such well-defined features and associations and so much a subject of cultural discourse. But one topic does not make an *Affektenlehre*.

On the other side, what Kramer counts on as the effect of the topic heard in that place—the representation of an "anti-European militancy"—is not something that is directly apprehended in the way that the first-movement exposition of K. 332 can be heard as "theater." If it evoked that response it would have been by way of an association, culturally constructed and learned. The proposition that "anti-European militancy" is a fixed association of the Turkish march topic is something that would have to be demonstrated. And if it were demonstrated, the music would not have to be heard at all, or to put it in terms introduced in chapter 1, the music would be transparent to its meaning. (Nicholas Cook begins the conclusion of his book on the Ninth Symphony with the observation that "Political interpretations of music substitute themselves for the original," and he ends it with an appeal to critics "to prevent the Ninth Symphony from being consumed by ideology."[15]) The historical material does not support the presumption that this image would have been evoked by the *Alla Marcia*. A few lines from Rice and a number of other circumstances will make that clear.

> The association of this music with the janissaries would be difficult for a Turk to make, just as it was in the chorus in *Die Entführung aus dem Serail*. The triangle's associative power among Europeans is particularly ironic given the fact that it never truly was a *mehter* (Turkish military) instrument. Horn fifths of the kind heard in the clarinet (mm. 345ff.) are often associated with pastoral scenes and the hunt, making the variation still more European. It may also be that both the Viennese audience and Beethoven himself were less familiar with *mehters* than their elders. During the gradual normalization of relations with the Ottoman Empire, *mehters* travelled throughout Europe as part of diplomatic retinues. This became less common by the close of the eighteenth century. The question of Beethoven's familiarity with Turkish music has not been—and perhaps cannot be—completely answered. The Ottoman Empire was in a decline and the music eventually went out of fashion—as did the clothing and candy (though not the coffee). . . . Moreover by 1824 the threat of the Ottoman Empire was minimal, and the centennial of the siege of Vienna was long over.[16]

Other historical circumstances contribute to the reservation with which Kramer's projections onto the *Alla Marcia* should be greeted. In the 1780s King Gustav III of Sweden had built in Haga Park in Stockholm a "Turkish pavilion" and a copper tent on the model of the luxurious tents of the Turkish pashas. (He also built a "Chinese pavilion" nearby.) In the same period "janizary pedals" and "Turkish stops" added to pianos became popular on the Continent. These "added all sorts of rattling noises to the normal piano performance. The pedal could cause a drumstick to strike the underside of the sound board [to simulate a bass drum], ring bells, shake a rattle, and even create the effect of a cymbal crash by hitting several bass strings with a strip of brass foil."[17] It seems hard to conceive that such whimsies would have been intended to evoke the "anti-European militancy" of an Oriental Other. Perhaps the *Alla Marcia* is even one of them? Then it would not be that "the Turkish topic came knocking at the door of the definitive Viennese master-work," but that it was cheerily called in.

"Turkish march" is just one of two topics that Kramer identifies in this section of the finale. The other is a "Dorian" topic, a projection onto the music of a "philhellenism" (Kramer), or "Graecophilia" (Schiller) that Kramer draws, again, from surrounding literature—in addition to Schiller, we find Winckelman, Goethe, Hölderlin, and August Schlegel. He does not claim that everyone recognizes this topic in the finale. Its musical features are $\frac{6}{8}$ meter contrasting with the $\frac{2}{4}$ the march music, the solo tenor with the male chorus, the lyrical style, and a harmonic relationship that I'll come to in a moment. The two topics "split the music into two separate aspects," which

correspond to two different models of manhood current in the early 19th century, one rooted in classical Greece, the other in Ottoman Turkey. The first model involves an ideal of fervent love and loyalty between comrades, which, under the banner of military fellowship, is allowed to assume a nearly explicit erotic quality. . . . The feeling-tone typical of the cult of Dorian companionship . . . can perhaps be heard most clearly in the distraught tritone-related section—on D minor in the key of A♭ minor. The second pertinent model of manhood involves controlled brutality and what Hegel called fanaticism, the superlative degree of single-mindedness. In general this is the manhood of the Other, powerful, ruthless, and fierce; it is a kind of concentrated dangerousness viewed with an unstable mixture of envy, awe, and revulsion. The topical mixture of Dorian and janissary masculinities in the Turkish march is consistent with the synthesizing "world-historical" impulse of the Ninth Symphony . . . [But] the Dorian ideal brought with it two difficulties. One was its eroticism. . . . Beethoven might accordingly have been trying to desexualize the Dorian topic by combining it with janissary music. . . . At the same time, he might also have been trying to temper any feeling of effeminacy that might attach to the Dorian ethos. . . . The second difficulty with Dorianism is its association with sacrificial death. . . . Perhaps Beethoven needs to intimate a Dorian vitalism because he is worried . . . by the lifeless im-

242 · *Interpretative Frames*

personality that may threaten the ideal of brotherhood from within ... Or perhaps ... he wants to suggest that the spirit of classical Greece can be reborn in central Europe despite the oppressive rule of modern Greece by the Turks. Whatever the reasons, he seeks to secure the triumph of Euro-pean values by mending a defect in European masculinity. He guarantees the invincibility of European brotherhood by endowing the brother-band with a measured, medicinal dose of concentrated danger, the masculinity of the Turkish Other.[18]

My purpose in citing this has been to reflect about what it is we expect and demand of musical hermeneutics. As I confront this account and the Ninth Symphony, I wonder what the relationship is between the contemplation of one and the experience of listening to the other. It is surely not that the one enriches or enhances or illuminates the other. Having been told about fervent love, loyalty, companionship, eroticism, effeminacy, vitalism, fanati-cism, single-mindedness, ruthlessness, and ferocity, I do not newly hear them individually and playing against one another in the music of the Turkish march. No, it is quite the opposite relation. The Turkish march, and especially the question, "Why is it there?" are the occasions for the development of a portrayal of the ideals and anxieties of a culture. How should that portrayal be evaluated? There is no question of its being considered as a guide to the apprehension of the Ninth Symphony. On the contrary, the Ninth Symphony is read as a text and a source for the development of that portrayal. It can be evaluated only on its coherence and appeal as a portrayal, and on its consis-tency with what can be learned about the history of that culture. But Kramer has declined to confront his account with the relevant historical material on the ground; he draws only on the writings of the philosophers and poets he cites—lightly: Hegel, Tolstoy, Byron (*Don Juan,* the dwarfs guarding the harem), and the writers already mentioned in connection with the "Dorian topic." That leaves his story standing on its own, take it or leave it. I referred above to Umberto Eco's book *The Limits of Interpretation,* in which he writes about the difference between interpreting a text critically—reading it in or-der to discover, along with our reactions to it, something of its nature—and using it, starting from it in order to move somewhere else, "even accepting the risk of misrepresenting it from the semantic point of view." Kramer's story is an instance of the second kind.

Allanbrook's identification of the topics concept as a "valuable tool for analysis" was published in the same year (1986) as the reprint of Cone's essay

"Schubert's Promissory Note," which was the first in a new wave of studies in the United States explicitly represented as musical hermeneutics.[19] The essay begins with an acknowledgement of Hermann Kretzschmar's formal initiation of the project that Cone himself takes up here. He calls Kretzschmar's "musical hermeneutics" the "dogmatic climax" of a long tradition of elucidatory commentary on music for amateur audiences. Kretzschmar placed himself in such a tradition. "Hermeneutics has been constantly practiced," he wrote, "if not in so comprehensive and systematic a manner, since the dawn of modern art." He was refering to concert program notes, a tradition with whose initiation he credited George Grove's program notes for the Crystal Palace concerts beginning in 1856 but that had begun already with Thomas Arne's concert programs in 1768, and also to music journalism—he singled out particularly Rochlitz's *Allgemeine musikalische Zeitung* from 1798. Kanne's 1824 review of the Ninth Symphony is part of that history.

Cone represents Kretzschmar's program simply: music has meaning. It is an art of expression. It should be possible to determine what it expresses and how. Kretzschmar is a figure who should be of more than passing interest to us just now, first because of the parallels in the circumstances of musical discourse in which the label "musical hermeneutics" surfaced rather suddenly in Kretzschmar's time and has, with like suddenness, surfaced in ours, interestingly enough, both times on the premise of the illusory, wish-fulfilling *Affektenlehre*.

Kretzschmar actually had a most distinguished career as a musicologist, composer, conductor, music director of several academic institutions, university professor, director of the Hochschule für Musik and the Institut für Kirchenmusik in Berlin, one of the founders of the Bach-Gesellschaft edition and general editor of the *Denkmäler deutscher Tonkunst*. In his academic positions he instituted concert series, for which he took to writing program notes. These he gathered together in collections that he called *Führer durch den Konzert Saal* (Guides through the Concert Hall), for which he later coined the label "musical hermeneutics." The collections were published in 1887, 1888, and 1890 and became extremely popular; the label first appeared in the title of an essay, "Anregungen zur Forderung musikalischer Hermeneutik" (Initiative for the Call for a Musical Hermeneutics, 1902, and repeated in a second essay, "Neue Anregungen zur Forderung musikalischer Hermeneutik: Satzästhetik," 1905). These essays provide a justification and theoretical foundation for the guide books after the fact, as Kretzschmar made explicit

in the foreword to his collected writings, published in 1911: "I came to hermeneutics as concert director through the requests of the subscribers that I
prepare them for unfamiliar or difficult works. My 'Guides' were born of such
introductions."[20]

What he writes in the foreword of 1911 provides the key to his conception of musical hermeneutics. Its goal is not the development of aesthetic-
philosophical or theoretical refinement; it is pedagogy, aimed at music lovers,
not specialists. There are two higher aims, aesthetic-educational and social-
political. The first is to enable the listener to "penetrate into the interior and
intimate world of the work itself and the soul of its composer [notice here the
thematic words of the Romantic aesthetics of both formalism and transcen-
dentalism] and wherever possible to [recognize] what connects the work to its
own time, to the musical context in which it came about, and to the spiritual
trends from which it arose [and here the leading ideas of *Kulturgeschichte*]."
And the second aim is to spread and deepen musical understanding and
appreciation among a broad public and trained musicians and music lovers, in the interest of raising the level of education and culture of ordinary
people, those whom Kretzschmar characterized as "folk," "classes with few
leisure hours at their disposal," "simple glass-blowers," in other words, artisans. In view of that purpose Kretzschmar's hermeneutic writing eschewed
the technical, which was consigned to appendices. But more: in his 1902
essay he blasted off at the "so-called formal aestheticians," with Hanslick
in the lead, warning against "the disgrace of a purely physical, animalistic
[elsewhere he says "mechanical"] music reception" that he associated with
formalism. "The most important musicians and music theorists" have, in all
times, taken heed "against formalism." The two strains come together when
he excoriates formalists for failing to say "a word about the purposes to which
the composer harnesses the technical means, no attempt to get to the heart
of the task, namely to help the [listener] towards a spiritual understanding
of the composition."[21]

The political-ideological tinge of Kretzschmar's aesthetic and pedagogical
program is better understood against the background of his professed sym-
pathies with the policies of Otto von Bismarck, the Iron Chancellor of the
German Empire until 1890. In the German politics of his time Bismarck was
a defender of the monarchy against liberal revolutionary groups. He acted on
the anticipation that the decisive power would rest with the working classes,
and it would be essential to exploit workers and artisans (recall Kretzschmar's

"ordinary glass-blowers") against the new elite of "culture and property," as he put it (the middle class). "The crown must place itself at the head of the movement by promoting the moral and material interests of the masses." Education played a prominent role in the competition for workers' support. The crown's liberal opponents formed *Arbeiterbildungsvereine* (worker-education societies). Bismarck flirted with the most radical elements. He boasted of receiving "the most respectful greetings from the reds here and abroad. They love us of the extreme right." He had frequent contact with the socialist Ferdinand LaSalle, who urged the monarchy to transform itself from a monarchy of the privileged classes into a social and revolutionary people's monarchy. Kretzschmar's "formalists" would have counted as members of "the elite of culture," and doubtless, of property. That was in large part what the polemic was about, over and above the aesthetic-philosophical debates of theorists. I wouldn't want to say that when Kretzschmar said "formalism" it was altogether in the sense of the *Pravda* review of Shostakovich's *Lady Macbeth* or Goebbels's speech for the Düsseldorf exhibit of "degenerate music," but there was something of that in it.

The idea of a "musical hermeneutics" was born in ideology and polemic. We cannot really understand Kretzschmar's hermeneutics except in the sense of its ideological purpose and the specific sense of the quarrel with formalism that this engendered. This history is one that is not shared by general hermeneutics. Superficially, it has come alive again in one branch of the recent revival of musical hermeneutics, in the quarrel with formalism, as we can tell from the mantra with which appraisals of the current state of musical interpretation have been frequently introduced. But the *Bildungs* ideology that cranked up that quarrel separates Kretzschmar from today's hermeneuts of all stripes; it could hardly be said that any of them aim for the musical education of today's counterparts of the simple glass-blower.

The subtitle of Cone's essay—"An Essay in Musical Hermeneutics"—is to be taken literally: the essay is an exercise in a kind of criticism long practiced by the author which, sniffing the air, he now identifies as "hermeneutics"— grounded in detailed analysis but moving "Beyond Analysis," to cite the title of an earlier essay of his.[22] The essay is a narrative account of Schubert's *Moment musical* in A♭, op. 94, no. 6, with commentary about the notes. The author's voice is like the omniscient voice of a novelist, commenting as he narrates. Samples: "the concluding phrase member dutifully remembering the demands of the true dominant"; "the E remains in the ear as a troubling element"; "a slight uneasiness with respect to the cadence on E"; "usurping a tonicization to which it had no right"; "the offer [of a ii⁶ chord] was spurned"; "irony in the insinuation of the problematic note once again into the descending line of bars 51–53 immediately after the emphatic proclamation of F minor. To be sure the note now seems docile"; "a recalcitrant applied dominant"; and finally, "Did the development in giving E its own head encourage it to incur still further obligations?"

These are Cone's premises: (1) A distinction adopted from the aesthetics of Wilson Coker's book *Music and Meaning* between two types of musical meaning: "congeneric meaning, comprising exclusively the relationship of part to part within a composition and of the composition to others perceived to be similar to it. . . . Extrageneric meaning is the supposed reference of a musical work to non-musical objects, events, moods, emotions, ideas, and so on." (2) A commitment to "the existence and relevance of extrageneric meaning." (3) The belief that "extrageneric meaning can be completely explained, [but] only in terms that take account of congeneric meaning." "If verbalization of true content is possible at all, it must depend in large part on close structural analysis."[23] Note that there is no reference to, or dependence on, any idea of an *Affektenlehre*.

A note on language. First, verbalization commonly means "putting in words." It is linked with explanation as an account of causal or logical relations in that you cannot say what the expression of the piece is until you can explain it on the grounds of close structural analysis. Both terms—verbalization and explanation—are links to the hermeneutic tradition: verbalization to the very original sense of "hermeneutics," bringing to understanding in language (speech); (causal) explanation to that same origin and to Wilhelm Dilthey's project of bringing history and all the human sciences to the rank of the natural sciences. Second, the unappealing word pair "congeneric-extrageneric" looks in form like Leonard Meyer's dichotomy of embodied versus referential meaning (in *Emotion and Meaning in Music*)[24] and Kofi Agawu's dichotomy of introversive versus extroversive semiosis (in *Playing With Signs*),[25] which he borrowed from Roman Jacobson. In their shared implication of the objective-subjective divide and their reference to "musical" and "extramusical" meaning they presume too much about the clarity of that general conception, the sharpness of the divide between the two sides, and the exactness with which one can speak of "musical meaning." Suspicion about whether this epistemology works at all arises from an effort to coordinate these sets of pairs in detail, even with respect to what would seem to be clear instances of extrageneric, referential, extroversive, extramusical meaning achieved through imitation—say, the wind machine in Strauss's *Alpine Symphony*. Why is that not embodied, musical, part of the musical structure, and so forth?

Consider a more involved case. With the appearance of the Commendatore's statue in the finale of *Don Giovanni*, Mozart conjures up a portentous, threatening, frightening, supernatural atmosphere. How? Through the two great tutti chords at the beginning of the scene, the statue's octave plunges and his steady chromatic ascent, the ponderous dotted rhythms of the strings, the blasts on the trombones, the rising and falling minor scales of the violins jacked up a half-step at a time. These are purely musical signs that yet together have in their meanings a very specific psychic state and dramatic condition. But that state and condition is musical and only musical; they are not imitative of or borrowed from some other domain, they are the expressive face of those musical gestures. It is only the impoverishment of language for the description of life that requires us to use a word like "portentous" to characterize situations in warfare, football, doctoral examinations, and music, among many others (see chapter 1). That does not mean that the word has been borrowed from its application in one of those domains for any of the others.

Cone's project is to "derive from the structural analysis of the composition an account of its expressive content . . . to show how [the congeneric interrelations of] Schubert's work account for [that is, explain] and cause their extrageneric significance."[26] There are two things to highlight here: the word "derive" as key to the logical nature of the relation, and the implication that "expressive content" and "extrageneric significance" are not experienced but deduced. But this can hardly be said of the language of Cone's narrative that I sampled just before. In acknowledgement of that, Cone writes that the analysis hasn't been "wholly objective," that "I have insinuated a few leading phrases to suggest to [the reader] the kind of expression I find [not deduce] in the work."

With the greatest respect and without the least suggestion that he is dissembling, I really do not believe Cone about this. His account ascribes expressive quality to features of the structure not only in the instance of describing them but in the very language of the description. I think this is not a rhetorical gesture to the reader, as he says, but a consequence of the fact that expressive quality is immanent in the structure, not derived from it. I read his account as a virtual portrayal of the way the work addresses him, as he opens up its world in response or, as he puts it, "as I apprehend the work." And I cannot help understanding the sequence and logic imposed after the fact on his account of his encounter with the work as an act of obedience to the imperatives of a discipline and to an epistemological tradition. In fact Cone has demonstrated in his language, in spite of himself, the fragility of the divide between his con- and extrageneric meanings and between objective and subjective apprehension. And so I think that in effect, his essay is even more an exercise in hermeneutics than he has explicitly announced.

Cone represents his opening of the work at six hierarchical levels or stages, and there is the hint that this would be normative for musical hermeneutics. They are not presented in the sharply stratified way that I am about to present them, but they function that way. The ideal first level, the objective, pure, structural analysis that yields congeneric meaning and uniquely defines the work is, as I've already observed, assumed but not presented. An unstated reason for this is that Cone must accomplish something that is essential to the hermeneutic enterprise: he must confront the work as strange. Hints of this are scattered here and there: "all is in order—but is it?"; talk of imbalance, obligations not discharged, uneasiness, nagging doubts, all of those puzzling things that provoke hermeneutics.

Stage 2 is presented in the qualitative descriptions of the note events that I have sampled. Stage 3 interprets, shapes those *aperçus* into a whole configuration in the passage beginning, "As I apprehend the work, it dramatizes the injection of a strange, unsettling element into an otherwise peaceful situation." In stage 4 this musical scenario is interpreted as the representation of "the psychic pattern embodied in the musical structure"; the "context . . . not the content . . . but the necessary vehicle of the content." Its elements are related "symbolically" to the corresponding elements of the "abstraction" (for example, "I assume the arrival of the foreign element to be symbolic of the occurrence of a disquieting thought to one of a tranquil, easygoing nature. . . . The trio . . . tries to forget the catastrophe," and so on). And in stage 5 this psychic pattern is given concrete content as Schubert's state of mind upon discovering that he is infected with syphilis. This interpretation is not, however, presented as "the meaning" of the work, but as one of innumerable possible expressive contents. The range of possibilities of expressive meaning Cone calls the piece's "expressive potential." Every stage of the analysis is an interpretation of the preceding stage, and there is always a many-to-one, never just a one-to-one relation between an interpretation at any stage and the interpretation at the next lower one. Each interpretation is recognized as one in a range of potential interpretations. That is, of course, with the exception of the first-stage structural analysis which, if it were given as such, must be uniquely related to the work. That exception aside, it seems quite a lot like the polyvocality of language we confronted in the first two chapters, which depends on a context to filter out the surplus meaning so that a univocal discourse can be left.

Then "the final step in my investigation [the sixth in my enumeration] . . . [is] an attempt to answer what is possibly a forbidden question: What context might the composer himself have adduced? What personal experiences might Schubert have considered relevant to the expressive significance of his own composition?" This is the strangest turn in the whole essay—not because of the specific expressive content that Cone has finally adduced, Schubert's horror at the discovery that he has syphilis—a suggestion that was greeted in the profession with something of a sense of shock—but because of what is implied about the order of the compositional process by this way of putting it: the composer, having first created a musical structure—the structure that is explicated through analysis—seeks to establish its expressive significance and, Cone hypothesizes, finds it in his discovery about his own condition— composition as a technique of psychological self-analysis. It seems to be put in this strange way in order to avoid the opposite interpretation, which is of a more familiar kind: that the composer is possessed by dark feelings as the result of his discovery, and these feelings are given expression in this piece and in much other music composed around that time. Putting it this way reverses the direction of causal explanation—from expressive content to the musical structure. That seems to be ruled out by the absolute priority with which Cone invests musical structure and its analysis.

Yet for a moment he teeters on the edge of such an interpretation: "Did Schubert's realization [of his having contracted syphilis and of its immanent dread] induce or at least intensify the sense of desolation and even dread that penetrates much of his music from then on?" That turns the direction of causal explanation around, from the mental state to the musical details, and it seems like another breach in the otherwise tightly held line of the essay. And we can sympathize with Cone for allowing it, despite its violation of his first principle.

250 · *Interpretative Frames*

But suppose we were to view this not as a contradiction but as an implicit recognition that the best understanding will come by allowing the explanation to move in both directions at once: analysis leads to questions answerable only through interpretation of expressive content; apprehension of expressive content leads to questions answerable only by analysis. This is nothing other than a hermeneutic circle operating in the interpretation of music. It allows us to reduce the opposition between explanation and interpretation that has been a troublesome problem in general hermeneutics. Although he tacitly manifests it, there is no place for such circular gathering up of understanding in the sort of linear, teleological program that Cone sets forth.

The openness to the listener's role in determining meaning that is signified by the generous conception of the "expressive potential" seems to be overridden by the declaration that the work's meaning is embodied in its tonal structure and the insistence that analysis of the tonal structure must uniquely map onto the work. This seems to be another contradiction. But these apparent contradictions arise out of the bundle of dichotomies into which the modern hermeneutic tradition was born and which that tradition has come to question, and that goes as well for the intolerance of contradiction altogether that obliges us constantly to file phenomena on one side or the other of those dichotomies, objective or subjective, explaining or understanding (interpreting), natural science or human science; in the musical domain formalism or elucidation of expressive meaning, structural analysis or interpretation, congeneric or extrageneric meaning, embodied or referential meaning, introversive or extroversive semiosis. To direct that questioning to the musical domain is, I believe, a principal task of musical hermeneutics.

I have found a way of expressing my discomfort with the apparatus on which this system depends by way of reflection on how language hooks onto the world. We could ask, "What would it be like if we did not have this reductionist epistemology woven into the fabric of our musical discourse?" And we could follow with the question, "What arguments do you have against saying that we should not pin our accounts of how music is to be understood on this web of binaries?" We would have even fewer answers to the second question because we have hardly tried to imagine answers to the first. I think it would be a relief to be free of the entanglement. We should say, "You used to think it was terribly important to be able to settle whether the significance of some musical utterance is congeneric or extrageneric, embodied or referential, whether our apprehension of it is objective or subjective, whether our verbalization about it is literal or metaphorical." But it isn't. It just gets in your way and makes you say contradictory and confusing things." We don't want to frame arguments against these dichotomies, we want to talk about music without invoking them, pro or con, and if they force themselves on us sometimes, we just have to live with them, as we have to live with so many things that get in our way but that we can't just eliminate. But tolerance is not affirmation.

POSTSCRIPT

At the risk of seeming to contravene my own skepticism about such dichotomies, I close by citing a paradigm that has been laid out in the form of a polarity in the ways that the significance of literature and its functions in society have been assessed. Although the paradigm occurs in a study that can seem far distant from the subjects of this chapter, the way each of its seemingly opposite practices can slip surreptitiously into unintended disguise as the other can help to reveal a dubiousness about the claimed culture-historical sensitivity of what is sometimes presented as "hermeneutic." And its very distance from the subjects of this chapter shows that the issue is far from new to the modern age.

In *The Book of Memory: A Study of Memory in Medieval Culture,* which has been of importance for chapter 6, Mary Carruthers distinguishes usefully between "fundamentalism" and "textualism," offering the following as a thumbnail illustration: "[S]ome Biblical scholars of the thirteenth century stressed the literal 'intention' of the text in order to redress what they saw as an excess of interpretative commentary on the part of earlier exegetes." Fundamentalism, she writes, "regards a work of literature as essentially not requiring interpretation. It emphasizes its literal form as independent of circumstance, audience, author . . . Legal scholars speak of 'originalists,' who believe that the original intention of a written document [such as the U.S. Constitution] is contained entirely in its words. The kinship of this position to religious fundamentalism is apparent." Under textualism, "literary works become institutions as they weave a community together by providing it with shared experience and a certain kind of language . . . Their meaning is thought to be implicit, hidden, polysemous, and complex, requiring continuing interpretation and adaptation. Taken to an extreme, of course, textualism can bury the original work altogether in purely solipsistic interpretation."[27]

Two points on which the boundary between the two dogmas can become permeable are Carruthers's observations that "the role of scholarship [under fundamentalism] is solely to identify the accumulations of interpretive debris and to polish up the original and simple meaning" (as one interpreter's "accumulated debris" may be another's "shared experience and language"), and that under textualism—and hermeneutic practice—the meaning of literary works may be, among other properties, "hidden" (but perhaps by "accumulated interpretative debris").

Sontag, in the essay cited earlier in this chapter, illustrates this equivocal status of meanings with interpretations ranging from Homer to Marx and Freud.

> The Stoics, to accord with their view that the gods had to be moral, allegorized away the rude features of Zeus and his boisterous clan in Homer's epics. What Homer *really* designated by the adultery of Zeus with Leto, they explained, was the union between power and wisdom [my emphasis] ... The most celebrated and influential modern doctrines, those of Marx and Freud, actually amount to elaborate systems of hermeneutics ... All observable phenomena are bracketed, in Freud's phrase, as *manifest content*. This manifest content must be probed and pushed aside to find the true meaning—the *latent content*—beneath.[28]

Manifest content or interpretative debris? Latent content or true meaning?

"Hermeneutics": textualist or fundamentalist? These deliberations continue into the next chapter.

12

FACILE METAPHORS, HIDDEN GAPS, SHORT CIRCUITS: *SHOULD* WE ADORE ADORNO?

Europeans began writing down music in the ninth century, as an aspect of the powerful orientation toward scripturality that characterized the Carolingian culture. Whether as a matter of chance coincidence or not (I think not), medieval writing *about* music began, as far as we know, in the same century and under the same cultural and political circumstances. To get a sense of what it was about music that the musically curious and informed thought should and could be described and explained, we can consult the oldest comprehensive—and widely transmitted—didactic manual about music that has come down to us from the Middle Ages, the *Musica enchiriadis* (Handbook on Music), written around 900 by an anonymous author.

> [W]e can judge whether the construction of a melody is proper, and distinguish the qualities of tones and modes and the other things of this art. Likewise we can adduce, on the basis of numbers, musical intervals or the sounding together of pitches and give some explanations of consonance and dissonance.

For a hint of what might have been meant by "qualities" in reference to music we can read a bit further:

> [It] is necessary that the *affects* of the subjects that are sung correspond
> to the *effect* of the song, so that melodies are peaceful in tranquil subjects,
> joyful in happy matters, somber in sad [ones], and harsh things are said or
> made to be expressed by harsh melodies [my emphases].[1]

Guido of Arezzo writes that for the cognoscenti, recognizing the "characters and individual features" of the modal patterns is like distinguishing people of Greek, Spanish, Latin, German, and French origin from one another. Thus the "broken leaps" of the authentic deuterus (mode), the "voluptuousness" of the plagal tritus, the "garrulousness" of the authentic tetrardus, and the "suavity" of the plagal tetrardus are distinctly recognizable. And he writes that this diversity of characters matches the diverse mental dispositions among different people, so that one prefers this mode whereas another prefers that one. Further, Guido compares this diversity of musical qualities and tastes with the diversity of phenomena that enter "the recess of the heart" through the other senses, the "windows of the body"—colors, odors, tastes. Finally, Guido reaches beyond this matter of affects and tastes to the effects or powers of music, reporting by way of examples on a madman cured of his madness by music and another man brought to the point of rape by one kind of music and then made to back off at the last moment by another kind.[2]

Guido's is a particularly colorful and replete spelling out of this medieval music concept, but in its core aspect it is an elaboration of the ancient concept according to which the cosmos, the human soul, and music are bound together through their regulation by the same proportions. This was familiarly expressed by Boethius (sixth century):

> When we hear what is properly and harmoniously united in sound in conjunction with what is harmoniously coupled and joined together within us and are attracted to it then we recognize that we ourselves are put together in its likeness.[3]

The certainty of this notion was beyond question or need for argument for the author of the *Musica enchiriadis* even though he could not fully articulate it. He wrote,

> [I]n what way music has so great an affinity and union with our souls—for
> we know we are bound to it by a certain likeness ["we know" this through

the inherited doctrine that is expressed by Boethius in the passage I've just quoted]—we cannot express easily in words.[4]

I interpret that as a way of saying that "we" cannot step outside ourselves to gain an objective view of this affinity.

This music concept was but an aspect of a medieval way of experiencing the self in relation to the world. Owen Barfield has written of "the organic universe of the Middle Ages" that had "beaten with the same heart as the human being." To the people of the Middle Ages, "the world was more like a garment they wore about them than a stage on which they moved." (Associated with this observation is Barfield's interesting interpretation of the lack of interest in visual perspective in medieval painting). Compared to us they "felt themselves and the objects around them and the words [we can add the music] that expressed these objects immersed together in a clear lake of meaning." They viewed man as "a microcosm within a macrocosm." In his relation to the world around him, "the man of the Middle Ages was less like an island, more like an embryo than we are."[5]

This is to say that properties and associations of music that we today would differentiate as technical, aesthetic, affective, rhetorical (effective), cultural, or sociological were all experienced at once as music, and in description folded into a continuous unified music concept. How different, then, is the modern—or modernist—conception that Charles Rosen accurately characterizes in the opening of his review "Should We Adore Adorno?": "No art appears as remote as music from the life and the society that produce it . . . The sounds of music . . . are artificial and set apart." By contrast, he writes, "Painting and sculpture reflect some aspects of the figures and objects or at least the forms and colors that we encounter; novels and poems convey experiences and aspirations that recall, however distantly, the world that we know."[6]

If we compare the two conditions—medieval and modern—it must be evident that the second is the result of a kind of parturition, a rending of the self from the world, the mind from the body, the senses from the intellect such as has been influential since the promulgation of the dualism preached by Descartes, which would make impossible Guido's image of the sweetness of sensual things entering the recess of the heart through the windows of the body. Barfield refers to this parturition as the foundation of the scientific revolution (see also the introduction to my book *Music and the Historical Imagination*).

Diderot provides Rosen an opening for the suggestion of an alternative with the former's observation that "even though the signs of music are more ephemeral and less easily definable than those of painting or literature, their emotional impact upon our senses is even greater." Whether knowingly or not, Diderot revives here the ancient doctrine that lay behind the medieval conception. As it was expressed by Aristotle in the *Politics*,

> [R]hythms and mele contain representations of anger and mildness, and also of courage and temperance and all their opposites and the other qualities . . . whereas the other objects of sensations contain no representation of ethoses . . . , though the objects of sight do so slightly, for there are forms that represent character, but only to a small extent.[7]

Insofar as music's emotional impact trumps its ineffability, Rosen implies, it must reveal something significant about the musicians who created it and the age, the culture, and the society in which it was made. That is the occasion for introducing Adorno, as the writer on music who "devoted more energy" to the challenge of understanding "the significance of music for the musicians who created it and the society in which it was produced" than any other.

There may be a presumption that Adorno showed the way to the healing of the breech that has been upon us through his conception of the world as an integrated totality of culture and society, whose manifestations are reflective of one another by virtue of underlying relations that bear on them all. That outlook enabled Adorno, like a man of the Middle Ages or a contemporary of Aristotle, to explicate musical processes or structures in the light of human comportment. A prime instance would be his posing of "the musical dialectics which in sonata form mediate between harmony (the general) and thematism (the particular) as a reflection of the conflict between society as a whole and a 'particular interest.'"[8] (Music's enactment of the conflict between the individual and the society in post-Enlightment Europe is perhaps the leading thread in Adorno's narrative of the history of central European music from Beethoven to Schoenberg that is the backdrop for the fifty percent or so of his prolix output that is concerned with music.)

Adorno larded his writing with such exegesis throughout his life. In the late *Minima moralia* he wrote,

> Beethoven's music, which works within the forms transmitted by society and is ascetic towards the expression of private feelings, resounds with the guided echo of social conflict, drawing precisely from the asceticism the

whole fullness and power of individuality. That of Richard Strauss, wholly at the service of individual claims and dedicated to the glorification of the self-sufficient individual, thereby reduces the latter to a mere receptive organ of the market, an imitator of arbitrarily chosen ideas and styles.[9]

These portrayals are issued with ease and without the slightest hint of doubt or clue to the grounds for them, as if reported by an uninvolved observer from a platform above the fray.

Rosen characterizes such bridges as "Adorno's attempt to unite art and society with a facile metaphor." He cites Carl Dahlhaus's similar characterization: "The verbal analogies perform the function of hiding a gap which the argument could not close."[10] But it is worth citing the rest of the passage in which Dahlhaus's sentence occurs:

> [Adorno] provokes the impatient objection that these are merely verbal analogies which have no basis in fact but owe their origin and a semblance of plausibility to a generously ambivalent use of words like "integration," "subject and object," or "general and particular." . . . Yet the blind spots are not simply an accidental defect. Rather, the contrast between the methods—between the formal-analytically individualizing and the sociologically generalizing procedure—returns as a flaw in the individual analysis . . .

There is yet another type of flaw created by the disequilibrium that is pointed out by Dahlhaus in the continuation:

> . . . a detailed analysis of motivic technique in the first of Schoenberg's Five Orchestral Pieces culminates in the observation that "the growth in complexity, as if according to the fundamental tenets of the contemporary sociology of Herbert Spencer, goes together with growing integration as its correlative." It remains unclear whether the digression into the sociological realm is meant to be merely an illustration of the connection between complexity and integration, or an allusion . . . to a sociological exegesis of Schoenberg's motivic technique. But in any case the "correlation" to which the sociological commentary refers is not peculiar to Op. 16. Rather, it is a feature common to all of Schoenberg's works since the time of the transition from tonality to atonality.[11]

This is to say that the excursion into the sociological realm contributes virtually nothing to the elucidation of the particular work that is its target; it is virtually meaningless. The flaw is unavoidable when there is such a many-to-one relationship between the specific musical and general sociological members of this sort of analogy.

Dahlhaus raises the question of meaning explicitly with another citation in the same passage:

> An assertion like the one that the musical dialectic between the rationality of compositional technique and the irrationality of expression represents a reflection and consequence of the social conflict between the rationality of the technical means and the irrationality of the "indigenous" ends, which are at cross purposes,[12] is simply impossible to understand. For even the most daring of psycho-analytical theories would find it hard to establish a link between the irrationality of the emotions and that of economic liberalism.

It is a comfort to be offered an alternative to the silly Pollyanna-like rationalization that is frequently offered, according to which Adorno's "difficult prose . . . is an attraction; it forces one to pay attention," as Rosen puts it.[13]

From "impatient objection" to outrage. Milan Kundera, in an essay "Improvisation in Homage to Stravinsky," cites Adorno's interpretation of the dissonances in Stravinsky's adaptations of works of Gesualdo, Pergolesi, and Tchaikovsky:

> These notes . . . become the marks of the *violence* the composer wreaks against the idiom, and it is that *violence* we relish about them, *that battering, that violation, so to speak of musical life.* Though dissonance may originally have been the expression of *subjective suffering,* its harshness shifts in value and becomes the sign of a *social constraint* . . . It may be that the widespread effect of these works of Stravinsky's is due in large part to the fact that inadvertently, and under color of *aestheticism, they in their own way trained men to something that was soon methodically inflicted on them at the political level* [Kundera's emphases].[14]

Kundera comments, "Let us recapitulate: a dissonance is justified if it expresses 'subjective suffering,' but in Stravinsky . . . that very dissonance is the sign of brutality: a parallel is drawn (by a brilliant short circuit of Adorno's thought) with political brutality: . . . the coming political oppression (which in this particular historical context can mean only one thing: fascism)."

Adorno's practice in the sociological interpretation of music might be thought to pursue the lead taken by Max Weber in his book *The Rational and*

Social Foundations of Music (written in 1911 and published ten years later).[15] This is an analysis of the historical development of music in terms of the increasing rationality of its technical basis (the tonal system, the system of meters, the regulation of multivoice composition) and of its social organization as an institution. This analysis Weber conducts in parallel with an analysis of the development of capitalism in terms of its rationalization. What Adorno did not observe, however, is Weber's caveat that the empirical history of music must analyze these factors without involving itself in the aesthetic evaluation of musical works of art.

Although he is one of many critics who have blown the whistle on this practice of Adorno's, Rosen chooses generously to side-step the issue. After all, the available responses to it are limited. Confronted with such exegesis one can adopt the practice under the illusion that one has somehow "historicalized" the music, or one can throw up one's hands and say, "I don't get it." The practice does not lend itself to confirmation or disconfirmation— a charge that would not have upset Adorno (as Rosen observes, Adorno shared with Oswald Spengler not only the thesis of the "decline of the West" but also a "preference of intuition to empirical research and theory"). It is even questionable whether the claims under such a practice have heuristic value.

Instead Rosen writes, "Perhaps the fundamental insight of Adorno was a recognition that works do not passively reflect the society in which they arise, but act within it, influencing it and criticizing it."[16] His language makes clear that he endorses this axiom, as well he might, for it would constitute a basis for a historiography in which things happen because of what people do (and fail to do). Adorno espouses such a historiography. But he seems not to have been able to desist from issuing such seemingly playful and essentially meaningless characterizations as this, which Rosen cites: "The functional interconnections present throughout Haydn's music give an impression of competence, active life and suchlike categories, which ominously call to mind the rising bourgeoisie."[17] But Adorno was dead serious, as he made clear in this propaedeutic that he published in 1932 in the *Zeitschrift für Sozialforschung* and reaffirmed in his *Introduction to the Sociology of Music:*

> Here and now, music can do nothing but *represent,* in its own structure, the social antimonies which also bear the guilt of its isolation. It will be the better the more deeply it can make its forms lend shape to the power

of those contradictions, and to the need to overcome them socially—the more purely the antimonies of its own formal language will *express* the calamities of the social condition and call for change in the cipher script of suffering. It does not behoove music to stare at society in helpless horror; its *social function* will be more exactly fulfilled if the social problems contained *in it in the inmost cells of its technique,* are *represented* in its own material and according to its own formal laws [my emphases].[18]

This question—passive reflection or interaction?—compares two incommensurables. The decoding of "passive reflection" in Adorno's writing is generally done from the standpoint of the present-day exegete, without much concern whether the proposed meanings would have been picked up by the composer's contemporaries. The analyses of interactions between music and society have at least the potential of generating a history, potentially subject to degrees of justification, as the meanings Adorno read out of scores, or more often oeuvres, are not.

This is to say that Adorno's interpretations are not either one or the other. Readings (translations) of musical detail and historical interpretation are mutually interdependent, something that is about as plain as can be in the passage about the meaning of dissonance in Stravinsky's arrangements of music by Gesualdo, Pergolesi, and Tchaikovsky. That passage, with its focus on the approach of authoritarianism that is played out in Stravinsky's music, links that music with the "12-tone constructivism," or, "the rigid apparatus of the twelve tone system"[19] of Schoenberg, in Adorno's disapproving view. Adorno's sociological reading of the twelve-tone system forced him into characterizations of the compositional procedure and its music that are as arbitrary and distorted as are the flawed interpretations of the music of the late Beethoven under the influence of his historical readings, as Rosen has demonstrated. But the top-down nature of his interpretation here is perhaps more striking, considering his closeness to Schoenberg and his disciples.

We read in the section "The Concept of Twelve-Tone Technique" of *Philosophy of Modern Music* the following characterizations:

> The twelve-tone technique demands that every composition be *derived from* such a "fundamental structure" or "row." This refers to an *arbitrarily* designated ordering of the twelve tones available to the composer in the tempered half-tone system. . . . Every tone of the composition is *determined* by this row: there is no longer a single "*free*" note.[20]

The emphases are mine, and they are intended to mark the fallaciousness of the respective terms. To say that every twelve-tone composition is derived from a row is as if we would say that every tonal piece is derived from a key, without implying that the row is the exact counterpart of a key. But like a key, a row sets certain sonic constraints, in one sense, and potentials, in another. That the ordering of tones in a row is arbitrary is to imply that it might equally well be determined by a throw of the dice or a sequence of letters randomly chosen from a telephone catalogue. The implication is confirmed in a footnote: "The twelve-tone composer resembles the gambler; he waits and sees what number appears and is happy if it is one offering musical meaning."[21] In another footnote Adorno writes,

> It is hardly a coincidence that the *mathematical* techniques of music originated in Vienna, the home of logical positivism [despised by Adorno]. The inclination towards numerical games is as unique to the Viennese intellect as is the game of chess in the coffee house [one wonders whether Adorno played chess].

And then, sure enough, this is explained by means of a kind of vulgar Marxism:

> While productive intellectual forces in Austria developed to the highest level of capitalist technique, material forces did not keep pace. For this very reason controlling calculation became the dream image of the Viennese intellectual . . .[22]

On July 27, 1932, Schoenberg wrote to Rudolf Kolisch, "I tried to convince Wiesengrund, and I can't say it often enough: my works are twelve note *compositions,* not *twelve note* compositions." On February 5, 1951, Schoenberg wrote to Joseph Rufer, "The first conception of a series always takes place in the form of a thematic character." How he meant these remarks can be read out of Rosen's book *Arnold Schoenberg.* "The series was, for Schoenberg, both a group of motifs and an organization of the tonal spectrum." "The series is . . . not a melody but a premelodic idea." "So intense was Webern's concentration on the motif that one may say that his motifs are not really derived from the series, they generate it."[23] This understanding of the place of the series in the ontology of the work has been borne out by numerous analyses, including my own of Berg's *Lulu* (see chpter 8). Whether it is that a series is abstracted from a concrete musical idea (or a complex of such ideas), or constructed to produce properties that a composer means at the outset to impose on a work, is moot. What is important is that Adorno's characterization of the ordering of the series as "arbitrary" is wrong, his insinuation that the process of twelve-tone composition is some sort of Viennese mathematical game is wrong, and his claim that the composition is determined by the series (implication: rather than by the artistic design of the composer) is wrong. It is all, shockingly, like the sort of banal journalistic polemic against twelve-tone composition that one could read regularly not so many years ago in various organs of the popular press.

Rosen writes, "For his view of the history of music and society, [Adorno] needed [the *Missa solemnis*] to fail." He also needed to present a distorted portrayal of twelve-tone composition than which he surely must have known better. It allowed him to depict twelve-tone composition as the triumph of the form or the method over the material, of the object over the subject, of the system over the creator, of the triumph of order.

> The new ordering of twelve-tone technique virtually extinguishes the subject . . . [M]usic becomes capable of restraining itself coldly and inexorably, and this is the only fitting position for music following its decline."[24]

Thus is completed a process that was immanent in music history "since the beginning of the bourgeois era," a "longing . . . to 'grasp' and to place all sounds into an order, and to reduce the magic essence of music to human logic." In a rare swerve outside the confines of the Beethoven-to-Schoenberg framework for his history, he continues, "Luther calls Josquin des Pres, who died in 1521, 'the master of notes who compelled the notes to his will, in contrast to other composers, who bent the will to the notes.'"[25] And here is where the Stravinsky and Schoenberg lines converge in his story of the decline of music into an authoritarian society.

A personal note: whatever I may think of Adorno's thesis of a tendency in Western society toward a state of authoritarianism, I do not hear it in the late music of Beethoven, in Stravinsky's transformations of music by Gesualdo, Pergolesi, and Tchaikovsky, or in Schoenberg's twelve-tone music. And I resist as a piece of authoritarianism in itself the dogma that this tendency is *in* that music.

It is a matter of some dispute whether Adorno was influenced by Oswald Spengler (Rosen claims Spengler's influence as an instance of Adorno's "derivative intelligence").[26] But I don't know that we have to attribute Adorno's extreme pessimism directly to Spengler's influence. For one thing, the idea of the decline of the West, which is writ large across Adorno's work, was in the air.[27] But more specifically, reading *Dialectic of Enlightenment* and *Minima moralia* one can get an impression of how the Nazi years had turned Adorno's criticism of capitalism into a vision of the decline of Western Civilization over a much longer span of time. And given his lifelong consuming engagement with music and his totalizing view of society and culture, one can well ask how could he *not* see that vision reflected in music history, regardless of whether that outcome is defensible on the evidence of hearing or on the logic of reason.

At the conclusion of his review, Rosen reflects on Adorno's historical view against the background of his biography: "His view of modern culture arises from the natural despair of one who lived through the terrible inflation in Germany of the 1920's, which ruined so many upper middle-class families. His attack on commercial interests betrayed him into an idealization of the past." Rosen asks, "What was this world whose disappearance could inspire in Adorno such profound and ironic nostalgia?" By way of answer he closes with a paragraph from *Minima moralia,* which he introduces with these words: "at one point his prose rises to a truly poetic evocation of the Golden Age, a world whose disappearance is a cause of poignant regret." I repeat Adorno's paragraph here because reading it does truly contribute to an understanding of the very enigmatic, and contradictory, character of his work. Also because Adorno deserves to be represented here by a specimen of his finest writing, beside the writing that I have cited with less enthusiasm.

> Rampant technology eliminates luxury, but not by declaring privilege a human right; rather, it does so by both raising the general standard of living and cutting off the possibility of fulfillment. The express train that in three nights and two days hurtles across the continent is a miracle, but traveling in it has nothing of the faded splendor of the *train bleu*. What made up the voluptuousness of travel, beginning with the goodbye-waving through the open window, the solicitude of amiable accepters of tips, the ceremonial of mealtimes, the constant feeling of receiving favors that take nothing from anyone else, has passed away, together with the elegant people who were wont to promenade along the platforms before the departure, and who will by now be sought in vain even in the foyers of the most prestigious hotels. That the steps of railway carriages have to be retracted intimates to the passenger of even the most expensive express that he must obey the company's terse regulations like a prisoner. Certainly, the company gives him the exactly calculated value of his fare, but this includes

nothing that research has not proved an average demand. Who, aware
of such conditions, could depart on impulse on a voyage with his mistress
as once from Paris to Nice?[28]

With a wider understanding of Adorno's pessimism about the course
of music's history within the context of his personal history and its engagement with world history, and of the way that doleful overview forced his
interpretations of individual musical works or oeuvres into congruence with
it, there might have been less enthusiasm for extracting from his work and on
his authority an autonomous practice of deciphering music on the strength
of sheer intuition, a practice with the bravado of tightrope walking without
a net.

I began by asking whether Adorno's holistic view of culture and society
constitutes the basis for a healing of the parturition that accompanied the
age of enlightenment. Considering the unconvincing way in which, in his
practice, phenomena of one domain (art) are transposed as phenomena
of another (commerce), I would have to say, hardly. It is a kind of artificial,
counterfeit holism, required for the story that Adorno had to tell. It falls too
far short of portraying our experience of music in the world as the alternative
we seek to the tradition of approaching music as an autonomous phenomenon—a tradition that was in fact explicitly embraced by Adorno himself as
a grounding principle of his complex views.[29]

Rosen never comes back around to answer the question of his title. I
believe most readers would conclude that, on balance, his review implies a
negative answer. It is all too true that "unfortunately Adorno's admirers often
treasure [I would add "and imitate"] the worst aspects of his work," as Rosen
writes. But it is unfortunate, too, that, with the exception of that striking
passage from *Minima moralia*, Rosen makes no mention of work of Adorno
that can inspire the admiration of even those of us who share his distaste for
the worst aspects.

In his essay "Homage to Adorno's 'Homage to Zerlina,'"[30] Berthold Hoeckner writes that "Adorno's 'Homage' may be no more than a sketch, but it
claims for itself no less than the quality of a master painting." He reproduces
this "bagatelle," as he calls it, so that we can see for ourselves, and stresses its
character as a late work. But he mentions in the same breath the breathtaking
essay "Schubert,"[31] written by Adorno in 1928, his twenty-fifth year, which
Adorno judged thirty-six years later to be his "first somewhat comprehensive

… work touching on the meaning of music." I read with the same pleasure the omnibus essay he published two years later in the Viennese journal *Anbruch* under the title "Hermeneutik," comprising a brief theoretical statement and a number of exemplary critical sketches.[32] Probably the best-known extended critical work in this "high-flying style" (Hoeckner) is Adorno's *Mahler: A Musical Physiognomy.*[33]

We might consider it another casualty of the Nazi era that Adorno on the whole had higher priorities when it came to writing about music—or perhaps better said, that work of this uniquely inspired character and eloquence of style had to compete for Adorno's attention with his high-flying (in a different sense) oracular ambitions in work that he could well have left to others—and lament the critical writing that he might otherwise have produced and inspired in his followers. In an indirect sense Adorno's work was a casualty of the very conditions that he diagnosed. At the same time we can be consoled by the fact that not all escapees from the Nazi horrors who took refuge amidst the commercialism of America allowed their work to be so embittered by the experience of both. Not all have shared Adorno's declaration that "To write a poem after Auschwitz is barbaric."[34]

PERMISSIONS ACKNOWLEDGMENTS

Chapter 1. "Language and the Interpretation of Music" was originally published in Jenefer Robinson, ed., *Music and Meaning* (Ithaca, N.Y.: Cornell University Press), 23–56.

Chapter 2. "Being at a Loss for Words" was originally published in *Archiv für Musikwissenschaft,* Jahrgang 64 Heft 4 (2007): 265–84.

Chapter 3. "Beethoven's 'Expressive' Markings" was originally published in *Beethoven Forum* 7 (1999): 89–111.

Chapter 4. "The Immanence of Performance in Medieval Song" was originally published in Robert Hatten, ed., *A Sounding of Signs: Modalities and Moments in Music, Culture, and Philosophy: Essays in Honor of Eero Tarasti on His 60th Anniversary* (Imatra, Finland: International Semiotics Institute, 2008), 139–51.

Chapter 5. "Early Recorded Performances of Chopin Waltzes and Mazurkas: The Relation to the Text" was originally published in the *Journal of the American Liszt Society* 51 (2002): 57–77. Reprinted by permission.

Chapter 8. "The Lulu Character and the Character of *Lulu*" was originally published in Leo Treitler, *Music and the Historical Imagination* (Cambridge, Mass.: Harvard University Press, 1989), 264–305.

Chapter 9. "History and Archetypes" was originally published in *Perspectives of New Music* 35 (1997): 115–27.

Chapter 10. "Gender and Other Dualities of Music History" was originally published in Ruth Solie, ed., *Musicology and Difference: Gender and Sexuality in Music Scholarship.* ©1993 by the Regents of the University of California. Published by the University of California Press, 23–45.

Chapter 11. "Hermeneutics, Exegetics, or What?" was originally published in Thomas Holme Hansen, ed., *13th Nordic Musicological Congress: Papers and Abstracts* (Aarhus: Department of Musicology, University of Aarhus, 2002), 48–64.

Chapter 12. "*Should* We Adore Adorno?" was originally published in Robert Curry, David Gable, and Robert Marshall, eds., *Variations on the Canon: Essays on Music from Bach to Boulez in Honor of Charles Rosen on His Eightieth Birthday* (Rochester, N.Y.: University of Rochester Press, 2008), 291–302.

NOTES

1. Language and the Interpretation of Music

1. Márquez, "Bon Voyage, Mr. President."

2. The text is published in Schumann, *The Musical World of Robert Schumann*, 112–13.

3. The full text of both inquiry and Mendelssohn's response are given in English translation in *Strunk's Source Readings in Music History*, 1193–201.

4. Wittgenstein, "The Blue Book," in *The Blue and Brown Books*, 25–26.

5. Dahlhaus, "Fragments of a Musical Hermeneutics," 8.

6. Page numbers to citations from Agawu, *Playing with Signs*, in the following paragraphs are noted in the main text.

7. Groden and Kreiswirth, *The Johns Hopkins Guide to Literary Theory*, s.v. "Semiotics."

8. Wittgenstein, *Culture and Value*, 40; and Kivy, *Sound Sentiment*, 12–17.

9. Calvino, *Under the Jaguar Sun*, 51.

10. Newcomb, "Sound and Feeling," 623.

11. Goodman, *Languages of Art*, 45–52.

12. *Random House Dictionary of the English Language*, s.v. "metaphor."

13. Davies, *Musical Meaning and Expression*, 125.

14. Sibley, "Making Music Our Own," 175.

15. Lakoff and Turner, *More Than Cool Reason*, 114–19.

16. Hanslick, *On the Musically Beautiful*, 30; Reid is cited in Kivy, *Music Alone*, 46.

17. Erickson, *Musica enchiriadis*, 31.

18. Panofsky, "Iconography and Iconology," 38.

19. Proust, *In Search of Lost Time*, vol. 1, *Swann's Way*, 294, 295–96.

20. Davidson, "What Metaphors Mean," 246.

21. For an overview of the range of approaches to this topic, see *Indiana Theory Review* 12 (1991), ed. Richard Littlefield.

22. Abbate, *Unsung Voices,* 53–56.

23. E.g., Plato *Republic* 3.393: "Then in this case [when the epic poet speaks in the voice of another] the narrative of the poet may be said to proceed by imitation?"

24. See Berger, "*Diegesis* and *Mimesis:* The Poetic Modes." Fred Everett Maus has written separately about "Music as Narrative" in *Indiana Theory Review* 12 (1991), and "Music as Drama" in *Music Theory Spectrum* 10 (1988).

25. Abbate, *Unsung Voices,* 53.

26. Homer, *The Odyssey,* 439–40.

27. This has been demonstrated in a masterful way in Cone, "Three Ways of Reading."

28. Nattiez, "Can One Speak of Narrativity in Music?"

29. For a précis and critique of Nattiez's theory and its influences, see Powers, "Language Models and Musical Analysis."

30. Keiler, "Two Views of Musical Semiotics," 139; Ruwet citation (trans. Keiler) from Ruwet, "Théorie et methodes dans les études musicales."

31. See Bielitz, *Musik und Grammatik.*

32. Powers, "Language Models and Musical Analysis," 49.

33. Johannes, *De musica,* in Babb, *Hucbald, Guido, and John on Music,* 116.

34. Powers, "Language Models and Musical Analysis," 50.

35. See Treitler, *With Voice and Pen,* 46–47; and Reckow, "Tonsprache."

36. Allanbrook, "Ear-Tickling Nonsense."

37. Sissman, *Haydn and the Classical Variation.*

38. White, "Commentary: Form, Reference, and Ideology in Musical Discourse," 293–95.

39. Ricoeur, "Narrative Time," 165.

40. Hatten, "Metaphor *in* Music," 373–91.

41. Black, "Metaphor"; Hausman, *Metaphor and Art.*

2. Being at a Loss for Words

1. Erickson, *Musica enchiriadis and Scolica enchiriadis,* 31.

2. Augustine *Retractationes* 1.12.

3. Ibid., *De magistro* 10.37.

4. Ibid., 11.36. All citations of and translations from Saint Augustine are based on Burnyeat, "Wittegenstein and Augustine *De magistro.*" I am grateful to the author for calling my attention to this essay.

5. In Babb, *Hucbald, Guido, and John,* 69.

6. Aurelian of Réôme, *The Discipline of Music,* 13.

7. Personal communication from Edward Nowacki to the author. The citations of Isidore are from *The Etymologies of Isidore of Seville,* 96.

8. See *Strunk's Source Readings,* 146, with attention to n. 12.

9. Gushee, "Aurelian of Réôme."

10. Austin, *How to Do Things with Words.*

11. Franklin, *On Bullshit.* The book runs to only sixty-seven pages and should be read through for an impression of Franklin's conception of "bullshit."

12. As cited in Lloyd, *The Revolutions of Wisdom,* 183–84. Lloyd cites the following further remark to make clear that this is a criticism of Empedocles: "[T]here is nothing in common between Homer and Empedocles except the meter, so it is right to call the first a poet but the second a natural philosopher rather than a poet."

13. Ibid., 185.

14. In Levin, "Aristotle's Theory of Metaphor," 41.

15. In Nemis, "Aristotle's Analogical Metaphor," 220.

16. Von Staden, "Science as Text, Science as History," 499.

17. Ibid., 510.

18. Ibid., 508.

19. Ibid., 507.

20. Augustine, *Confessions,* trans. Robert S. Pine-Coffin, 1.8.13; Wittgenstein, *The Blue and Brown Books,* 77. For the following account Burnyeat's essay (see n. 4, above) has been most helpful.

21. Wittgenstein, *Philosophical Investigations,* 2.

22. This no-longer-familiar metaphor is explained by John Ciardi in *A Browser's Dictionary* (s.v. "Stalking horse"): "In politics, a candidate put forward to hide the candidacy of another, in whose favor he will withdraw." In this case Wittgenstein has set up Augustine's description by way of floating a theory that had earlier been his own but that it is his purpose in the *Philosophical Investigations* to disown. In its earliest use the phrase refers to "a horse trained to walk toward a deer while concealing a hunter who walked behind it, because deer will not take alarm at a riderless horse."

23. In Wittgenstein, *The Blue and Brown Books,* 75.

24. Ibid., *Philosophical Investigations,* par. 1.

25. Ibid., in *The Blue and Brown Books,* 77.

26. Augustine *De magistro* 11.36.

27. Wittgenstein, *Philosophical Investigations,* par. 13.

28. Ibid., *Tractatus logico-philosophicus,* 4.01.

29. Ibid., *Philosophical Investigations,* par. 340.

30. Ibid., par. 19.

31. Ibid., par. 7.

32. Von Staden, "Science as Text, Science as History."

33. In Babb, *Hucbald, Guido, and John,* 70.

34. Polanyi, *Personal Knowledge: Toward a Post-Critical Philosophy.*

35. Wittgenstein, *Philosophical Investigations,* par. 78.

36. This summary is based on three studies: Schooler and Engotler-Schooler, "Verbal Overshadowing of Visual Memories"; Schooler, Ohlsson, and Brooks, "Thoughts beyond Words"; and Schooler, Fiore, and Brandimonte, "At a Loss from Words."

37. Schooler, Ohlsson, and Brooks, "Thoughts beyond Words."

38. Schooler, Fiore, and Brandimonte, "At a Loss from Words."

39. Lehrer, *Wine and Conversation,* epigraph.

40. Wittgenstein, *Philosophical Investigations,* par. 610.

41. In Forster, *Abinger Harvest,* 105.

3. Beethoven's "Expressive" Markings

1. *New Harvard Dictionary of Music,* s.v. "Largo."

2. Ibid., s.v. "Mesto."

3. In *Strunk's Source Readings,* 662.

4. *New Harvard Dictionary of Music,* s.v. "Performance marks."

5. "Tender expression in music. It isn't to be characterized in terms of degrees of loudness or tempo any more than a tender facial expression can be described in terms of the distribution of matter." In Wittgenstein, *Culture and Value,* 89e. For a rare discussion of the potential contribution to the consideration of musical expression in Wittgenstein's thought, see Hanfling, "I Heard a Plaintive Melody."

6. Finscher, "Zur Interpretation," 83: "Wie, in welchem Masse, mit welchen Mitteln findet Beethovens Vortragsbezeichnung *Largo e mesto* ihre Entsprechung im musikalischen Material and Prozess des Satzes?"

7. This "picture of the essence of human language" is Wittgenstein's characterization, given in his *Philosophical Investigations* of the view of language that he had presented in his first book, *Tractatus logico-philosophicus* (see chap. 2, section 4 of this book).

8. Finscher, "Zur Interpretation," 83–84.

9. Panofsky, "The History of Art," 16.

10. Ibid., 12–14.

11. The following remarks about Schenker's conception of musical content have been informed by four pieces of writing to which I am indebted: Calcagno, "Heinrich Schenker's Analyses of Beethoven," and *"Wie war ein Beethoven musikalisch?";* Snarrenberg, "Tones and Words"; Snarrenberg, *Schenker's Interpretive Practice;* and Guck, "Analytical Fictions." On the wide reception of Schenker in the United States, see Rothstein, "The Americanization of Schenker."

12. Schenker, *Five Graphic Music Analyses (Fünf Urlinie-Tafeln),* and *Neue musikalische Theorien and Phantasien,* vol. 3 of *Der freie Satz;* trans. by Ernst Oster as *Free Composition (Der Freie Satz).*

13. Bent, *Music Analysis in the Nineteenth Century,* 1, 11. On this point, see Keiler, "The Origins of Schenker's Thought," where the author speaks of the "teleological

straightjacket that has limited the study of the intellectual background of Schenker's work to a consideration of the mature period alone." Keiler's study is altogether indispensable for this subject.

14. Forte, introduction to Schenker, *Free Composition,* xviii.

15. Schenker, *Beethovens neunte Sinfonie,* trans. by John Rothgeb as *Beethoven's Ninth Symphony;* and *Erläuterungsausgabe der letzten fünf Klaviersonaten.*

16. Ibid., *Erläuterungsausgabe,* Op. 109, 1:56–57. I read this somewhat in the sense of Wittgenstein's conception of the life of language. For example, "if we had to name anything which is the life of the sign, we should have to say that it was its *use.*" "The Blue Book," in *The Blue and Brown Books,* 4.

17. Ibid., *Erläuterungsausgabe,* Op.109, 1:50.

18. Cone, *The Composer's Voice,* 18.

19. Schenker, *Beethovens neunte Sinfonie,* 48–49, 80, xiv.

20. Ibid., *Erläuterungsausgabe,* Op. 110, 3:67.

21. This conception of the place of programs in music's ontology is closest to that presented by Dahlhaus in his essay "Thesen über Programmusik."

22. "Töne sind Wesen, die einander verstehen, so wie wir den Ton. Jeder Accord schon mag ein Tonverständniss unter einander seyn, und als bereits gebildete Einheit zu uns kommen. Accord wird Bild von Geistergemeinschaft, Liebe, Freundschaft, u.s.w. Harmonie Bild and Ideal der Gesellschaft. Es muss schlechterdings kein menschliches Verhältniss, keine menschliche Geschichte geben, die sich nicht durch Musik ausdrücken liesse. . . . Der hier sprechende Geist ist derselbe, wie der unsere. . . . Ausserdem [haben wir] am Tone und an der Musik unser Bild und Ebenbild. . . . Im Tone gehen wir mit unsers Gleichen um . . . Alles Leben ist Musik, und alle Musik als Leben selbst-zum wenigsten sein Bild. . . . Aber [die Musik] müsste zum *absoluten* Complement des Menschengeschlechts erhoben werden können, und Jedem wäre ihr Verständniss leicht zu öffnen. Alles, was in eines Menschen Gedanken kommen kann, vermag er auch auszusprechen, and was der Mensch aussprechen kann, spricht auch der *Ton* aus . . . Mensch und Ton sind durchaus gleich unerschupfbar, and gleich unendlich in ihrem Werk und ihrem Wesen. Des Menschen Wesen und Wirken ist Ton, ist Sprache. Musik ist gleichfalls Sprache, allgemeine; die erste des Menschen. Die vorhandenen Sprachen sind Individualisirungen der Musik; nicht individualiserte Musik, sondern, die zur Musik sich verhalten, wie die einzelnen Organe zum organisch Ganzen." Ritter, *Faksimiledruck nach der Ausgabe von 1810,* 233–36; my translation. I am indebted to Kristina Muxfeldt for bringing this text to my attention.

23. "Herzlich freut mich die selbe Ansicht, welche sie mit mir theilen in Ansehung der noch aus der *Barbarey* der Musick her rührenden Bezeichnungen des Zeitmaasses denn nur z.B. was kann widersinniger seyn als *Allegro* welches ein fur allemal *Lustig* heisst, u. wie weit entfernt sind wir oft von diesem Begriffe dieses

Zeitmaasses, so dass das Stück selbst das Gegentheil der Bezeichnung sagt." Brandenburg, *Briefwechsel Gesamtausgabe,* no. 1196, 4:130; my translation. The practice of tempo indications goes back to the seventeenth century; one can't tell which ages Beethoven counted as "barbarous." See *New Harvard Dictionary of Music,* 838–39.

24. Letter of August 19, 1826, in Brandenburg, *Briefwechsel Gesamtausgabe,* no. 2187, 6:269. The extensive literature on the uncertain status of Beethoven's metronome marks in general does not really affect this interpretation of the marking at the beginning of the "Hammerklavier." On the authenticity of the source for that indication, see Paolone, "L'originale autografo."

25. "Ein anderes ist es mit den Karakter des Stücks bezeichnenden Wortern, solche können wir nicht aufgeben, da der Takt eigentlich [nur] mehr der Körper ist, *diese aber schon* selbst *Bezug auf den Geist des Stückes haben.*" Ibid., no. 1196, 4:330; my translation.

26. *New Harvard Dictionary of Music,* s.v. "Performance marks."

27. Ibid., s.v. "Allegro."

28. "Auf meine einstmals an Beethoven gerichtete Frage, warum er bei einem oder dem anderen Satze seiner Sonaten nicht gleich die poetische Idee angedeutet habe, indem sich eine solche dem sinnigen Hörer gewissermassen von selbst aufdringe? antwortete er: 'Dass jene Zeit, in welcher er seine Sonaten geschrieben, poetischer als jetzt (1823) gewesen; daher solche Andeutungen damals überflüssig waren. Jedermann, fuhr er fort, fühlte damals aus dem *Largo* der dritten Sonate in D, op. 10, den geschilderten Seelenzustand eines Melancholischen heraus, mit allen den verschiedenen Nuancen von Licht and Schatten im Bilde der Melancholic and ihrer Phasen, ohne dass eine Aufschrift den Schlüssel dazu liefern musste.'" Schindler, *Beethoven as I Knew Him,* 406.

29. For an overview of this phenomenon, see Wiora, "Religioso," in *Triviale Zonen in der Religiösen Kunst,* 1–12.

30. Nietzsche, *Human, All Too Human,* 89.

31. Mendel and Reissmann, *Musikalisches Conversations-Lexicon,* s.v. "Religiös"; cited in Wiora, *Triviale Zonen.*

32. Nottebohm, *Zweite Beethoveniana,* 163.

33. Ibid., 189.

34. This and subsequent citations to Hanslick in the following paragraphs are from Hanslick, *On the Musically Beautiful,* trans. Geoffrey Payzant, 48–49.

35. Bamberger, "The Musical Significance of Beethoven's Fingerings," 237 and 245.

36. Ibid., 246.

37. Ibid.

38. This important detail has been secured by Lewis Lockwood in "On Beethoven's Sketches and Autographs," 38.

39. Bamberger, "The Musical Significance of Beethoven's Fingerings," 246 n. 21, 270 n. 44

40. At last someone has surveyed such enigmatic notational signs and regarded them as intentional rather than editorial or typographical errors, composers' slips, or other ways of dismissing them as exceptions to the norms of notation. See Poli, *The Secret Life of Musical Notation.* I'm grateful to Jim Samson for drawing my attention to this book.

41. Dahlhaus, "Fragments of a Musical Hermeneutics," 6.

42. Ibid., 8.

4. The Immanence of Performance in Medieval Song

1. Ingarden, *The Work of Music and the Problem of Its Identity.*
2. Dahlhaus, *Esthetics of Music,* 12.
3. Van Gulik, *The Lore of the Chinese Lute,* vii.
4. DeWoskin, *A Song for One or Two,* 128.
5. Ibid., 132.
6. Humboldt, *Gessamelte Schriften,* 6:147.
7. In Babb, *Hucbald, Guido, and John,* 74.
8. Ibid., 137. I have changed the last word in the translation from "say," restoring the counterpart of the Latin original, *sonar.* This can be a little object lesson in allowing distant cultures to choose words that manifest *their* way of perceiving, even if it doesn't make sense to us.
9. The examples of medieval song can be heard on the CD accompanying Treitler, *With Voice and Pen.*
10. For sources, edition, and translation of Rudel, "Laquand li jorn," see Treitler, *With Voice and Pen,* 474 n. 17.
11. Butterfield, "Brush with Genius."
12. Benjamin, *Gesammelte Schriften,* 538.

5. Early Recorded Performances of Chopin Waltzes and Mazurkas

1. Zak, *The Poetics of Rock.*
2. Stravinsky, *The Poetics of Music,* 5.
3. Reckow, *Der Musiktraktat des Anonymus 4,* 46.
4. Vladimir de Pachmann, RCA ARM-0260. This and other early recordings cited in this chapter are identified by original shellac discs. Many have been digitally remastered and issued as compact disc recordings.
5. In Schonberg, *The Great Pianists,* 332.
6. Ibid.
7. Eigeldinger, *Chopin: Pianist and Teacher,* 87. However, in the same report Eigeldinger writes that Chopin's way of enacting that idea was to "compress the

first four bars almost into two bars." Then perhaps what those four written-out measures denote is something like "spin out that figure until you are ready to strike out into the piece."

8. Pachmann, RCA-LMY 10.

9. The performances can be heard on the following recordings: Paderewski, RCA Camden CAL-310; Cortot, Hunt CD 510; Rachmaninoff, RCA VIC 1534.

10. Debussy, *Monsieur Croche*, 22.

11. Eigeldinger, *Chopin: Pianist and Teacher*, 74–75, 76–79, 86–87, 212–13, 217, 221, 235. In the matter of Chopin's textual variation, the most thorough studies and suggestive interpretations have been presented in Kallberg, "The Problem of Repetition and Return," and "Are Variants a Problem?"

12. See Kallberg, "Chopin in the Marketplace," 543.

13. Butt, *Playing with History*, 117.

14. Pirrotta, "Church Polyphony a propos of a New Fragment at Foligno," 124.

15. Rankin, "Between Oral and Written," 2.

16. This is described in Treitler, *With Voice and Pen*, chap. 3.

17. Butt, *Playing with History*, 121.

18. Hanslick, *On the Musically Beautiful*, 48–49.

19. "The Concert of M. Chopin from Warsaw," in *Strunk's Source Readings*, 1123–25.

20. See Butt, *Playing with History*, 68–69, for a discussion of this polarity.

21. Quoted from the translation in Arato and Gebhard, *The Essential Frankfurt School Reader*, of "Über den Fetischcharakter in der Musik and die Regression des Hörens," *Zeitschrift für Sozialforschung* 7 (1938). My attention was drawn to this by John Butt's *Playing with History*.

22. Schonberg, *The Great Pianists*, 377–78.

23. Hofmann, *Piano Playing*, 20.

24. Schonberg, *The Great Pianists*, 378.

25. Butt, *Playing with History*, presents the most recent and the most thoroughly thought-out account of this discourse that we have.

26. Busoni, "Sketch of a New Aesthetics of Music," 85.

27. Calvino, *If on a Winter's Night a Traveller*.

28. Forkel, "A General History of Music," in *Strunk's Source Readings*, 1012.

29. Kallberg, "The Problem of Repetition and Return," 1.

30. Ibid., "Are Variants a Problem?" 267.

31. Ibid., 260.

32. This subject is discussed in Treitler, *With Voice and Pen*, chap. 12. See also the section "Notation as Example" in chap. 4 of Butt, *Playing with History*, 109–14.

33. Listenius, *Musica ab authore denuo multisque novis regale et exemplis adaucta*. Listenius's "opus perfectus et absolutus" is more often translated to the seeming cognates "perfect and absolute." But both Latin words have the sense of "finished,"

and that makes more sense of the distinction that Listenius was getting at and that is discussed with respect to both the visual and the musical arts in chap. 7 of the present volume. That it was a distinction recognized in both arts in close temporal proximity seems significant.

34. See Nelson Goodman, *Languages of Art.*
35. Thomas Kuhn, *The Structure of Scientific Revolutions.*

6. What Kind of Thing Is Musical Notation?

1. Modern works that have particularly informed this chapter are Barrett, "Reflections on Music Writing"; Carruthers, *The Book of Memory*; Colish, *The Mirror of Language*; Gombrich, *Art and Illusion*; Harris, *The Origin of Writing*; Havelock, *Preface to Plato*; Modrak, *Aristotle's Theory of Language and Meaning*; Tanay, *Noting Music, Marking Culture*; Treitler, *With Voice and Pen.*
2. As reported in Treitler, *With Voice and Pen,* chaps. 13 and 14.
3. Tanay, *Noting Music, Marking Culture,* ix.
4. Colish, *The Mirror of Language,* 8.
5. Carruthers, *The Book of Memory,* 8.
6. Ibid., 15.
7. Cicero, *Partitiones oratorie,* 26; cited in Carruthers, *The Book of Memory,* 18.
8. Hucbald, *De harmonica institutione,* in Babb, *Hucbald, Guido, and John on Music,* 37.
9. Treitler, *With Voice and Pen,* chap. 13.
10. Plato *Cratylus* 423b ff, 427c–d, 428e, 434b, 439a; Colish, *The Mirror of Language,* 12.
11. Plato *Cratylus* 439b, 439c.
12. Colish, *The Mirror of Language,* 12.
13. Gombrich, *Art and Illusion,* 141.
14. Harris, *The Origin of Writing,* 24.
15. Havelock, *Preface to Plato,* vii.
16. Gombrich, *Art and Illusion,* 4.
17. Tanay, *Noting Music, Marking Culture,* 6.
18. Harris, *The Origin of Writing,* 5.
19. Plato, *The Republic* 10.600.
20. Colish, *The Mirror of Language,* 15.
21. Aristotle *De interpretatione* 1.4–6; trans. in Modrak, *Aristotle's Theory of Language and Meaning,* 8.
22. Modrak, *Aristotle's Theory,* 8, 13.
23. Cited in Harris, *The Origin of Writing,* 114–15.
24. Cited in Harris, *The Origin of Writing,* 76.
25. Gombrich, *Art and Illusion,* 362–63.
26. Ibid., 366.

27. Ibid., 191.

28. Bercow and Schisgal, *Two of a Kind,* introduction.

29. Plato *Cratylus* 424e, 434a–b.

30. Priscianus, *Institutiones grammaticae* 1.2.4; cited in Harris, *The Origin of Writing,* 114–15.

31. John of Salisbury, *Metalogicon,* book 1, chap. 13, p. 202.

32. *Encyclopedia Britannica,* 11th edition (1911), 28:852.

33. *Musica enchiriadis,* "Beginning of the Handbook on Music," in *Strunk's Source Readings,* 189, 193. See the translator's note about the tentative state of the words "pitches" and "sounds" in the translation.

34. In *Strunk's Source Readings,* 149.

35. Augustine *Confessions* 10.9, trans. Robert S. Pine-Coffin, p. 217.

36. See Carruthers, *The Book of Memory,* 169–70 and n. 54.

37. Aurelian, *The Discipline of Music,* 45.

38. In Barrett, "Reflections on Music Writing," 91.

39. Aurelian, *The Discipline of Music,* 46. For a general treatment of the subject of memory in medieval music practice see Busse Berger, *Medieval Music and the Art of Memory.*

40. In *Strunk's Source Readings,* 189, 193.

41. In Babb, *Hucbald, Guido, and John,* 36.

42. In *Strunk's Source Readings,* 190.

43. In ibid., 264.

44. In I. J. Gelb, *A Study of Writing,* 13.

45. Derrida, *Of Grammatology,* 28.

46. Harris, *The Origin of Writing,* 93.

47. Ibid., 118.

48. Picket, *The Acoustics of Speech Communication,* 6–7.

49. Paul, *Principles of the History of Language,* 38, 39.

50. Smith, *Understanding Reading;* see especially chap. 10.

51. This conception is fundamental to Robert Hatten's theory of gesture in his *Interpreting Musical Gestures, Topics, and Tropes.* I cite two interconnectred passages: "The concept of gesture (like that of time itself) is endlessly fascinating, because it touches upon a competency that is fundamental to our existence as human beings—the ability to recognize the significance of energetic shaping through time" (p. 93); and "Gestures may be inferred from musical notation, given knowledge of the relevant musical style and culture" (p. 93).

52. Tanay, *Noting Music, Marking Culture,* 6.

53. Carruthers, *The Book of Memory,* 18.

54. Black, *Models and Metaphors,* 241.

55. This characterization, generalizing from the concepts underlying the terms cited above by Carruthers, terms central but not in identical ways to the

epistemologies of both Plato and Aristotle, takes account of a caveat sounded by Richard McKeon in his essay "Literary Criticism and the Concept of Imitation in Antiquity," 127: "To elaborate the full significance of the term 'imitation' . . . more is required than the simple enumeration of the list of other words equivalent to it or used in its explication." McKeon, and Carruthers, should be consulted for the necessary differentiations.

56. Barrett, "Reflections on Music Writing," 92–93.

57. Ibid., 89–90.

58. In Gombrich, *Art and Illusion,* 63.

59. Ibid., 77.

60. Ibid., 155–56.

61. Ibid., 3.

62. Haar, "Music as Visual Language," 265–84.

63. Ibid., 280–81.

64. Ibid., 267.

65. The painting was included in the exhibition Watteau, Music, and Theater, at the Metropolitan Museum of Art, New York, 2009, curated by Katherine Baetjer and Georgia Cowart; exhibition catalogue edited by Baetjer. Cowart called my attention to the painting and conveyed her interpretation of it to me in a personal communication.

66. Single leaf of a gradual, Pierpoint Morgan Library, Ms. M.653.1.

67. In a book that appeared just as I was proofreading the copyedited manuscript of this one, Roberto Poli engages such seeming notationl anomolies in suggestive ways in *The Secret Life of Musical Notation.*

68. Bent, "Notation."

69. Carruthers, *The Book of Memory,* 32 and n. 43.

70. Powers, in *New Harvard Dictionary of Music,* s.v. "Rhythm."

71. Ibid.

72. Halle, "On Meter and Prosody"; and Keyser, "The Linguistic Basis of English Prosody" and "Old English Prosody."

73. This practice, known today as "modal rhythm," will be familiar to most readers. I rehearse it here in a somewhat uncommon interpretation—resonant with the linguistic approach of Halle and Keyser—that suits my general purpose in this chapter. The interpretation is presented in detail in Treitler, "Regarding Rhythm and Meter."

74. Johannes de Garlandia, *De musica mensurabili,* chap. 6, chap. 1.

75. Ibid., chap. 4.

76. All the citations from Franco of Cologne up to "The rule . . ." are from *Strunk's Source Readings,* 229.

77. Ibid., 241.

78. Ibid., 239.

79. All citations in the remainder of this paragraph are in ibid., 229.

80. Bispham, "Rhythm in Music," 126, 130. I encountered this reference in the first chapter of Gary Tomlinson's work in progress, *1,000,000 Years of Music: A History*. I am grateful to Tomlinson for making this draft available to me.

81. This sentence is encountered in the website *Brainy Quote* (www.brainy-quote.com; accessed November 14, 2010), which does not identify sources. I cannot vouch for its authenticity, but about its aptness I have no doubt.

82. Schenker, *Erläuterungsausgabe der letzten fünf Klaviersonaten*, op. 109, 1:56–57.

7. Sketching Music, Writing Music

1. Onions, Burchfield, and Friedrichsen, *Oxford Dictionary of English Etymology*, s.v. "sketch."

2. Klein, *Klein's Comprehensive Etymological Dictionary*, s.v. "sketch."

3. Rosand, *Drawing Acts*, 52. I am indebted to this book and to personal communications from its author for this section of the present chapter.

4. Vasari, in Rosand, *Drawing Acts*, 53.

5. Ibid.

6. Goethe, "The Collector and His Circle," 70.

7. Rosand, *Drawing Acts*, 53.

8. Jacobssson and Treitler, "Sketching Archetypes."

9. See Owens, *Composers at Work*.

10. Pierre Bonnard: The Late Interiors, exhibition at the Metropolitan Museum of Art, New York, January 27–April 19, 2009.

11. See Johnson, "Beethoven Scholars and Beethoven Sketches," for the reasoning opposing the use of sketches as guides in analysis.

12. An outstanding, encouraging exception is Richard Kramer's book *Unfinished Music*.

13. Lockwood, "On Beethoven's Sketches and Autographs, 34.

14. Ibid., 38.

15. Nottebohm, *Beethoveniana*, and *Zweite Beethoveniana*. I cite these phrases as cliches.

16. See Atkinson, "From *Vitium* to *Tonus acquisitus*."

17. Galassi, *Picasso's Variations on the Masters*. The study includes many reproductions from all the series except that based on *Le Californie*.

18. Ibid., 13–14. I have changed the translation somewhat because the French use of *interprétation* in reference to music normally has the sense of "performance."

19. Ibid., 146.

20. Schiller, *Der Briefwechsel zwischen Schiller und Goethe*, 365; my translation.

21. The example is taken from Kallberg, *Chopin at the Boundaries*, 219.

8. The Lulu Character and the Character of *Lulu*

The work on this subject has benefited in numerous ways from conversations with the great drama critic Jan Kott, who was my colleague at Stony Brook University when I wrote the first version of this essay.

1. Pierre Boulez, program booklet to *Alban Berg: Lulu,* Teresa Stratas, Orchestre de L'Opéra de Paris, dir. Pierre Boulez, Deutsche Grammophon Gesellschaft 3308345-48 (1979), 4–5.

2. See Hall, "Role and Form in Berg's Sketches for *Lulu,*" and *A View of Berg's* Lulu *through the Autograph Sources.*

3. Kraus, *Literatur and Lüge,* 9; my translation.

4. Ibid., 12.

5. See Jarman, "Dr. Schön's Five-Strophe Aria," in his *The Music of Alban Berg,* 95–101.

6. Rothe, *Frank Wedekinds Dramen,* 57.

7. The first three pitches of Schön's and Alwa's rows in their untransposed and prime positions constitute A-major and A-minor triads, respectively, in the second inversion—they are differentiated by $C_\sharp$ and $C_\natural$.

8. Lochhead, "Lulu: Structural Principles."

9. Perle, *The Operas of Alban Berg,* vol. 2, *Lulu,* 34.

10. See "*Wozzeck* and the Apocalypse," in Treitler, *Music and the Historical Imagination,* 242–63.

11. Kott, "Ionesco, or a Pregnant Death," in his *The Theater of Essence,* 99; also the essay "Witkiewicz, or the Dialectic of Anachronism" in the same collection, where Kott writes "a time is coming in which only farce will have the appearance of tragedy" (pp. 80–81).

12. Fechter, *Frank Wedekind,* 56, 58–59; my translation.

13. Berg's decision to make the orchestral voice in the D-minor interlude of *Wozzeck* suddenly his own is questioned by Joseph Kerman and Igor Stravinsky. The suggestion from both is that the interjection of a direct expression of the composer's own feelings for the first and only time so late in the opera radically disrupts and thereby weakens the dramatic transaction. Should we not read in Berg's musical commentaries on the deaths of both his leading ladies expressions not only of compassion but also of remorse? And are they not further signs of his ambivalence? See Kerman, *Opera as Drama,* 230–33. Stravinsky's critique is quoted in Craft, *Stravinsky: Chronicle of a Friendship,* 32–34. I am grateful to David Gable for calling my attention to those passages.

14. Kott, "Ionesco, or a Pregnant Death," in *The Theater of Essence.*

15. Jarman, *The Music of Alban Berg,* 234.

16. Baudelaire, *Les fleurs du mal,* 5–6.

17. Patrice Chereau, in program booklet to *Alban Berg: Lulu* (see n. 1, this chapter), 15.

18. Cited in Franz, "The Process of Individuation," 180.

19. Wedekind, "Lulu—The Role of My Life,"

20. Mudocci was born Evangeline Muddock in 1872 in England, nine years after Munch's birth. Shortening her given name to Eva and lengthening her family name to Mudocci contributed to an identity more consonant with her sensuous appearance and her artistic life (and afterlife). She was a professional violinist, touring in Paris when she met Munch. An exhibition in the summer of 2010 at the Metropolitan Museum of Art in New York of the work of Henri Matisse displayed an etching identified as a portrait of Eva Mudocci. Hilary Spurling, in *Matisse the Master,* makes the connection, writing of the "relentless practicing [on the violin] that drove Matisse to the brink of exhaustion . . . Music provided the outlet for Matisse that he could no longer find in painting, as [in 1914] the weeks that were to have decided the fate of France stretched into months with no end in sight . . . Matisse dashed off a whole series of etchings of young string players, including . . . Eva Muddoci [she would have been forty-two] whose passionate playing spoke directly to Parisians in this first winter of the war" (p. 167). Eva died in 1952, two years before Matisse. For her last appearance in the art world she joined Marilyn Monroe, Elizabeth Taylor, Greta Garbo, and Jane Fonda in the female pantheon of Andy Warhol, by way of Munch's portrayal of her as *Madonna.*

21. Carlyle, preface to Goethe, *Wilhelm Meister's Apprenticeship and Travels,* ix.

22. See Bril, *Lilith, ou la mère obscure,* and Koltuv, *The Book of Lilith.* Jewish tradition regarding the origins of Lilith and Eve is reported in Schneider, *Jewish and Female.* I am obliged to Joseph Straus for calling my attention to the latter source.

23. Bennett, "Maschinist Hopkins."

24. Berg's letter is cited in Perle, *The Operas of Alban Berg,* vol. 2, *Lulu,* 40.

25. The classic treatment of this subject is in Praz, *The Romantic Agony,* chap. 4, "La Belle Dame Sans Merci." See also Kingsbury, "The Femme Fatale and Her Sisters."

26. See Franz, "The Process of Individuation," 177–88.

27. A very rich interpretation of the Pierrot figure is given in Starobinski, *Portrait de l'artiste en saltimbanque.*

28. Wedekind, "Lulu—The Role of My Life," 7.

9. History and Archetypes

1. The attraction of this archetype for our own time was demonstrated by a recent news report about the researches of a Cornell University entomologist on the meaning of firefly flashes. The males of each species flash in a fixed pattern, which is recognized by the females of the species waiting on the ground, who respond with their own fixed pattern, which brings the males down to them for sexual union. But the males face a hazard in the ability of females of different spe-

cies to imitate one anothers' response patterns. When they do so, the males of the species whose female patterns are being imitated descend in the expectation of copulation, but instead they are killed and eaten by those females. The report was headlined "Firefly Femmes Fatales."

2. See chap. 8, n. 1.

3. Susan McClary called attention to this weakness—correctly, I now see—in her review of my book *Music and the Historical Imagination*, in *Notes* 48 (1991): 38–40.

4. Bourdieu, *Outline of a Theory of Practise*, 79.

5. Showalter, *Sexual Anarchy*, 10.

6. Dijkstra, *Idols of Perversity*.

7. Ibid., 193–94.

8. Godeau is equally skeptical in her review of Dijkstra's book (Godeau, "Misogynist Masquerade). As her title hints, she suggests that the misogyny is in the book itself, which she sees as a "voyeur's feast."

9. In Dijkstra, *Idols of Perversity*, 137.

10. Kramer, "*Carnaval*, Cross Dressing, and the Woman in the Mirror," 305.

11. Ibid., 315–16.

12. Jérome-Joseph de Momigny, from *A Complete Course of Harmony and Composition*, in *Strunk's Source Readings*: "The style of this *Allegro Moderato* is noble and pathetic. I decided that the best way to have my readers recognize its true expression was to add words to it. But since these verses, if one can call them that, were improvised, as it were, they ought not to be judged in any other regard than that of their agreement with the sense of the music." (p. 827).

13. See Morgan, "The Eternal Return."

14. Showalter, *Sexual Anarchy*, 78.

15. Richard Wagner, from *The Artwork of the Future*, in *Strunk's Source Readings*, 1085–112.

10. Gender and Other Dualities of Music History

1. Boethius, from *De institutione musica libri quinque*, in *Strunk's Source Readings*, 138–39.

2. Treitler, *Music and the Historical Imagination*, 11–12.

3. Rousseau, *Dictionnaire de musique* (Paris, 1768) includes an article entitled "Plainchant"; see Rousseau, *A Complete Dictionary of Music*, 95–105.

4. An overview of the positions that have been taken is presented in Hucke, "Gregorian and Old Roman Chant."

5. Stäblein, "Die Entstehung des gregorianischen Chorals," 11.

6. Ibid., *Die Gesänge des altrömischen Graduale*, 38.

7. Ibid., 13, 17. In the Latin citations Stäblein is quoting a ninth-century writer on ecclesiastical matters, Walafried Strabo (*De rebus ecclesiasticis* 22).

8. Stäblein, *Die Gesänge des altrömischen Graduale,* 14.

9. Ibid.

10. For an introduction to this background and its relation to the church-musical traditions, see Treitler, *With Voice and Pen,* chap. 6.

11. I quote from the English translation of Rousseau, *A Complete Dictionary of Music,* 64–65. I think my interpolation of "ancient" before Greek is not problematic. Unlike his followers John Hawkins and Charles Burney, Rousseau had no interest in bringing the Byzantine Greeks into the story.

12. See Gombrich, *The Ideas of Progress,* 12–34. Gombrich writes here about Rousseau's forerunner and exact counterpart as historian of the figurative arts, Johann Joachim Winckelmann, who set up a dualism virtually identical with Rousseau's: "the noble simplicity," "purity," and "quiet grandeur of Greek statues" on one side, the "corruption," "artificiality," "affectation," and "*effeminacy*" of the works of artists like Bernini, on the other (Winckelmann, *Thoughts on the Imitation of Greek Works;* my emphases; Gombrich refers to this work as "the famous manifesto of classicism"). "Corrupt" and "effeminate" are so closely associated in this usage that they become virtually synonymous.

13. I take this distinction from White, *The Content of the Form,* ix.

14. Wagner, *Einführung in die gregorianische Melodien,* vol. 3, *Gregorianische Formenlehre,* 398.

15. Ferretti, *Estetica gregoriana, ossia Trattato delle forme musicali del canto gregoriano,* vii–viii. That a treatise on musical forms would constitute the extension of the title "Gregorian aesthetic" is as significant as is the fact that a theory of form, in Wagner's title, would constitute a science of style. Regarding the influence of these aesthetic issues on the analysis of chant, see Treitler, *With Voice and Pen,* chap. 7.

16. Wagner, *Einführung in die gregorianische Melodien,* vol. 3, *Gregorianische Formenlehre,* 398, 403.

17. Apel, *Gregorian Chant,* 362.

18. See Treitler, "The Politics of Reception."

19. Webern, *Der Weg zur neuen Musik,* 23.

20. Said, *Orientalism,* 1–2.

21. Ibid., "Orientalism Reconsidered," 103.

22. Beginning with Rousseau's article (*A Complete Dictionary of Music,* 66–67), the theme of corruption and the desire for the restoration of the pure tradition is concretized in a creation myth about Gregorian chant that has its origins in the ninth century and a transmission into the twentieth. See Treitler, *With Voice and Pen,* chap. 6. Conrad Donakowski has interpreted the theme of the restoration of plainchant in the context of changes in European thought from the Enlightenment to the Romantic era; see Donakowski, "A Musical Return to the State of Nature."

23. Bernal, *Black Athena,* vol. 1, *The Fabrication of Ancient Greece,* 1.

24. Ibid., 29.

25. Ibid., 1–2.

26. Kiesewetter, *Geschichte der europäisch-abendländischen oder unsrer heutigen Musik*, 1.

27. See Stocking, *Race, Culture, and Evolution*, 44: "[The ramifications of] the nineteenth-century notion of race could—and should—be followed into various areas of social, historical, literary, philological, biological, and political thought, as well as into the 'external' reality of European expansion, slavery, nationalism, and all the manifold events and processes which help to define men's thinking regarding human differences." See also Brown, *Western Music and Race*.

28. Eichenauer, *Musik und Rasse*. Bibliographic details for the other titles can be found in Eichenauer.

29. Ibid., 37; my translation of this and the following quotations from Eichenauer.

30. Ibid.

31. Ibid., 67, 87 n. 1, 89.

32. Ibid., 89.

33. Ibid.

34. McClary, "Getting Down Off the Beanstalk," in *Minnesota Composers Forum Newsletter* (February 1987): unpaginated; see McClary, *Feminine Endings*, 124–25, and 128–30 for a revised version of these paragraphs. As to "the phallus of the classical Greek column," in *The Reign of the Phallus: Sexual Politics in Ancient Athens*, classicist Eva C. Keuls provides reason for caution. Her book opens thus: "In the case of a society dominated by men who sequester their wives and daughters, denigrate the female role in reproduction, erect monuments to the male genitalia, have sex with the sons of their peers, sponsor public whorehouses, create a mythology of rape, and engage in rampant saber-rattling, it is not inappropriate to refer to a reign of the phallus. Classical Athens was such a society" (p. 1). Then to the point: "In speaking of 'the display of the phallus,' I am not referring, as Freudians do, to symbols that may remind us of the male organ, such as bananas, sticks, or Freud's own cigar [or architectural columns, we might add]. In Athens no such coding was necessary.... Athenian men habitually displayed their genitals, and their city was studded with statues of gods with phalluses happily erect" (p. 2). This raises again the question of the preceding chapter about where the gender coding originates, whether in the artistic tradition itself or in the writing of the critic.

35. As described by McClary, "Narrative Agendas in 'Absolute' Music," 332.

36. Ibid., 338–39.

37. Eichenauer, *Musik und Rasse*, 13.

38. The background of the essentialism of race is described in Stocking, *Race, Culture, and Evolution*. Literature regarding the history of the essentialism of gender is cited in Solie, "Whose Life?"

39. Hanslick, *On the Musically Beautiful,* 46, 64.

40. Kretzschmar, *Führer durch den Konzertsaal,* vol. 1, 253.

11. Hermeneutics, Exegetics, or What?

1. In Sontag, *Against Interpretation and Other Essays,* 3–14.

2. Ibid., 5.

3. Kramer, "Tropes and Windows," 1–20.

4. Cone, "Schubert's Promissory Note."

5. Kramer, "Tropes and Windows," 2.

6. Geertz, "From the Native's Point of View," 482.

7. Eco, *The Limits of Interpretation.*

8. Kramer, "The Harem Threshold," 78.

9. Tovey, *Essays in Musical Analysis: Symphonies,* 122. Kanne's review was printed in the *Vienna Allgemeine musikalische Zeitung* 8 (1824): 149–51, 157–60, 173–74, and reprinted in *Ludwig van Beethoven—Die Werke im Spiegel seiner Zeit— Gesammelte Konzertberichte und Rezensionen bis 1830,* ed. Stefan Kuntze, 474–85; references to Turkish music are on pp. 480–81.

10. Buelow, "Rhetoric: Topics."

11. Allanbrook, *Rhythmic Gesture in Mozart,* 2, 6.

12. A thorough study is Rice, "Representations of Janissary Music."

13. Mozart, *Letters of Mozart,* 176.

14. Ibid., 198.

15. Cook, *Beethoven Symphony No. 9,* 100, 105.

16. Rice, "Representations of Janissary Music," 80–81.

17. Dolge, *Pianos and Their Makers,* 35.

18. Kramer, "The Harem Threshold," 89.

19. Cone's essay is reprinted in *Schubert: Critical and Analytical Studies,* ed. Walter Frisch. In Germany the renewed attention to musical hermeneutics had begun in 1973 in a symposium on the subject in Frankfurt, with a publication entitled *Beiträge zur musikalischen Hermeneutik,* edited by Carl Dahlhaus.

20. Bibliographic details in *Riemann Musik Lexikon,* s.v. "Kretzschmar."

21. Kretzschmar, "Anregungen zur Forderung musikalischer Hermeneutik," v–vi; my translation.

22. Cone, "Beyond Analysis"; with reply by David Lewin, "Behind the Beyond," and Cone, "Mr. Cone Replies."

23. Cone, "Beyond Analysis," 23–24.

24. Meyer, *Emotion and Meaning in Music.*

25. Agawu, *Playing with Signs.*

26. Cone, "Beyond Analysis," 25.

27. Carruthers, *The Book of Memory,* 13–14.

28. Sontag, "Against Interpretation," 6–7.

12. Facile Metaphors, Hidden Gaps, Short Circuits

1. In Erickson, *Musica enchiriadis*, 31–32.
2. Guido of Arezzo, *Micrologus*, in Babb, *Hucbald, Guido, and John on Music*, 69.
3. Boethius, *Fundamentals of Music*, 9–10.
4. Erickson, *Musica enchiriadis*, 31.
5. Barfield, *Saving the Appearances*, 78.
6. Rosen, "Should We Adore Adorno?"
7. In *Strunk's Source Readings in Music History*, 29.
8. Adorno, *Klangfiguren*, 24; my translation.
9. Ibid., *Minima moralia*, 49.
10. Rosen, "Should We Adore Adorno?"
11. Dahlhaus, "The Musical Work of Art as a Subject of Sociology," 243.
12. Adorno, "Zur Vorgeschichte der Reihenkomponisten," in *Klangfiguren*, 16.
13. Rosen, "Should We Adore Adorno?" I have seen this peculiar idea attributed to George Lichtheim in his writing about Adorno but have not been able to confirm that.
14. In Kundera, "Improvisation in Homage to Stravinsky," 78–79.
15. Weber, *The Rational and Social Foundations of Music*.
16. Rosen, "Should We Adore Adorno?"
17. Ibid.
18. Adorno, *Introduction to the Sociology of Music*, 70.
19. In Rosen, "Should We Adore Adorno?"
20. Adorno, *Philosophy of Modern Music*, 60ff.
21. Ibid., n. 30.
22. Ibid., n. 24.
23. Rosen, *Arnold Schoenberg*, 81, 78.
24. Adorno, *Philosophy of Modern Music*, 69.
25. Ibid., 64–65. Adorno culled this bit of early music history from Richard Batka, *Allgemeine Geschichte der Musik*. Altogether, what he mentions here is a well-worn cliché of flimsy music history popularizations. Pertinent to the present subject is a judgment of the music of Ockeghem in Cecil Gray, *The History of Music*. According to Gray, Ockeghem was "a pure cerebralist, almost exclusively preoccupied with intellectual problems. . . . Expression was for him a secondary consideration, if indeed it existed for him at all. He seems to have had something of the mentality of Arnold Schoenberg today: the same ruthless disregard of merely sensuous beauty, the same unwearying and relentless pursuit of new technical means for their own sake. He is the schoolmaster, the drill sergeant of music." This passage was brought to my attention by Lawrence Bernstein's fine study of zealous and creative music historiography, "'Singende Seele' or 'unsingbar'?" The passage from Gray is cited on p. 4 n. 3.

26. Rosen, "Should We Adore Adorno?" writes that Spengler's "influence on Adorno is not mentioned by his admirers because [Spengler] is no longer intellectually respectable." Another influence about which one can say the same is that of Alfred Lorenz, the author of *Das Geheimnis der Form bei Richard Wagner.* See Carl Dahlhaus, "Soziologische Dechiffrierung von Musik-zu Th. W. Adornos Wagnerkritik." Regarding the disagreement about Spengler's influence, see Rosen's reply to correspondence in the *New York Review of Books,* February 13, 2003.

27. See Herman, *The Idea of Decline in Western History,* with numerous references to Adorno.

28. Adorno, *Minima moralia;* as cited in Rosen, "Should We Adore Adorno?"

29. See, for example, his lecture, "On the Problem of Musical Analysis," 2.

30. Hoeckner, "Homage to Adorno's 'Homage to Zerlina,'" 510–22.

31. Adorno, "Schubert (1928)."

32. Ibid., "Hermeneutik."

33. Ibid., *Mahler: A Musical Physiognomy.*

34. Ibid., "An Essay on Cultural Criticism and Society," 19. The phrase occurs in the opening sentence of the essay: "The critique of culture is confronted with the last stage in the dialectic of culture and barbarism: to write a poem after Auschwitz is barbaric, and that corrodes also the knowledge which expresses why it has become impossible to write poetry today."

BIBLIOGRAPHY

Abbate, Carolyn. *Unsung Voices: Opera and Musical Narrative in the Nineteenth Century*. Princeton, N.J.: Princeton University Press, 1992.

Adorno, Theodor W. "An Essay on Cultural Criticism and Society." In *Prisms*. Cambridge, Mass.: MIT Press, 1967.

———. "Hermeneutik." *Anbruch* 12 (1930): 235–38.

———. *Introduction to the Sociology of Music*. New York: Continuum, 1988.

———. *Klangfiguren*. Frankfurt am Main: Suhrkamp Verlag, 1959.

———. *Mahler: A Musical Physiognomy*. Translated by Edmund Jephcott. Chicago: University of Chicago Press, 1992.

———. *Minima moralia: Reflections from a Damaged Life*. Frankfurt am Main: Suhrkamp Verlag, 1951; New York, 1974.

———. "On the Problem of Musical Analysis." Introduction and translation by Max Paddison. *Music Analysis* 1 (1982): 169–87.

———. *Philosophy of Modern Music*. New York: Continuum, 1985.

———. "Schubert (1928)". Translated by Jonathan Dunsby and Beate Perrey. *19th-Century Music* 29, no. 1 (2005): 3–14.

Agawu, Kofi. *Playing with Signs: A Semiotic Interpretation of Classic Music*. Princeton, N.J.: Princeton University Press, 1993.

Allanbrook, Wye Jamison. "Ear-Tickling Nonsense: A New Context for Musical Expression in Mozart's 'Haydn' Quartets." *St. John's Review* 38 (1988): 1–24.

———. *Rhythmic Gesture in Mozart:* Le Nozze di Figaro *and* Don Giovanni. Chicago: University of Chicago Press, 1986.

Apel, Willi. *Gregorian Chant*. Bloomington: Indiana University Press, 1958.

Arato, Andrew, and Erike Gebhard, eds. *The Essential Frankfurt School Reader*. Oxford: Basil Blackwell, 1978.

Atkinson, Charles. "From *Vitium* to *Tonus acquisitus:* On the Evolution of the Notational Matrix of Medieval Chant." *Cantus Planus* (1990): 181–97.

Augustine, Saint. *Confessions*. Translated by Robert S. Pine-Coffin. Harmondsworth, Middlesex: Penguin Books, 1961.

Aurelian of Réôme. *The Discipline of Music*. Translated by J. Ponte. Colorado Springs: Colorado College Music Press, 1968.

Austin, J. L. *How to Do Things with Words*. 2nd ed. Cambridge, Mass.: Harvard University Press, 1975.

Babb, Warren, trans. *Hucbald, Guido, and John on Music: Three Medieval Treatises*. Edited by Claude V. Palisca. New Haven, Conn.: Yale University Press, 1978.

Baetjer, Katharine, ed. *Watteau, Music, and Theater*. Exhibition catalogue. New York: Metropolitan Museum of Art, 2009.

Bamberger, Jeanne. "The Musical Significance of Beethoven's Fingerings in the Piano Sonatas." *Music Forum* 4 (1976): 237–80.

Barfield, Owen. *Saving the Appearances: A Study in Idolatry*. 2nd ed. Middeltown, Conn.: Wesleyan University Press, 1988.

Barrett, Sam. "Reflections on Music Writing: Coming to Terms with Gain and Loss in Early Music Song." In *Vom Preis des Fortschritts: Gewinn und Verlust in der Musikgeschichte*, edited by Andreas Haug and Andreas Dorschel, 89–109. Vienna, London, New York: Universal Edition, 2008.

Batka, Richard. *Allgemeine Geschichte der Musik*. Stuttgart: C. Gruninger, Klett und Hartmann, 1900–1915.

Baudelaire, Charles. *Les fleurs du mal*. Translated by Richard Howard. Boston: D. R. Godine, 1982.

Beiträge zur musikalischen Hermeneutik. Edited by Carl Dahlhaus. Studien zur Musikgeschichte des 19. Jahrhunderts. Regensburg: G. Bosse, 1975.

Benjamin, Walter. *Gesammelte Schriften*. Edited by Rolf Tiedermann and Hermann Schwappenhäser. Frankfurt am Main: Suhrkamp Verlag, 1991.

Bennett, Clive. "Maschinist Hopkins: A Father for Lulu?" *Musical Times* 127 (1986): 481–84.

Bent, Ian. *Music Analysis in the Nineteenth Century*. Cambridge: Cambridge University Press, 1994.

———. "Notation." In *The New Grove Dictionary of Music and Musicians*, edited by Stanley Sadie. London: Macmillan, 1980.

Bercow, Larry, and Zachary Schisgal. *Two of a Kind: Dogs That Look Like Their Owners*. New York: Warner Books, 1999.

Berger, Karol. "*Diegesis* and *Mimesis*: The Poetic Modes and the Matter of Artistic Presentation." *Journal of Musicology* 12 (1994): 407–443.

Bernal, Martin. *Black Athena: The Afroasiatic Roots of Classical Civilization*. Vol. 1, *The Fabrication of Ancient Greece 1785–1985*. New Brunswick, N.J.: Rutgers University Press, 1987.

Bernstein, Lawrence. "'Singende Seele' or 'unsingbar'? Forkel, Ambros, and the Forces behind the Ockeghem Reception during the Late 18th and 19th Centuries." *Journal of Musicology* 23, no. 1 (2006): 2–61.

Bielitz, Mathias. *Musik und Grammatik: Studien zur mittelalterlichen Musiktheorie.* Munich: Musikverlag Katzbichler, 1977.

Bispham, John. "Rhythm in Music: What Is It, Who Has It, and Why." *Music Perception* 24 (2006): 125–34.

Black, Max. "Metaphor." *Proceedings of the Aristotelian Society,* n.s., 55 (1954–55): 273–74.

———. *Models and Metaphors.* Ithaca, N.Y.: Cornell University Press, 1962.

Boethius. *Fundamentals of Music.* Translated by Calvin M. Bower, edited by Claude V. Palisca. New Haven, Conn.: Yale University Press, 1989.

———. *De institutione musica libri quinque.* Translated by William Strunk, Jr. and Oliver Strunk. Revised by James McKinnon. In *Strunk's Source Readings in Music History,* rev. ed., ed. Leo Treitler, 137–42. New York: W. W. Norton, 1998.

Bourdieu, Pierre. *Outline of a Theory of Practice.* Cambridge: Cambridge University Press, 1977.

Brandenburg, Sieghard. *Briefwechsel Gesamtausgabe: Ludwig van Beethoven.* Munich: G. Henle, 1996–98.

Bril, Jacques. *Lilith, ou la mère obscure.* Paris: Payot, 1981.

Brown, Julie, ed. *Western Music and Race.* Cambridge: Cambridge University Press, 2007.

Buelow, George. "Rhetoric." In *The New Grove Dictionary of Music and Musicians,* edited by Stanley Sadie. London: Macmillan, 1980.

Burnyeat, M. F. "Wittgenstein and Augustine *De magistro.*" In *The Augustinian Tradition,* edited by Gareth B. Matthews, 286–302. Philosophical Traditions 8. Berkeley: University of California Press, 1999.

Busoni, Ferruccio. "Sketch of a New Aesthetics of Music." In *Three Classics in the Aesthetics of Music.* New York: Dover, 1962.

Busse Berger, Anna Maria. *Medieval Music and the Art of Memory.* Berkeley: University of California Press, 2005.

Butt, John. *Playing with History: The Historical Approach to Musical Performance.* Cambridge: Cambridge University Press, 2002.

Butterfield, Andrew. "Brush with Genius." *New York Review of Books.* April 26, 2007.

Cahn, Peter, and Ann-Katrin Heimer, eds. *De Musica et Cantu: Festschrift Helmut Hucke.* Hildesheim: Georg Olms Verlag, 1993.

Calcagno, Mauro. "Heinrich Schenker's Analyses of Beethoven: An Exercise in Musical Hermeneutics." Revision of the author's *"Wie ar ein Beethoven musikalisch?"* presented to the Nineteenth Annual Meeting of the Society for Music Theory, Baton Rouge, La., 1996.

———. *"Wie war ein Beethoven musikalisch?* Content, Form, and Time-Consciousness in Heinrich Schenker (1895–1913)." Term paper for seminar "Questions and Answers about Musical Meaning," Yale University, 1995.

Calvino, Italo. *If on a Winter's Night a Traveller*. New York: Knopf, 1993.
———. *Under the Jaguar Sun*. Translated by William Weaver. New York: Harcourt Brace Jovanovich, 1988.
Carruthers, Mary. *The Book of Memory: A Study of Memory in Medieval Culture*. 2nd ed. Cambridge: Cambridge University Press, 2008.
Ciardi, John. *A Browser's Dictionary*. Pleasantville, N.Y.: Akadine Press, 1997.
Clanchy, M. T. *From Memory to Written Record, England 1066–1307*. Cambridge, Mass.: Harvard University Press, 1979.
Coker, Wilson. *Music and Meaning*. New York: Free Press, 1972.
Colish, Marcia. *The Mirror of Language: A Study in the Medieval Theory of Knowledge*. New Haven, Conn.: Yale University Press, 1968.
Cone, Edward T. "Beyond Analysis." *Perspectives of New Music* 6 (1967–68): 33–61. Reply by David Lewin, "Behind the Beyond," *Perspectives of New Music* 7 (1968–69): 59–69; "Mr. Cone Replies," 70–72.
———. *The Composer's Voice*. Berkeley and Los Angeles: University of California Press, 1974.
———. "Schubert's Promissory Note: An Essay in Musical Hermeneutics." *19th-Century Music* 5, no. 3 (1982): 233–41. Reprinted in *Schubert: Critical and Analytical Studies*, edited by Walter Frisch, 13–30. Lincoln: University of Nebraska Press, 1986.
———. "Three Ways of Reading a Detective Story—or a Brahms Intermezzo." In *Music: A View from Delft*, edited by Robert P. Morgan, 77–94. Chicago: University of Chicago Press, 1989.
Cook, Nicholas. *Beethoven Symphony No. 9*. Cambridge: Cambridge University Press, 1993.
Craft, Robert. *Stravinsky: Chronicle of a Friendship*. New York: Knopf, 1972.
Dahlhaus, Carl. *Esthetics of Music*. Translated by William W. Austin. Cambridge, New York: Cambridge University Press, 1982.
———. "Fragments of a Musical Hermeneutics." Translated by Karen Painter. *Current Musicology* 50 (1992): 5–20.
———. "The Musical Work of Art as a Subject of Sociology." In *Schoenberg and the New Music: Essays by Carl Dahlhaus*, translated by Derrick Puffett and Alfred Clayton, 234–47. Cambridge: Cambridge University Press, 1989.
———. "Soziologische Dechiffrierung von Musik: zu Th. W. Adornos Wagnerkritik." *International Review of the Aesthetics and Sociology of Music* 1 (1970): 137–48.
———. "Thesen über Programmusik." In *Beiträge zur musikalischen Hermeneutik*, 187–204. Studien zur Musikgeschichte des 19. Jahrhunderts. Regensburg: G. Bosse, 1975.
Davidson, Donald. "What Metaphors Mean." In *Inquiries into Truth and Interpretation*, 246–64. New York: Oxford University Press, 1984.

Davies, Stephen. *Musical Meaning and Expression*. Ithaca, N.Y.: Cornell University Press, 1995.

Debussy, Claude. *Monsieur Croche:Dilletante Hater*. In *Three Classics in the Aesthetics of Music*. New York: Dover, 1962.

Derrida, Jacques. *Of Grammatology*. Translated by Gayatri Chakravorty Spivak. Baltimore: Johns Hopkins University Press, 1976.

DeWoskin, Kenneth. *A Song for One or Two: Music and the Concept of Art in Early China*. Ann Arbor, Mich.: Center for Chinese Studies, 1982.

Dijkstra, Bram. *Idols of Perversity: Fantasies of Feminine Evil in Fin-de-Siècle Culture*. New York: Oxford University Press, 1986.

Dolge, Alfred. *Pianos and Their Makers: A Comprehensive History of the Development of the Piano*. New York: Dover Publications, 1911.

Donakowski, Conrad. "A Musical Return to the State of Nature." In *A Muse for the Masses: Ritual and Music in an Age of Democratic Revolution, 1770–1870*, 135–52. Chicago: University of Chicago Press, 1977.

Eco, Umberto. *The Limits of Interpretation*. Bloomington: Indiana University Press, 1990.

Eichenauer, Richard. *Musik und Rasse*. Munich: J. L. Lehmans Verlag, 1932.

Eigeldinger, Jean-Jacques. *Chopin: Pianist and Teacher as Seen by His Pupils*. Translated by Krysia Osostowicz and Naomi Shohet. Edited by Ray Howat. Cambridge: Cambridge University Press, 1986.

Erickson, Raymond, trans. *Musica enchiriadis and Scolica enchiriadis*. Edited by Claude V. Palisca. New Haven, Conn.: Yale University Press, 1995.

Fechter, Paul. *Frank Wedekind: Der Mensch und das Werk*. Jena: Erich Lichtenstein, 1920.

Ferretti, Dom Paolo. *Estetica gregoriana, ossia Trattato delle forme musicali del canto gregoriano*. Rome: Pontificio Istituto di Musica Sacra, 1934.

Fétis, François-Joseph. "The Concert of Monsieur Chopin from Warsaw." In *Strunk's Source Readings in Music History*, rev. ed., edited by Leo Treitler. New York: W. W. Norton, 1998.

Finscher, Ludwig. "Zur Interpretation des langsamen Satzes aus Beethovens Klaviersonate Opus 10 Nr. 3." In *International Musicological Society, Report of the Eleventh Congress: Copenhagen 1972*, edited by Henrik Glahn, Soren Sorensen, and Peter Ryom, 1:82–85. Copenhagen: Edition Wilhelm Hansen, 1972.

Forster, E. M. *Abinger Harvest*. New York: Harcourt, Brace and Co., 1936.

Franklin, Harry. *On Bullshit*. Princeton, N.J.: Princeton University Press, 2005.

Franz, M. L. von. "The Process of Individuation." In *Man and His Symbols*, edited by Carl G. Jung, 157–254. New York: Dell Publications, 1964.

Galassi, Susan Grace. *Picasso's Variations on the Masters: Confrontations with the Past*. New York: Harry N. Abrams, 1996.

Geertz, Clifford. "From the Native's Point of View: On the Nature of Anthropological Understanding." In *Symbolic Anthropology: A Reader in the Study of Symbols and Meanings,* edited by Janet L. Dolgin, David S. Kemnitzer, and David M. Schneider, 420–92. New York: Columbia University Press, 1977.

Gelb, I. J. *A Study of Writing.* Chicago: University of Chicago Press, 1963.

Godeau, Abigail Solomon. "Misogynist Masquerade." Review of *Idols of Perversity,* by Bram Dijkstra. *Public* 3 (1990): 87–101.

Goethe, Johann Wolfgang von. "The Collector and His Circle." In *Propyläen II, ii: Goethe on Art,* 31–72. Selected, edited, and translated by John Gage. Berkeley: University of California Press, 1980.

———. *Wilhelm Meister's Apprenticeship and Travels.* 2nd ed. Translated by Thomas Carlyle. Boston: Houghton Mifflin, 1839.

Gombrich, E. H. *Art and Illusion: A Study in the Psychology of Pictorial Representation.* Princeton, N.J.: Princeton University Press, 1969.

———. *The Ideas of Progress and Their Impact on Art.* New York: The Cooper Union School of Art and Architecture, 1971.

Goodman, Nelson. *Languages of Art.* 2nd ed. Indianapolis: Hackett, 1981.

Gray, Cecil. *The History of Music.* London: K. Paul, Trench, Kubner, 1928.

Groden, Michael, and Martin Kreiswirth, eds. *The Johns Hopkins Guide to Literary Theory and Criticism.* Baltimore: Johns Hopkins University Press, 1994.

Guck, Marion. "Analytical Fictions." *Music Theory Spectrum* 16 (1994): 217–30.

———. "Rehabilitating the Incorrigible." In *Theory, Analysis, and Meaning in Music,* edited by Anthony Pople, 57–76. Cambridge: Cambridge University Press, 1995.

Gulik, Robert Hans van. *The Lore of the Chinese Lute: An Essay in Ch'in Ideology.* Rev. ed. Tokyo and Rutland, Vt.: Sophia University, 1969.

Gushee, Lawrence. "Aurelian of Réôme." In *The New Grove Dictionary of Music and Musicians,* edited by Stanley Sadie. London: Macmillan, 1980.

Haar, James. "Music as Visual Language." In *Meaning in the Visual Arts: Views from the Outside: A Centennial Commemoration of Erwin Panofsky (1892–1968),* edited by Irving Lavin, 265–84. Princeton, N.J.: Institute for Advanced Study, 1995.

Hall, Patricia. "Role and Form in Berg's Sketches for *Lulu.*" In *Alban Berg: Historical and Analytical Perspectives,* edited by R. Morgan and D. Gable, 235–60. New York: Oxford University Press, 1989.

———. *A View of Berg's* Lulu *through the Autograph Sources.* Berkeley: University of California Press, 1996.

Halle, Morris. "On Meter and Prosody." In *Progress in Linguistics,* edited by M. Bierwisch and K. Heidolph, 64–80. The Hague: Mouton, 1970.

Hanfling, Oswald. "'I Heard a Plaintive Melody.'" In *Wittgenstein Centenary Essays,* edited by A. Phillips Griffths, 117–34. Royal Institute of Philosophy Lecture Series 28, Cambridge: Cambridge University Press, 1991.

Hanslick, Eduard. *On the Musically Beautiful: A Contribution towards the Revision of the Aesthetics of Music.* Translated by Geoffrey Payzant. Indianapolis, Ind.: Hackett, 1986.

Harris, Roy. *The Origin of Writing.* LaSalle, Ill.: Open Court, 1986.

Hatten, Robert. *Interpreting Musical Gestures, Topics, and Tropes: Mozart, Beethoven, Schubert.* Bloomington: Indiana University Press, 2004.

———. "Metaphor in Music." In *Musical Signification: Essays in the Semiotic Theory and Analysis of Music,* edited by Eero Tarasti, 373–91. Berlin and New York: Mouton de Gruyter, 1995.

Haug, Walter, and Burghart Wachinger, eds. *Traditionswandel und Traditionsverhalten.* Tübingen: M. Niemeyer, 1991.

Hausman, Carl. *Metaphor and Art: Interactionism and Reference in the Verbal and Nonverbal Arts.* Cambridge: Cambridge University Press, 1989.

Havelock, Eric A. *Preface to Plato.* Cambridge, Mass.: Harvard University Press, 1963.

Herman, Arthur. *The Idea of Decline in Western History.* New York: Free Press, 1997.

Hess, Thomas B., and Linda Nochlin, eds. *Woman as Sex Object: Studies in Erotic Art, 1730–1970.* New York: Newsweek, 1972.

Hoeckner, Berthold. "Homage to Adorno's 'Homage to Zerlina.'" *Musical Quarterly* 87 (2004): 510–22.

Hofmann, Josef. *Piano Playing.* 1908. New York: Dover Publications, 1976.

Homer. *The Odyssey.* Translated by Robert Fagles. New York: Penguin Books, 1996.

Hucke, Helmut. "Gregorian and Old Roman Chant." In *The New Grove Dictionary of Music and Musicians,* edited by Stanley Sadie. London: Macmillan, 1980.

Humboldt, Wilhelm von. *Gesammelte Werke.* 6 vols. Edited by K. H. Brandes. Berlin: Albert Leitzman, 1903–06.

Indiana Theory Review 12 (Spring–Fall 1991). Special issue on narrative theory, edited by Richard Littlefield.

Ingarden, Roman. *The Work of Music and the Problem of Its Identity.* Translated by Adam Czerniawski. Edited by Jean G. Harrell. Berkeley: University of California Press, 1986.

Isidore of Seville. *The Etymologies of Isidore of Seville.* Translated by Stephen A. Barney et al. Cambridge: Cambridge University Press, 2006.

Jacobssson, Ritva, and Leo Treitler. "Sketching Archetypes." In *De Musica et Cantu: Studien der Kirchenmusik und der Oper: Helmut Hucke zum 60. Geburtstag,* edited by Peter Cahn and Ann-Katrin Heimer, 157–202. Hildesheim: Georg Olms Verlag, 1993.

Jarman, Douglas. *The Music of Alban Berg.* Berkeley: University of California Press, 1979.

Johannes de Garlandia. *De mensurabili musica: Kritische Edition mit Kommentar und Interpretation der Notationslehre.* Edited by Erich Reimer. Beihefte zum Archiv für Musikwissenchaft 10–11. Wiesbaden: F. Steiner, 1972.

John of Salisbury. *Metalogicon.* Edited by C. C. Webb. Oxford: Oxford University Press, 1929.

Johnson, Douglas. "Beethoven Scholars and Beethoven Sketches." *19th-Century Music* 2, no. 1 (1978): 3–17.

Kallberg, Jeffrey. "Are Variants a Problem? Composers' Intentions in Editing Chopin." In *Chopin Studies* 3, edited by Jim Samson, 257–67. Cambridge: Cambridge University Press, 1990.

———. *Chopin at the Boundaries: Sex, History, and Musical Genre.* Cambridge: Cambridge University Press, 1996.

———. "Chopin in the Marketplace: Aspects of the International Music Publishing Industry in the First Half of the Nineteenth Century." *Notes* 39 (1983): 535–69, 795–824.

———. "The Problem of Repetition and Return in Chopin's Mazurkas." In *Chopin Studies* 1, edited by Jim Samson, 1–23. Cambridge: Cambridge University Press, 1988.

Kanne, Friedrich. Review of Beethoven's Ninth Symphony. *Allgemeine musikalische Zeitung* 8 (1824): 149–51, 157–60, 173–74. Reprinted in *Ludwig van Beethoven—Die Werke im Spiegel seiner Zeit—Gesammelte Konzertberichte und Rezensionen bis 1830,* edited by Stefan Kuntze, 474–85. Laaber: Laaber Verlag, 1987.

Keiler, Allan. "The Origins of Schenker's Thought: How Man Is Musical." *Journal of Music Theory* 33 (1989): 273–98.

———. "Two Views of Musical Semiotics." In *The Sign in Music and Literature,* edited by Wendy Steiner, 138–68. Austin: University of Texas Press, 1981.

Kerman, Joseph. *Opera and Drama.* New York: Vintage, 1956.

Keuls, Eva. *The Reign of the Phallus: Sexual Politics in Ancient Athens.* New York: Harper and Row, 1985.

Keyser, S. J. "The Linguistic Basis of English Prosody." In *Modern Studies in English,* edited by S. Schane and D. Reibel, 379–94. Englewood Cliffs, N.J.: Prentice Hall, 1969.

———. "Old English Prosody." *College English* 30 (1969): 331–56.

Kiesewetter, Raphael Georg. *Geschichte der europäisch-abendländischen oder unsrer heutigen Musik.* Translated by Robert Muller. London, 1848; repr. 1973.

Kingsbury, Martha. "The Femme Fatale and Her Sisters." In *Woman as Sex Object: Studies in Erotic Art, 1730–1970,* edited by Thomas B. Hess and Linda Nochlin, 182–205. New York: Newsweek, 1972.

Kivy, Peter. *Music Alone: Philosophical Reflections on the Purely Musical Experience.* Ithaca, N.Y.: Cornell University Press, 1990.

————. *Sound Sentiment*. Philadelphia: Temple University Press, 1989.

Klein, Ernest. *Klein's Comprehensive Etymological Dictionary of the English Language*. Amsterdam: Elsevier, 1971.

Koltuv, Barbara Black. *The Book of Lilith*. York Beach, Me.: Nicolas-Hays, 1986.

Kott, Jan. *The Theater of Essence*. Evanston, Ill.: Northwestern University Press, 1984.

Kramer, Lawrence. "*Carnaval*, Cross Dressing, and the Woman in the Mirror." In *Musicology and Difference: Gender and Sexuality in Music Scholarship*, edited by Ruth Solie, 305–25. Berkeley: University of California Press, 1993.

————. "The Harem Threshold: Turkish Music and Greek Love in Beethoven's *Ode to Joy*." *19th-Century Music* 22, no. 1 (1998): 78–90.

————. "Tropes and Windows: An Outline of Musical Hermeneutics." In *Music as Cultural Practice, 1800–1900*, 1–20. Berkeley: University of California Press, 1990.

Kramer, Richard. *Unfinished Music*. New York: Oxford University Press, 2009.

Kraus, Karl. *Literatur und Lüge*. Munich: Kösel, 1958.

Krausz, Michael, ed. *The Interpretation of Music: Philosophical Essays*. Oxford: Clarendon Press 1993.

Kretzschmar, Hermann. "Anregungen zur Förderung musikalischer Hermeneutik." In *Gesammelte Aufsätze aus dem Jahrbüchern der Musikbibliothek Peters von Hermann Kretzschmar*. Leipzig: C. F. Peters, 1911

————. *Führer durch den Konzertsaal*. Vol. 1. Leipzig: Breitkopf und Härtel, 1932.

Kuhn, Thomas. *The Structure of Scientific Revolutions*. Chicago: University of Chicago Press, 1970.

Kundera, Milan. "Improvisation in Homage to Stravinsky." In *Testaments Betrayed*, translated by Linda Asher, 53–75. New York: Harper Collins, 1995.

Lakoff, George, and Mark Turner. *More Than Cool Reason*. Chicago: University of Chicago Press, 1989.

Lavin, Irving. *Meaning in the Visual Arts: Views from the Outside: A Centennial Commemoration of Erwin Panofsky (1892–1968)*. Princeton, N.J.: Institute for Advanced Study, 1995.

Lehrer, Adrienne. *Wine and Conversation*. Bloomington: Indiana University Press, 1983.

Levin, Samuel. "Aristotle's Theory of Metaphor." *Philosophy and Rhetoric* 15 (1982): 24–46.

Liddell, Henry George, and Robert Scott. *Greek-English Lexicon*. Oxford: Clarendon Press, 1996.

Lippman, Edward. *A History of Western Music Aesthetics*. Lincoln: University of Nebraska Press, 1992.

Listenius, Nicolai. *Musica ab authore denuo multisque novis regale et exemplis adaucta*. 1549. Rochester, N.Y.: University of Rochester Press, 1966.

Lloyd, G. E. R. *The Revolutions of Wisdom.* Berkeley: University of California Press, 1989.

Lochhead, Judy. "Lulu: Structural Principles." Unpublished essay, 1972.

Lockwood, Lewis. "On Beethoven's Sketches and Autographs: Some Problems of Definition and Interpretation." *Acta Musicologica* 42 (1970): 32–47.

Márquez, Gabriel Garcia. "Bon Voyage, Mr. President." *The New Yorker,* September 1993.

Marsten, Nicholas. "Sketch." In *The New Grove Dictionary of Music and Musicians,* edited by Stanley Sadie. London: Macmillan, 1980.

Maus, Fred Everett. "Music as Drama." *Music Theory Spectrum* 10 (1988): 54–74.

———. "Music as Narrative." *Indiana Theory Review* 12 (1991): 1–34.

McClary, Susan. "Getting Down Off the Beanstalk: The Presence of a Woman's Voice in Janika Vandervelde's Genesis II." *Minnesota Composers Forum Newsletter,* February, 1987. Revised version in McClary, *Feminine Endings: Music, Gender, and Sexuality,* 112–31. Minneapolis: University of Minnesota Press, 1991.

———. "Narrative Agendas in 'Absolute' Music: Identity and Difference in Brahms' Third Symphony." In Ruth Solie, *Musicology and Difference,* 326–44. Berkeley: University of California Press, 1993.

———. Review of *Music and the Historical Imagination,* by Leo Treitler. *Notes* 48 (1991): 838–40.

McKeon, Richard. "Literary Criticism and the Concept of Imitation in Antiquity." In *Critics and Criticism: Essays in Method by a Group of the Chicago Critics,* abridged ed., edited by R. S. Crane, 117–45. Chicago: University of Chicago Press, 1952.

Mendel, Hermann, and August Reissmann. *Musikalisches Conversations-Lexikon.* Leipzig, 1890.

Meyer, Leonard. *Emotion and Meaning in Music.* Chicago: University of Chicago Press, 1956.

Modrak, Deborah K. W. *Aristotle's Theory of Language and Meaning.* Cambridge: Cambridge University Press, 2001.

Momigny, Jérome-Joseph de. *A Complete Course of Harmony and Composition.* Extract in *Strunk's Source Readings in Music History,* rev. ed., edited by Leo Treitler. New York: W. W. Norton, 1998.

Morgan, Robert P. "The Eternal Return: Retrograde and Circular Form in Berg." In *Alban Berg: Historical and Analytical Perspectives,* edited by Robert P. Morgan and David Gable, 111–41. New York: Oxford University Press, 1991.

Mozart, Wolfgang Amadeus. *Letters of Mozart.* Edited by Hans Mersman. New York: Dorset Press, 1986.

Nägeli, Hans-Georg. *Vorlesungen über Musik zum Berücksichtigung der Dilletanten.* Stuttgart, 1876.

Nattiez, Jean-Jacques. "Can One Speak of Narrativity in Music?" *Journal of the Royal Musical Association* 115 (1990): 240–57.

———. *Fondements d'une sémiologie de la musique.* Paris: Seuil, 1975.

———. *Proust as Musician.* Cambridge: Cambridge University Press, 1989.

Nemis, Steve. "Aristotle's Analogical Metaphor." *Arethusa* 21 (1988): 215–26.

Newcomb, Anthony. "Sound and Feeling." *Critical Inquiry* 10, no. 4 (1984): 614–43.

New Harvard Dictionary of Music. Edited by Don Michael Randel. Cambridge, Mass.: Harvard University Press, 1986.

Nietzsche, Friedrich. *Human, All Too Human: A Book for Free Spirits.* Translated by Marion Faber, Stephen Lehman, and Arthur C. Danto. Lincoln: University of Nebraska Press, 1984.

Nottebohm, Gustav. *Beethoveniana.* Leipzig: Peters, 1872.

———. *Zweite Beethoveniana.* Leipzig: J. Rieter-Biedermann, 1887.

Onions, C. T., R. W. Burchfield, and G. W. S. Friedrichsen, eds. *Oxford Dictionary of English Etymology.* Oxford: Clarendon Press, 1966.

Owens, Jesse Ann. *Composers at Work: The Craft of Musical Composition 1450–1600.* New York and Oxford: Oxford University Press, 1997.

Panofsky, Erwin. "The History of Art as a Humanistic Discipline." In *Meaning in the Visual Arts: Papers in and on Art History,* 1–25. New York: Doubleday Anchor, 1955.

———. "Iconography and Iconology: An Introduction to the Study of Renaissance Art." In *Meaning in the Visual Arts: Papers in and on Art History,* 26–54. New York: Doubleday Anchor, 1955.

Paolone, Ernesto. "L'originale autografo della lettera del 16 apr. 1819 di L. van Beethoven, inviata a F Ries con le indicazioni metronomiche della 'Hammerklavier-Sonate' Op. 106." *Nuova rivista musicale italiana* 15 (1981): 181–96.

Paul, Hermann. *Principles of the History of Language.* Translated by H. A. Strong. London: Swan Sonnenschein, 1890.

Perle, George. *The Operas of Alban Berg.* Vol. 2, *Lulu.* Berkeley: University of California Press, 1985.

Pickett, J. M. *The Acoustics of Speech Communication.* Upper Saddle River, N.J.: Allyn and Bacon, 1999.

Pirrotta, Nino. "Church Polyphony a propos of a New Fragment at Foligno." In *Music and Culture in Italy from the Middle Ages to the Baroque,* 124–39. Cambridge, Mass.: Harvard University Press, 1984.

Plato. *Cratylus.* Translated by H. N. Fowler. London: Loeb Classical Library, 1926.

Polanyi, Michael. *Personal Knowledge: Toward a Post-Critical Philosophy.* Chicago: University of Chicago Press, 1958.

Poli, Roberto. *The Secret Life of Musical Notation: Defying Interpretive Traditions.* Milwaukee: Amadeus Press, 2010.

Powers, Harold. "Language Models and Musical Analysis." *Ethnomusicology* 24 (1980): 1–60.

Praz, Mario. *The Romantic Agony.* London: Oxford University Press, 1970.

Proust, Marcel. *In Search of Lost Time.* Vol. 1, *Swann's Way.* Translated by C. K. Scott-Moncrieff and Terence Kilmartin. Revised by D. J. Enright. New York: Modern Library, 1992.

Random House Dictionary of the English Language. 2nd ed., unabridged. Edited by Stuart Berg Flexner. New York: Random House, 1987.

Rankin, Susan. "Between Oral and Written: Twelfth-Century Italian Sources of Polyphony." In *Un millennio di polifonia liturgica tra oralità e scrittura,* edited by G. Cattin and F. A. Gallo, 75–98. Quaderni di "Musica e Storia" 3. Bologna: Società editrice il mulino; Venice: Fondazione Ugo e Olga Levi, 2002.

Reckow, Fritz. *Der Musiktraktat des Anonymus 4.* Teil 1: Edition. Wiesbaden: F. Steiner, 1967.

———. "Tonsprache." In *Handwörterbuch der musikalischen Terminologie.* Wiesbaden: Steiner, 1976.

Rice, Eric. "Representations of Janissary Music (Mehter) as Musical Exoticism in Western Compositions, 1670–1824." *Journal of Musicological Research* 19 (1999): 41–88.

Ricoeur, Paul. "Narrative Time." In *On Narrative,* edited by W. J. T. Mitchell, 165–90. Chicago: University of Chicago Press, 1980.

Riemann Musik Lexikon: Zwölfte völlig neubearbeitete Auflage, edited by Wilibald Gurlitt. Mainz: B. Schott's Söhne, 1975.

Ritter, Johann Wilhelm. *Faksimiledruck nach der Ausgabe von 1810, mit einem Nachwort von Heinrich Schipperges.* Heidelberg: Lambert Schneider, 1969.

Rosand, David. *Drawing Acts: Studies in Graphic Expression and Representation.* New York: Cambridge University Press, 2002.

Rosen, Charles. *Arnold Schoenberg.* New York: Viking Press, 1975.

———. "Should We Adore Adorno?" Review of *Philosophy of Modern Music, Essays on Music,* and *Beethoven: The Philosophy of Music,* by Theodor W. Adorno. *New York Review of Books,* October 24, 2002.

Rothe, Friedrich. *Frank Wedekinds Dramen: Jugendstil und Lebensphilosophie.* Stuttgart: J. B. Metzler, 1968.

Rothstein, William. "The Americanization of Schenker." *In Theory Only* 9 (1986): 5–17. Reprinted in *Schenker Studies,* edited by Hedi Siegel, 193–203. Cambridge: Cambridge University Press, 1990.

Rousseau, Jean-Jacques. *A Complete Dictionary of Music.* Translated by William Waring. London: J. Murray, 1779.

Ruwet, Nicolas. "Théorie et methodes dans les études musicales: Quelques remarques retrospectives et preliminaries." *Musique en jeu* 17 (1975): 11–36.

Said, Edward. *Orientalism.* New York: Pantheon Books, 1978.

———. "Orientalism Reconsidered." *Cultural Critique* 1 (1985): 89–107.

Saussure, Ferdinand de. *Course in General Linguistics.* Translated by Roy Harris. LaSalle, Ill.: Open Court, 1983.

Schane, S., and D. Reibel, eds. *Modern Studies in English.* Englewood Cliffs, N.J.: Prentice Hall, 1969.

Schapiro, Meyer. *Meyer Schapiro Abroad: Letters to Lillian and Travel Notebooks.* New York: Columbia University Press, 2009.

Schenker, Heinrich. *Beethovens neunte Sinfonie: Eine Darstellung des musikalischen Inhaltes unter fortlaufender Berücksichtigung auch des Vortrages und der Literatur.* Vienna: Universal Edition, 1912.

———. *Beethoven's Ninth Symphony.* Translated and edited by John Rothgeb. New Haven, Conn.: Yale University Press, 1992.

———. *Counterpoint: A Translation of Kontrapunkt.* Book 1. Translated by John Rothgeb and Jurgen Thym. New York: Schirmer Books, 1987.

———. *Erläuterungsausgabe der letzten fünf Klaviersonaten Beethovens.* 4 vols. Vienna: Universal Edition, 1913–21.

———. *Five Graphic Music Analyses (Fünf Urlinie-Tafeln).* Edited by Felix Salzer. Introduction by Allan Forte. New York: Dover, 1969.

———. *Free Composition (Der freie Satz).* Translated and edited by Ernst Oster. New York: Longman, 1979.

———. *Neue musikalische Theorien and Phantasien.* Vol.3, *Der freie Satz.* Vienna: Universal Edition, 1935. 2nd ed., edited by Oswald Jonas. Vienna: Universal Edition, 1956.

Scher, Peter Paul, ed. *Music and Text: Critical Inquiries.* Cambridge: Cambridge University Press, 1992.

Schiller, Friedrich. *Der Briefwechsel zwischen Schiller und Goethe.* Edited by S. Seidel. Vol. 2. Leipzig: Insel-Verlag, 1984.

Schindler, Anton. *Beethoven as I Knew Him: A Biography.* Edited by Donald W. MacArdle. Translated by Constance S. Jolly. Chapel Hill: University of North Carolina Press, 1966.

Schneider, Susan Weidman. *Jewish and Female.* New York: Simon and Schuster, 1984.

Schonberg, Harold C. *The Great Pianists.* New York: Simon and Schuster, 1987.

Schooler, Jonathan, and Tanya Y. Engotler-Schooler. "Verbal Overshadowing of Visual Memories: Some Things Are Better Left Unsaid." *Cognitive Psychology* 22 (1990): 36–71.

Schooler, Jonathan, Stephen Fiore, and Marie Brandimonte. "At a Loss for Words: Verbal Overshadowing of Perceptual Memories." *The Psychology of Learning and Motivation* 37 (1997): 291–335.

Schooler, Jonathan, Stella Ohlsson, and Kevin Brooks. "Thoughts beyond Words: When Language Overshadows Insight." *Journal of Experimental Psychology: General* 122, no. 2 (1993): 166–83.

Showalter, Elaine. *Sexual Anarchy: Gender and Culture at the Fin de Siècle*. New York: Penguin Books, 1991.

Schumann, Robert. *The Musical World of Robert Schumann*. Translated, edited, and annotated by Henry Pleasants. New York: St. Martin's Press, 1965.

Sibley, Frank. "Making Music Our Own." In *The Interpretation of Music*, edited by Michael Krausz, 165–76. Oxford: Clarendon Press, 1993.

Sissman, Elaine. *Haydn and the Classical Variation*. Cambridge, Mass.: Harvard University Press, 1993.

Smith, Frank. *Understanding Reading: A Psycholinguistic Analysis of Reading and Learning to Read*. New York: Holt, Rinehart and Winston, 1971.

Snarrenberg, Robert. *Schenker's Interpretive Practice*. Cambridge: Cambridge University Press, 1997.

———. "Tones and Words in Schenker's Representation of Content." Paper presented to the Society for Music Theory, New York, 1995.

Solie, Ruth. "The Living Work: Organicism and Musical Analysis." *19th-Century Music* 4, no. 2 (1980): 147–56.

———. *Musicology and Difference: Gender and Sexuality in Music Scholarship*. Berkeley: University of California Press, 1993.

———. "Whose Life? The Gendered Self in Schumann's *Frauenliebe* Songs." In *Music and Text: Critical Inquiries*, edited by Steven Paul Scher, 219–40. Cambridge: Cambridge University Press, 1991.

Sontag, Susan. "Against Interpretation." In *Against Interpretation and Other Essays*, 3–14. New York: Delta, 1961.

Sparling, Hilary. *Matisse the Master: A Life of Henri Matisse. The Conquest of Color, 1909–1954*. New York: Knopf, 2007.

Stäblein, Bruno. "Die Entstehung des gregorianischen Chorals." *Die Musikforschung* 27 (1974): 5–17.

———. *Die Gesänge des altrömischen Graduale Vat. lat. 5319*. Monumenta Monodica Medii Aevi 2. Kassel: Bärenreiter Verlag, 1970.

Starobinski, Jean. *Portrait de l'artiste en saltimbanque*. Geneva: Albert Skira, 1970.

Stocking, George W. *Race, Culture, and Evolution: Essays in the History of Anthropology*. Chicago: University of Chicago Press, 1982.

Stravinsky, Igor. *The Poetics of Music in the Form of Six Lessons*. Cambridge, Mass.: Harvard University Press, 1974.

Strunk's Source Readings in Music History. Rev. ed., edited by Leo Treitler. New York: W. W. Norton, 1998.

Tanay, Dorit. *Noting Music, Marking Culture: The Intellectual Context of Rhythmic Notation, 1250–1400*. American Institute of Musicology: Hänsler Verlag, 1999.

Taruskin, Richard. *Oxford History of Western Music*. 6 vols. Oxford: Oxford University Press, 2004.

Tovey, Donald Francis. *Essays in Musical Analysis: Symphonies and Other Orchestral Works*. London, New York: Oxford University Press, 1981.

Traub, A. "Zur Kompositionslehre im Mittelalter." (German translation of Guido, *Micrologus*, and Johannes, *De Musica*, with introduction and commentary.) *Beiträge zur Gregorianik* 17 (1994): 57–90.

Treitler, Leo. *Music and the Historical Imagination*. Cambridge, Mass.: Harvard University Press, 1989.

———. "On the Structure of the Alleluia Melisma: A Western Tendency in Western Chant." In *With Voice and Pen: Coming to Know Medieval Song and How It Was Made*. Oxford: Oxford University Press, 2007.

———. "The Politics of Reception: Tailoring the Present as Fulfillment of a Desired Past." *Journal of the Royal Musical Association* 116 (1991): 280–98.

———. "Regarding Rhythm and Meter in the *Ars antiqua*." *The Musical Quarterly* 65 (1979): 524–58.

———. *With Voice and Pen: Coming to Know Medieval Song and How It Was Made*. Rev. ed. Oxford: Oxford University Press, 2007.

Von Staden, Heinrich. "Science as Text, Science as History: Galen on Metaphor." *Clio medica: Acta Academia Internationalis Historiae Medicinae* 28 (1995): 499–518.

Wagner, Peter. *Einführung in die gregorianische Melodien*. Vol. 3, *Gregorianische Formenlehre: Eine choralische Stilkunde*. Leipzig: Breitkopf und Härtel, 1921.

Wagner, Richard, *The Artwork of the Future*. Extract, translated by Oliver Strunk. In *Strunk's Source Readings in Music History*, rev. ed., edited by Leo Treitler, 1097–112. New York: W. W. Norton, 1998.

Weber, Max. *The Rational and Social Foundations of Music*. Carbondale: Southern Illinois University Press, 1969.

Webern, Anton. *Der Weg zur neuen Musik*. Vienna: Universal Edition, 1960.

Wedekind, Tilly. "Lulu—The Role of My Life." *Theater Quarterly* 1 (1971): 3–7.

White, Hayden. "Commentary: Form, Reference, and Ideology in Musical Discourse." In *Music and Text: Critical Inquiries*, edited by Peter Paul Scher, 288–319. Cambridge: Cambridge University Press, 1992.

———. *The Content of the Form: Narrative Discourse and Historical Representation*. Baltimore: Johns Hopkins University Press, 1990.

Winckelmann, Johann Joachim. *Thoughts on the Imitation of Greek Works in Painting and Sculpture*. Dresden, 1755; English edition, London, 1765.

Wiora, Walter, ed. *Triviale Zonen in der religiösen Kunst des 19. Jahrhunderts*. Vitorio Klosterman, 1971.

Wittgenstein, Ludwig. "The Blue Book." In *The Blue and Brown Books*, dictated in English to Cambridge students and edited by Rush Rhees, 1958. New York: Harper and Row, 1960. References in the notes are to the 1960 edition.

———. "The Brown Book." In *The Blue and Brown Books*. New York: Harper and Row, 1960.

———. *Culture and Value*. Edited by G. H. von Wright and Heikki Nyman. Translated by Peter Winch. Chicago: University of Chicago Press, 1980.

———. *Philosophical Investigations*. 1953. Translated by G. E. M. Anscomb. Oxford: Basil Blackwell, 1958. References in the notes are to the 1958 edition.

———. *Tractatus logico-philosophicus*. Translated by David Pears and Brian McGuiness. London: Routledge, 1974.

Zak, Albin. *The Poetics of Rock*. Berkeley: University of California Press, 2001.

INDEX

settings, 178–181, *180, 181;* sexuality theme, 177–178, *178,* 193–194, 204; as tragic farce, 191–192

Madonna, 182
Madonna (Munch), 196, *197*
Mahler: A Musical Physiognomy (Adorno), 265
Marquez, Gabriel Garcia, 3–4, 19
Maschinist Hopkins (Brand), 201
Matisse, Henri, *80,* 81, 282n20
Mature theory doctrine, 55
Mazurka op. 33, no. 4 (Chopin), 51
Mazurka op. 67, no. 1 (Chopin), 98, *98*
Mazurka op. 67, no. 4 (Chopin), 85
McClary, Susan, 231, 285n34
McComb, Karen, 15
McKeon, Richard, 278n55
Mendelssohn, Felix, 5, 6, 29
Mesto, 16, 50–53, 57, 66
Metaphor: Adorno, 257; in Aristotle, 36–37, 42, 47; described, 14–22, 26, 30–31; Galen on, 42; in Guido, 36–37, 42, 43, 271n12; Hanslick on, 17, 42, 53; justification of, 37–39; in musical notation, 127–129, *130, 131;* Plato, 38–39; stalking horse, 39, 271n22; visual, 42–43, *43;* Wittgenstein on, 31
"Metaphor in Music" (Hatten), 30
Meteorologica (Aristotle), 36
Metronome marks, 58
Meyer, Leonard, 246
Meyer Schapiro Abroad: Letters to Lillian and Travel Notebooks (Schapiro), 166
Michelangelo di Lodovico Buonarroti, 12
Micrologus (Guido of Arezzo), 33, 34, 36–37, 42, 43, 75
Mies, Paul, 64

Mikrokosmos (Bartók), 28–30, 51
Mimesis principle, 113–125, *118, 119,* 127, 147
Ming dynasty, 73–74
Minima moralia (Adorno), 256–264
Minute Waltz (D♭-Major Waltz op. 64, no. 1) (Pachmann), 86–89, *87, 88,* 93, *93*
Mnemonics, 108–113, *109,* 117, 128
Modal rhythm, 147–148, 154–160, *155, 157, 160,* 279n73
Modalities of musical meaning: allegory, 43–44; diegetic *vs.* mimetic modes, 24–25; duality in, 18–19; embodying, exemplifying, 7–8, 12; as exemplification, 14–17; expression, 9–11, 22–23; instability, 8; literal meaning, 16–18; metaphor (*See* Metaphor); narrative voice, 23–30; representing, 9; sources for, 7; symbolizing, denoting, 7–9
Models and Metaphors (Black), 31, 127
Modrak, Deborah K. W., 116
Moment musical in A♭, op. 94, no. 6 (Schubert), 245–249
More Than Cool Reason (Lakoff/Turner), 17, 53
Mosel, Ignaz von, 58
Mozart, Wolfgang, 13, 25, 30, 238–239, 247
Mudocci, Eva, 196, 282n20
Munch, Edvard, 196, *197, 198, 202, 207*
Murs, Jehan de, 124, 132
Musée Condé manuscript, 131
Music: Aurelian classification of, 34–35; cognitive contents of, 29–30, 253–256; composition *vs.* performance, 61–63; as constituent hierarchy, 27–28; decline of into authoritarian society, 261–262, 287n25, 288n26; duality in, 53–54;

LEO TREITLER is Distinguished Professor of Music Emeritus, CUNY Graduate Center, and Fellow, American Academy of Arts and Sciences. Born 1931 in Dortmund, Germany, Treitler emigrated to the United States in 1938, and received his higher education at the University of Chicago (AB, MA) and Princeton (PhD). He has held principal teaching positions at the University of Chicago, Brandeis University, Stony Brook University, and the CUNY Graduate Center.